LIBRARY OF HEBREW BIBLE/ OLD TESTAMENT STUDIES

566

Formerly Journal for the Study of the Old Testament Supplement Series

T & T CLARK • LIBRARY OF BIBLICAL STUDIES •

MEDIATING BETWEEN HEAVEN AND EARTH

Communication with the Divine in the Ancient Near East

edited by

C.L. Crouch
Jonathan Stökl
Anna Elise Zernecke

t&t clark

Published by T&T Clark International
A Continuum imprint
The Tower Building, 11 York Road, London SE1 7NX
80 Maiden Lane, New York, NY 10038

www.continuumbooks.com

Visit the T & T Clark blog at www.tandtclarkblog.com

British Library Cataloguing-in-Publication Data
A catalogue record for this book is available from the British Library.

ISBN: 978-0-567-46162-9

Typeset and copy-edited by Forthcoming Publications Ltd. (www.forthpub.com)
Printed and bound in the United States of America

CONTENTS

ILLUSTRATIONS

ACKNOWLEDGMENTS

The editors would all like to thank the editors of the Library of Hebrew Bible/Old Testament Studies for accepting our manuscript into the series, and Andrew Mein in particular for his regular advice and assistance. Jonathan Stökl would like to acknowledge the support of the European Research Council starting grant project BABYLON at University College London, which allowed him the time to do his share of the editorial work. Carly Crouch would like to express her thanks to Fitzwilliam College, Cambridge, where she was Research Fellow during the time in which this volume was planned and took shape. Anna Zernecke would like to thank Prof. Dr. Sebastian Grätz at Johannes Gutenberg-Universität Mainz for giving her the time to work on the volume. We are also grateful to the committee of the European Association for Biblical Studies for allowing our research group, "Israel in the Ancient Near East," to operate within the auspices of the Association, to Rainer Albertz for his encouragement, and to the members of the panel at the group's first session, at the 2010 meeting in Tartu, Estonia, where the idea for this volume was born and where many of the papers were first read.

C. L. Crouch, Jonathan Stökl and Anna Zernecke
Nottingham, London and Mainz
November 2011

ABBREVIATIONS

AB	Anchor Bible
ABL	*Assyrian and Babylonian Letters Belonging to the Kouyunjik Collection of the British Museum*. Edited by Robert Francis. London, 1892–1914
ADAIK	Abhandlungen des Deutschen Archäologischen Instituts, Abteilung Kairo
AfO	*Archiv für Orientforschung*
AfOB	Archiv für Orientforschung Beihefte
ALASPM	Abhandlungen zur Literatur Alt-Syrien-Palästinas und Mesopotamiens
ANEM	Ancient Near East Monographs
ANET	*Ancient Near Eastern Texts Relating to the Old Testament*. Edited by J. B. Pritchard. 3d ed. Princeton, 1969
AO	Der Alte Orient
AOAT	Alter Orient und Altes Testament
ARM	Archives Royales de Mari
BA	*Biblical Archaeologist*
BagF	Bagdader Forschungen
BagM	*Baghdader Mitteilungen*
BAM	Franz Köcher, *Die babylonisch-assyrische Medizin in Texten und Untersuchungen*. Berlin 1963–80
BASOR	*Bulletin of the American Schools of Oriental Research*
BHT	Beiträge zur historischen Theologie
BibOr	Biblica et Orientalia
BiOr	*Bibliotheca Orientalis*
BWANT	Beiträge zur Wissenschaft vom Alten und Neuen Testament
BWL	W. G. Lambert, *Babylonian Wisdom Literature*. Oxford, 1969 (repr. 1996)
CAD	*The Assyrian Dictionary of the Oriental Institute of the University of Chicago*. Edited by Ignace J. Gelb, Erica Reiner et al. Chicago, 1956–2010
CBQMS	Catholic Biblical Quarterly Monograph Series
CDA	*A Concise Dictionary of Akkadian*. Edited by J. Black, A. George, and N. Postgate. 2d (corrected) printing. Wiesbaden, 2000
CH	Codex Hammurapi/Hammurabi
CII	Corpus Inscriptionum Iranicarum
CIS	*Corpus inscriptionum semiticarum, ab Academia inscriptionum et litterarum humaniorum conditum atque digestum*. Paris, 1889

CLAM	Mark E. Cohen, *The Canonical Lamentations of Ancient Mesopotamia*. Potomac, 1988
CM	Cuneiform Monographs
FAT	Forschungen zum Alten Testament
FM	Florilegium Marianum
FOTL	Forms of the Old Testament Literature
FRLANT	Forschungen zur Religion und Literatur des Alten und Neuen Testaments
HBS	Herders biblische Studien
HKAT	Handkommentar zum Alten Testament
HO	Handbuch der Orientalistik
HSM	Harvard Semitic Monographs
HThKAT	Herders Theologischer Kommentar zum Alten Testament
HTR	*Harvard Theological Review*
HUCA	*Hebrew Union College Annual*
IPIAO	Ikonographie Palästinas/Israels und der Alte Orient
JANER	*Journal of Ancient Near Eastern Religions*
JAOS	*Journal of the American Oriental Society*
JCS	*Journal of Cuneiform Studies*
JNES	*Journal of Near Eastern Studies*
JSJSup	Supplements to the Journal the Study of Judaism
JSOT	*Journal for the Study of the Old Testament*
JSOTSup	Journal for the Study of the Old Testament: Supplement Series
JSSEA	*Journal of the Society of the Study of Egyptian Antiquities*
K	Museum siglum of the British Museum in London (Kuyunjik)
KAI	*Kanaanäische und aramäische Inschriften*. H. Donner and W. Röllig. 2d ed. Wiesbaden, 1966–69
KAR	Keilschrifttexte aus Assur religiösen Inhalts
KTU	Manfried Dietrich, Oswald Loretz, Joaquín Sanmartín. *The Cuneiform alphabetic texts: from Ugarit, Ras Ibn Hani and other places (KTU)*. 2d ed. ALASPM 8. Münster, 1995
LAPO	Littératures anciennes du Proche-Orient
LBAT	A. Sachs, T. Pinches, and J. Strassmaier, *Late Babylonian Astronomical and Related Texts*. London, 1955
LSS	Leipziger semitistische Studien
MC	Mesopotamian Civilizations
MNABU	Mémoires de Nouvelles assyriologiques brèves et utilitaires
NABU	*Nouvelles assyriologiques brèves et utilitaires*
OBE	*Old Babylonian Extispicy: Omen Texts in the British Museum*. U. Jeyes. Istanbul, 1989
OBO	Orbis Biblicus et Orientalis
OBO.SA	Orbis Biblicus et Orientalis: Series Archaeologica
OLA	Orientalia Lovaniensia Analecta
OLB	Orte und Landschaften der Bibel
Or	*Orientalia (New Series)*
OTL	Old Testament Library

PRT	*Politisch-religiöse Texte aus der Sargonidenzeit.* E. G. Klauber. Leipzig, 1913
RA	*Revue d'assyriologie et d'archéologie orientale*
RB	*Revue Biblique*
SAA	State Archives of Assyria
SAACT	State Archives of Assyria Cuneiform Texts
SAALT	State Archives of Assyria Literary Texts
SAAS	State Archives of Assyria Studies
SBB	Stuttgarter biblische Beiträge
SBL	Society of Biblical Literature
SBLSymS	Society of Biblical Literature Symposium Series
SBLWAW	Society of Biblical Literature Writings from the Ancient World
SBS	Stuttgarter Bibelstudien
SEPOA	Société pour l'Étude du Proche-Orient Ancien
SJOT	*Scandinavian Journal of the Old Testament*
StOr	Studia Orientalia
StP.SM	Studie Pohl: Series maior
TAPS	Transactions of the American Philosophical Society
TCBAI	Transactions of the Casco Bay Assyriological Institute
ThB	Theologische Bücherei
ThWAT	*Theologisches Wörterbuch zum Alten Testament.* Edited by G. J. Botterweck, H.-J. Fabry und H. Ringgren. 9 vols. Stuttgart, 1989
TUAT	*Texte aus der Umwelt des Alten Testaments.* Edited by Otto Kaiser. Gütersloh, 1984–
UBL	Ugaritisch-biblische Literatur
UF	*Ugarit-Forschungen*
VAT	Vorderasiatische Abteilung. Tontafeln (siglum for texts in the Vorderasiatisches Museum, Berlin
VTSup	Supplements to Vetus Testamentum
WMANT	Wissenschaftlichen Monographien zum Alten und Neuen Testament
WVDOG	Wissenschaftliche Veröffentlichungen der Deutschen Orient-Gesellschaft
WZKM	*Wiener Zeitschrift für die Kunde des Morgenlandes*
WZKMS	Wiener Zeitschrift für die Kunde des Morgenlandes: Sonderband
ZAR	*Zeitschrift für altorientalische und biblische Rechtsgeschichte*
ZARB	Beihefte zur Zeitschrift für altorientalische und biblische Rechtsgeschichte

LIST OF CONTRIBUTORS

Jan Dietrich, Aarhus Universitet

Erhard S. Gerstenberger, Philipps-Universität Marburg

Anne Katrine de Hemmer Gudme, Københavns Universitet and University of Exeter

Nils P. Heeßel, Ruprecht-Karls-Universität Heidelberg

Herbert Huffmon, Drew University, Madison, N.J.

Margaret Jaques, Universität Zürich

Alan Lenzi, University of the Pacific, Stockton, Calif.

Jonathan Stökl, University College London

Anna Elise Zernecke, Johannes Gutenberg-Universität Mainz

INTRODUCTION

This volume originated in the 2010 meeting of the Israel in the Ancient Near East research group of the European Association of Biblical Studies in Tartu, Estonia, and includes a number of the papers presented to the group on that occasion as well as several further contributions.

The object of the original conference session as well as this volume was to examine ancient Near Eastern perspectives on mediation between the divine and earthly realms, taking a broad definition of mediation in order to allow a multi-faceted discussion of the wide variety of religious practices used to communicate with deities and to interpret the divine response. These practices include intuitive divination (prophecy), technical divination and prayers, and the project was undertaken in the hope that it would encourage the study of prayers, technical divination and prophetic communication in conversation with each other, rather than as independent and unrelated phenomena. In a departure from previous scholarship, the present volume thus brings together the study of prophecy, as an intuitive form of divination, with the study of technical methods of divination and other forms of institutionalised human–divine communication, such as prayer.

The advantage of such an approach is that it allows the phenomena of divine–human communication to be studied with one eye on the means by which the divine communicates to human beings through divination—both technical and intuitive—and one eye on the means by which human beings communicate with the divine—through prayer. This dual perspective on the study of divine–human–divine communication enables a better appreciation of the ways in which communication and the relationship between heaven and earth were conceived in the ancient Near East.

This volume has accordingly aimed to bring together experts in the study of ancient prayers as well as experts on intuitive and technical divination. We begin with Anne Katrine de Hemmer Gudme's study of the dedicatory inscriptions from the YHWH sanctuary on Mount Gerizim ("Out of Sight, Out of Mind? Dedicatory Inscriptions as Communication with the Divine"), in which she argues that the physicality of the inscription itself acts as a means of ongoing communication with the deity, with the inscriptions' presence before the deity serving as a continual reminder of the worshipper and thereby effecting the deity's remembrance and a relationship with the deity.

The hermeneutics of technical divination in Mesopotamia is explored by Nils P. Heeßel in "The Hermeneutics of Mesopotamian Extispicy: Theory vs. Practice." Paying particular attention to the Neo-Assyrian evidence, Heeßel examines the theory of extispicy as expounded in the omen texts as compared to the practice of extispicy as it appears in the reports and explores possible explanations for the imperfect correlation between these two categories of texts.

Potential challenges to the technical methods of interpreting the divine will are examined in "The Curious Case of Failed Revelation in *Ludlul Bēl Nēmeqi*: A New Suggestion for the Poem's Scholarly Purpose," in which Alan Lenzi proposes that part of the purpose of this lengthy composition was to present an explanation of why technical divinatory activities might not always work as desired and, in particular, to explain how a supplicant might succeed in resolving their problem outside the divinatory system without at the same time undermining it.

In a related paper Herbert Huffmon addresses the perennial problem of how the ancients distinguished among conflicting divine messages, focusing on the concept of false prophecy in the deuteronomistic literature and suggesting that the exclusive worship of YHWH rendered this an especially potent issue ("The Exclusivity of Divine Communication in Ancient Israel: False Prophecy in the Hebrew Bible and the Ancient Near East").

In juxtaposition to this, Jonathan Stökl questions the distinctiveness of biblical prophetic activity in "(Intuitive) Divination, (Ethical) Demands and Diplomacy in the Ancient Near East." Stökl argues that the ethical aspect of divinatory communications outside the Hebrew Bible has been largely overlooked and that these activities are involved in foreign politics to a degree not generally acknowledged.

The final four essays address the human side of communication with the divine. In the first of these Erhard S. Gerstenberger sketches out three different "Modes of Communication with the Divine in the Hebrew Psalter": the supplications of a distraught petitioner, the joyous praise of the community and the late-stage development of the internal meditation.

In her essay, "'To Talk to One's God': Penitential Prayers in Mesopotamia," Margaret Jaques examines the corpus of penitential prayer texts and their relationship to other, ritual texts, using the prayers' appearances to elucidate the changing nature of the divine–human relationship and the development of the idea of a personal god.

In “How to Approach a Deity: The Growth of a Prayer Addressed to Ištar,” Anna Elise Zernecke studies the relationship of two copies of the same prayer (Ištar 2). She shows the way that prayer grew from an older and shorter version to the longer version, a process in which the prayer grew from a short hymn of and plea to the goddess into an intricately structured prayer of lament and supplication which puts greater emphasis on the individual person who prays.

In “Psalm 72 in Its Ancient Syrian Context,” Jan Dietrich argues for a Levantine orientation for Ps 72, referring to textual and iconographic sources to contend that the conceptual nexus between justice, fertility and the king is present in the west as much as in the Mesopotamian sources.

The editors hope that these studies will instigate a broader conversation of the myriad means by which the humans of the ancient Near East attempted to communicate with their gods, with the human and divine activities to this end viewed in relation.

Out of Sight, Out of Mind? Dedicatory Inscriptions as Communication with the Divine

Anne Katrine de Hemmer Gudme

The purpose of the present study is to treat dedicatory inscriptions containing a version of a remembrance formula as examples of communication with the divine. In the following, it will be argued that dedicatory inscriptions communicate with a deity not only by means of the written message they carry, but also by means of their mere existence: their materiality and presence in the sanctuary close to the divine presence itself.

Communication with the divine can be described as "vertical communication," based on the assumption that deities dwell in heaven.[1] Along the same lines, "horizontal communication" is communication with the surrounding society. In what follows I will analyze dedicatory inscriptions as both horizontal and vertical forms of communication. As examples I will use the dedicatory inscriptions from the YHWH sanctuary on Mount Gerizim.

1. In the Hebrew Bible and in most ancient cults communication and interaction with the divine technically takes place on both the vertical and horizontal axes. In the case of the sanctuary as described in Exod 25–40 we have a vertical axis described by the smoke rising up from the altar of burnt offerings in front of the tent of meeting and a horizontal axis described by the bread placed in "the holy" in front of the deity, who resides in the "holy of holies." See H. J. Lundager Jensen, *Den Fortærende Ild: Strukturelle analyser af narrative og rituelle tekster i Det Gamle Testamente* (Aarhus: Aarhus Universitetsforlag, 2000), 288–91. Lundager Jensen discerns between the theo-topology of the tabernacle (horizontal) and the topology of the altar (vertical). According to the former YHWH dwells in the temple, and according to the latter YHWH dwells in heaven. Bearing in mind that YHWH cannot necessarily be approached exclusively on a vertical axis, I will nonetheless use the terms "horizontal" and "vertical" communication here for illustrative purposes.

Mount Gerizim is situated on the West Bank near present-day Nablus. During the excavation which was carried out on the site between 1982 and 2006, a Yahwistic sanctuary from the Persian and Hellenistic periods and a city from the Hellenistic period were uncovered.[2] The sanctuary shows signs of two main building phases. The first phase is the construction of the Persian-period sacred precinct in the mid-fifth century B.C.E.[3] This structure occupies the highest spot on the mount and was the first structure to be built on the excavated parts of Mount Gerizim. Only further excavation will show if there are earlier structures on the main summit. The Persian-period sanctuary was active for approximately 250 years until the second building phase which dates to the early second century B.C.E., during the reign of Antiochus III, when an enlarged sanctuary and precinct were built on top of the Persian-period structure. There are no signs of abandonment or discontinuity between the Persian and Hellenistic periods.[4] In fact, it seems that efforts have been made to continue the sacrificial cult in the precinct during the construction of the second building phase.[5]

Mount Gerizim is both historically and today the centre of worship for the Samaritan community and therefore the temple on Mount Gerizim is frequently associated with "Samaritan" worship and religion, seen as distinct from Judaism and the Yahwism practiced in Judah in the Persian and Hellenistic periods.[6] However, there is nothing distinctly "Samaritan" about the sanctuary or the worship on Mount Gerizim in the Persian and Hellenistic periods.[7] What is clear about the temple on Mount Gerizim

2. A Late Roman-period citadel and a Byzantine church of Mary Theotokos were also uncovered, and a Roman Temple to Zeus on Tell er-Ras north of the city re-excavated; see Y. Magen, "The Dating of the First Phase of the Samaritan Temple on Mount Gerizim in Light of the Archaeological Evidence," in *Judah and the Judeans in the Fourth Century B.C.E.* (ed. O. Lipschits, G. N. Knoppers and R. Albertz; Winona Lake, Ind.: Eisenbrauns, 2007), 157–211, and *Mount Gerizim Excavations*. Vol. 2, *A Temple City* (Judea and Samaria Publications 8; Jerusalem: Israel Antiquities Authority, 2008).

3. Magen, "Dating," 180, and *Temple City*, 103, 167.

4. Magen, "Dating," 157–66, and *Temple City*, 97–203.

5. Magen, *Temple City*, 118.

6. R. Pummer, "Samaritanism: A Jewish Sect or an Independent Form of Yahwism?," in *Samaritans: Past and Present: Current Studies* (ed. M. Mor and F. V. Reiterer; Berlin: de Gruyter, 2010), 1–24; Y. Magen, *The Samaritans and the Good Samaritan* (Judea and Samaria Publications 7; Jerusalem: Israel Antiquities Authority, 2008).

7. Cf. B. Becking, "Do the Earliest Samaritan Inscriptions Already Indicate a Parting of the Ways?," in Lipschits, Knoppers and Albertz, eds., *Judah and the Judeans in the Fourth Century B.C.E.*, 213–22.

is that it is a Yahwistic sanctuary.[8] The sacred precinct shows no signs of worship of deities other than YHWH and it appears to conform to regulations for the cult known from the Pentateuch both with regard to a ban on images, purification rules for priests and the assemblage of sacrificial bones found on the mountain.[9] Furthermore, the Samarian onomasticon from the Persian and Hellenistic periods does not differ from the Judean onomasticon in the same period.[10] Therefore, it seems preferable to talk about Samarian Yahwistic worship in the temple on Mount Gerizim rather than "Samaritan" worship. The dedicatory inscriptions from Gerizim offer us a unique window into Yahwistic votive practice in Hellenistic-period Palestine.[11]

The assemblage of dedicatory inscriptions from Mount Gerizim contains roughly 380 inscriptions and inscription fragments, written in Aramaic using either lapidary Aramaic or Proto-Jewish script.[12] The inscriptions follow either a long or a short version of the same dedicatory formula. The short version is "that which offered (זי הקרב) Personal Name [PN] son of PN (from Geographical Name [GN]) for himself, his wife and his sons (על נפשה על אנתתה ועל בנוהי)." The long version

8. The deity on Mount Gerizim is addressed as *yhwh* (inscription no. 383), *ʾdny* and *ʾlhʾ* (Y. Magen, H. Misgav and L. Tsfania, *Mount Gerizim Excavations*. Vol. 1, *The Aramaic Hebrew and Samaritan Inscriptions* (Judeaea and Samaria Publications 2; Jerusalem: Israel Antiquities Authority, 2004), 22–23, 254.

9. Magen, *Temple City*, 141–64; M. Kartveit, *The Origin of the Samaritans* (Leiden: Brill, 2009), 257.

10. Pummer, "Samaritanism," 14–15, with references; I. Hjelm, "Changing Paradigms: Judean and Samarian Histories in Light of Recent Research," in *Historie og Konstruktion. Festskrift til Niels Peter Lemche I anledning af 60 års fødselsdagen den 6. September 2005* (ed. M. Müller and T. L. Thompson; Copenhagen: Museum Tusculanums, 2005), 161–79 (170).

11. I use the term "votive practice" in the broadest sense of the term, meaning simply "gifts to the gods." See the discussion in A. K. de H. Gudme, "Barter Deal or Friend-Making Gift? A Reconsideration of the Conditional Vow in the Hebrew Bible," in *The Gift in Antiquity* (ed. M. Satlow; Oxford: Blackwell, forthcoming).

12. For a definition of the two scripts, see Magen, Misgav and Tsfania, *Inscriptions*, 37–40 with references. Two inscriptions, nos. 150 and 151, seem to be written in Hebrew, using Proto-Jewish script, see ibid., 141–42. Nine other inscriptions, written in Paleo-Hebrew script, have been discovered at the site; see ibid., 26, 253–61. The Aramaic, Hebrew and Samaritan inscriptions were published by the excavators in 2004. Prior to this 36 of the inscriptions were published in *Atiqot* in 1997 (J. Naveh and Y. Magen, "Aramaic and Hebrew Inscriptions of the Second-Century BCE at Mount Gerizim," *Atiqot* 32 [1997]: 9*–17*). Both of these publications are preliminary and a final publication of the inscriptions remains forthcoming; see Magen, *Temple City*, ix–x.

begins in the same way but adds the ending “for good remembrance before the god in this place” (לדכרן טב קדם אלהא באתרא דנה).[13] The inscriptions are all private inscriptions in the sense that they refer to donations made on the initiative of private individuals on behalf of themselves and their families.[14] The majority of the donors are male although a few female donors appear in the corpus as well. In a few rare cases the donation has been made jointly by husband and wife. The beneficiaries mentioned in the inscriptions always belong to the family of the votary and in most cases they are the votary’s “wife and sons.”[15]

A good example of a full version of the short formula is inscription no. 2. The inscription is written in lapidary script on a rectangular stone block that measures 83 centimetres high by 32 centimetres wide by 29 centimetres deep. The inscription consists of two lines; unfortunately, the right side of the stone is damaged so that the first letters in each line are broken off. Nevertheless, the rest of the inscription makes it easy to reconstruct the whole: “[That which] ([ד̊/די]) offered (הקרב) *Šby* for himself (על נפשה) for his [w]ife ([על א]נתתה) and his sons (ובנוהי).”[16]

A good example of an abbreviated version of the short formula is inscription no. 3. The inscription is written in lapidary script on a pillar whose ends are broken. The pillar fragment measures 99 centimetres high and has a diameter of 42.5 centimetres. The inscription consists of five complete lines: “That which offered (די הקרב) Ḥaggai son of Qimi from Kfar Ḥaggai.”[17]

The inscriptions are carved on building and paving stones. With only one exception (no. 223), none of the inscriptions were found *in situ* due to the destruction and rebuilding of the site. The excavators estimate that the hundreds of inscriptions found so far may only be a small part of a corpus which could have originally numbered in the thousands. Since none of the inscriptions were found *in situ* they cannot be dated on the basis of stratigraphy and their original location cannot be determined

13. Magen, Misgav and Tsfania, *Inscriptions*, 16.

14. B. H. McLean describes private inscriptions as follows: “Private inscriptions are largely the product of the peripheral workshops. Though some are quite formal in style, they generally tend to have more errors and be more heterogeneous in style, especially in multilingual and multicultural contexts, such as Asia Minor and Palestine” (B. H. McLean, *An Introduction to Greek Epigraphy of the Hellenistic and Roman Periods from Alexander the Great Down to the Reign of Constantine [323 B.C.–A.D. 337]* [Ann Arbor: University of Michigan Press, 2002], 181–82).

15. Magen, Misgav and Tsfania, *Inscriptions*, 20–21, 61–65.

16. Ibid., 50.

17. Ibid., 51–52.

with certainty. The excavators date the Aramaic inscriptions to the Hellenistic period.[18]

The quality of the inscribed stones does give some indication of where the inscriptions might have been situated in the sacred precinct, as the inscriptions were all carved on white limestone ashlars, all roughly similar in size and apparently part of the same structure. It is possible that the inscriptions were all carved on stones which were part of an inner wall encompassing the inner courtyard and separating the external precinct from the inner precinct which was only accessible to priests.[19]

The Gerizim inscriptions are all clearly dedicatory inscriptions. They contain a Haphel form of the root קרב, which means "to bring near" or "to offer," referring to a donation of some sort.[20] Unfortunately, only two of the inscriptions explicitly identify the object of dedication as "this stone" (אבנה דה).[21] The vast majority of the inscriptions contain the beginning of the dedicatory formula, "that which offered" (*זי הקרב*), but they do not reveal to what the relative pronoun זי refers. Joseph Naveh suggests that we should understand the inscribed stone as the offering in every case at Mount Gerizim.[22] This is of course a possibility and it would be very much in line with Mark Lidzbarski's classic description of dedicatory inscriptions:

> In den meisten Fällen wird der geweihte Gegenstand in der Inschrift nicht erwähnt; das is ja auch nicht nötig, da er es in der Regel selbst ist, der die Inschrift trägt und also vor den Augen des Lesers steht.[23]

18. In the general description of the inscriptions they leave room for the possibility that some of the inscriptions may date back to the Persian-period precinct, while in the conclusion they seem to lean towards the Hellenistic period (third to second centuries B.C.E.) (ibid., 14, 41).

19. Ibid., 14–16; Magen, *Temple City*, 145, 147–48, 153–55.

20. Magen, Misgav and Tsfania, *Inscriptions*, 17; Naveh and Magen, "Aramaic and Hebrew Inscriptions," 11*–13*. The combination of the relative pronoun *zy* with the verb *qrb* is also attested in the fifth-century B.C.E. Aramaic dedicatory inscriptions from Tell el-Mashkuta in Lower Egypt; see J. C. L. Gibson, *Textbook of Syrian Semitic Inscriptions*. Vol. 2, *Aramaic Inscriptions Including Inscriptions in the Dialect of Zenjirli* (Oxford: Clarendon, 1975), 122–23, and I. Rabinowitz, "Aramaic Inscriptions of the Fifth Century B.C.E. from a North-Arab Shrine in Egypt," *JNES* 15 (1956): 1–9.

21. Nos. 147 and 148; see Magen, Misgav and Tsfania, *Inscriptions*, 137–39.

22. Naveh and Magen, "Aramaic and Hebrew Inscriptions," 13*–14*.

23. M. Lidzbarski, *Handbuch der Nordsemitischen Epigraphik nebst Ausgewählten Inschriften. I. Text* (Weimar: Felber, 1898), 151. It should be noted that Lidzbarski does not categorize "Memorialinschriften" as dedicatory or votive inscriptions (*Handbuch*, 165–69).

Naveh goes on to draw a parallel to the construction of the city wall in Neh 3.[24] This parallel should not be taken too far, however, since by implication it ties the dedicatory inscriptions exclusively to the construction phase of the temple wall on Mount Gerizim, and this is contradicted by the material itself since at least some of the stones were not originally prepared for an inscription, but the inscriptions were added only after the stones were set in place in the wall.[25] Therefore, rather than the building stones themselves, the dedicatory formula most likely refers to a gift of sacrifices or money, or the equivalent of money, dedicated to the deity and eternalized with an inscription.[26] An offering, however, could be understood to equal the value of a stone and to thereby give the donor and his beneficiaries the "right of dedication" to a certain stone and the right to have an inscription commemorating the gift made on this stone.[27]

In return for the gift the worshipper requests that the deity may remember him positively. In 52 of the inscriptions a counter-gift of "good remembrance" (דכרן טב) is requested in return for the gift given.[28] The phrase "for good remembrance" or "to be remembered for good" is common in Semitic inscriptions and graffiti.[29] In sanctuary settings similar to what we have on Mount Gerizim, inscriptions containing a version of a remembrance formula have been found in Assur, Hatra, Jebel Ramm, Palmyra, Sumatar Harabesi and in a number of synagogue inscriptions as well.[30] The majority of these inscriptions date to the first

24. Naveh and Magen, "Aramaic and Hebrew Inscriptions," 13*–14*. Cf. H. Eshel, "Hellenism in the Land of Israel From the Fifth to the Second Centuries BCE in Light of Semitic Epigraphy," in *A Time of Change: Judah and Its Neighbours in the Persian and Early Hellenistic Periods* (ed. Y. Levin; LSTS 65; London: T&T Clark International, 2007), 16–124. But see the critique of this interpretation in Magen, Misgav and Tsfania, *Inscriptions*, 17–18.

25. Naveh and Magen, "Aramaic and Hebrew Inscriptions," 10*; Magen, Misgav and Tsfania, *Inscriptions*, 14–16.

26. Magen, Misgav and Tsfania, *Inscriptions*, 17–18.

27. Such a practice would to some extent mirror the practice of redemption in Lev 27, where dedications of land and sacrifices are given an "exchange value."

28. Nos. 147–98; Magen, Misgav and Tsfania, *Inscriptions*, 137–71. The fragmentary nature of many of the inscriptions renders it impossible to know whether the actual number of inscriptions containing the term "good remembrance" is in fact higher or lower than 52.

29. John F. Healey, "'May He Be Remembered for Good': An Aramaic Formula," in *Targumic and Cognate Studies: Essays in Honour of Martin McNamara* (ed. K. J. Cathcart and M. Maher; JSOTSup 230; Sheffield: Sheffield Academic, 1996), 177–86; Magen, Misgav and Tsfania, *Inscriptions*, 18–19.

30. A majority of these can be found in *CIS* II. The "remembrance inscriptions" have not been treated extensively, but see Healey, "'May He Be Remembered for

and second centuries C.E. and B.C.E. The main difference between the Gerizim inscriptions and the other Semitic inscriptions containing a version of a remembrance formula is that the Gerizim inscriptions all contain a verb of dedication, referring to the offering made, which identifies them beyond doubt as dedicatory inscriptions. The vast majority of the other inscriptions merely contain an invocation, the names of worshippers and a request to be remembered for good.[31] However, in light of their sanctuary setting the case for interpreting them as dedicatory inscriptions appears very strong.[32]

If we look to the Hebrew Bible it is quite clear that to be remembered (for good) by YHWH is to be taken care of. This is expressed by the parallelism in Ps 8:5—"What is man that you remember (תזכרנו) him and mankind that you care (תפקדנו) for him?"—and by several narrative examples: YHWH *remembers* Noah in the ark and makes the waters withdraw in Gen 8:1, YHWH *remembers* the childless Rachel and opens her womb in Gen 30:22 and in 1 Sam 1:19 YHWH *remembers* Hannah and she conceives Samuel. As Brevard S. Childs puts it, "God's remembering has not only a psychological effect, but an ontological as well."[33] To be remembered by YHWH is thought to have a tangible beneficial effect for the one remembered. On the other hand, not to be remembered by YHWH is described as similar to death: "like the slain who lie in the grave, whom you do not remember anymore (לא זכרתם עוד)" (Ps 88:6).

The religious practice reflected in the inscriptions from Mount Gerizim is the practice of giving gifts to YHWH; worshippers came to the sanctuary on the mountain and offered sacrifices, money or other valuables and they and their gifts were commemorated with an inscription in the wall surrounding the sanctuary. This practice finds a mythological foundation in the narrative about the construction of the sanctuary in

Good,"' for an excellent introduction and discussion and W. Schottroff, *"Gedenken" im Alten Orient und im Alten Testament: Die Wurzel Zakar im Semitischen Sprachkreis* (WMANT 15; Neukirchen–Vluyn: Neukirchener Verlag, 1964), 58–89. See also Lidzbarski, *Handbuch*, 165–69. Naveh's article, "Graffiti and Dedications," *BASOR* 235 (1979): 27–30, is very brief but the author does mention several important aspects and occurrences of remembrance inscriptions.

31. Some of the inscribed dedicatory altars from Palmyra are an exception to this rule. See the following inscriptions in D. R. Hillers and L. Cussini, *Palmyrene Aramaic Texts* (Baltimore: The Johns Hopkins University Press, 1996), 0319; 0333; 0339; 0346; 0347; 0408; 0448; 0449; 0451; 0454; 1432; 1433; 1435; 1451; 1455; 1546; 1625; 1677; 1680; 1681b; 1681c; 1694a; 1706; 1741; 1743; 1744a; 1744b; 1744c; 1917; 1918; 1919; 2752 and 2814.

32. Cf. Lidzbarski, *Handbuch*, 148.

33. B. S. Childs, *Memory and Tradition in Israel* (London: SCM, 1962), 33.

Exod 25 (cf. Exod 35), where YHWH commands the Israelites to bring gifts (תרומה) for the construction and furnishing of the desert tabernacle.[34]

Giving gifts to the gods in many ways resembles gift-giving between humans; the exchange of gifts is initiated in order to create a lasting and beneficent relationship between the two exchanging parties.[35] Gift-giving is an invested social act and it always entails the risk of being rejected. If the gift came with no obligation attached and therefore also with no risk, it would lose its social power and its ability to create bonds between people.[36] Accounts of failed sacrifices or gifts refused by the gods are rare, but when they do occur the consequences for the sacrificers are usually grave. One of the best-known examples of a rejected sacrifice is Cain's gift (מנחה) in Gen 4.[37] When offering a gift one offers a part of oneself in hope of friendship; rejection can be painful.[38]

A gift-giving relationship between a human being and a deity is clearly an asymmetrical relationship and thus there is no expectation of even a rough equivalence between the objects exchanged.[39] As Robert Parker aptly puts it, "Gods give to humans what they desperately need—health, property, life itself—whereas humans give to gods what they do not need and are not benefited by, a mere luxury as it were, marks of

34. Cf. 2 Kgs 12; 2 Chr 24 and Ezra 8. Magen, Misgav and Tsfania, *Inscriptions*, 17–18; M. Satlow, "Giving for a Return: Jewish Votive Offerings in Late Antiquity," in *Religion and the Self in Antiquity* (ed. D. Brakke, M. Satlow and S. Weitzman; Bloomington: Indiana University Press, 2005), 91–108 (96–97); S. Japhet, *I & II Chronicles: A Commentary* (Louisville, Ky.: Westminster John Knox, 1993), 841–45.

35. R. Osborne, "Hoards, Votives, Offerings: The Archaeology of the Dedicated Object," *World Archaeology* 36 (2004): 1–10 (3); F. Van Straten, "Gifts for the Gods," in *Faith, Hope and Worship: Aspects of Religious Mentality in the Ancient World* (ed. H. S. Versnel; Leiden: Brill, 1981), 65–151 (65, 76); J. Bodel, "'Sacred Dedications': A Problem of Definitions," in *Dediche Sacre Nel Mondo Greco-Romano: Diffusione, funzioni, tipologie* (ed. J. P. Bodel and M. Kajava; Acta Instituti Romani Finlandiae 35; Rome: Institutum Romanum Finlandiae, 2009), 17–30 (18); C. Grottanelli, "Do ut Des?," *Scienze Dell'antichità: Storia Archeologia Antropologia* 3–4 (1989–90): 45–54 (46).

36. P. Bourdieu, *The Logic of Practice* (trans. R. Nice; Cambridge: Polity, 1980), 99.

37. See F. S. Naiden, "Rejected Sacrifice in Greek and Hebrew Religion," *JANES* 6 (2006): 186–90. Cf. Grottanelli, "Do ut Des?," 53.

38. Grottanelli, "Do ut Des?," 46.

39. J. van Baal, "Offering, Sacrifice and Gift," *Numen* 23 (1976): 161–78 (164); J.-M. Bremer, "The Reciprocity of Giving and Thanksgiving in Greek Worship," in *Reciprocity in Ancient Greece* (ed. C. Gill, N. Postlethwaite and R. Seaford; Oxford: Oxford University Press, 1998), 127–37 (133).

honour."[40] The gods may appreciate and even desire the gifts and honour offered to them by humans, but they are not dependent on them. It is the difference between "need to have" and "nice to have."[41] Thus, the objective of giving gifts to the gods is to create a lasting relationship with the deity.[42] This goal is further supported by the materiality of durable votive objects, such as dedicatory inscriptions. By leaving an eternal memento of the act of giving, one creates a visible and tangible link with the deity. The dedicatory inscription converts the occasional sacrifice or gift into a permanent relationship.[43] The dedicatory inscription is intended to remind the deity of the gift given, but it also serves as a reminder of the worshipper himself and lends him a physical presence in the sanctuary, in the place where the deity is assumed to be residing.[44]

This practice corresponds well with the portrayal of YHWH's memory in the Hebrew Bible. YHWH's remembrance is described as being dependent on or at least affected by material mementos or memory aids. For example, in Gen 9 YHWH places his bow in the sky as a sign to remind himself of his covenant with Noah: "When the bow is in the clouds, I will see it and remember (לזכר) the everlasting covenant between God and every living creature of all flesh that is on the earth" (Gen 9:16). Similarly, in the Pentateuch a number of ritual acts and objects are said to serve as reminders (זכרן) of the Israelites before YHWH. This focus on remembrance particularly in the so-called priestly writings in the Pentateuch led Gerhard von Rad to propose that the purpose of the cult in the Hebrew Bible could be described simply as an

40. R. Parker, "Pleasing Thighs: Reciprocity in Greek Religion," in Gill, Postlethwaite and Seaford, eds., *Reciprocity in Ancient Greece*, 105–26 (122).

41. The misconception that the gods need and are dependent on sacrifices has been astutely treated in D. Ullucci, "The End of Animal Sacrifice" (Ph.D. diss., Brown University, 2009), 44–49.

42. Cf. Grottanelli, "Do ut Des?," 48.

43. M. Beard, "Writing and Religion: Ancient Literacy and the Function of the Written Word in Roman Religion," in *Literacy in the Roman World* (Journal of Roman Archaeology Supplementary Series 3; Ann Arbor, Mich.: Journal of Roman Archaeology, 1991), 35–58 (48); Satlow, "Giving for a Return," 94.

44. Cf. J. B. Connelly, "Standing Before One's God: Votive Sculpture and the Cypriot Religious Tradition," *BA* 52 (1989): 210–18 (211); C. Renfrew, *The Archaeology of Cult: The Sanctuary at Phylakopi* (London: Thames & Hudson, 1985), 23; J. N. Postgate, "Text and Figure in Ancient Mesopotamia: Match and Mismatch," in *The Ancient Mind: Elements of Cognitive Archaeology* (ed. C. Renfrew and E. B. W. Zubrow; Cambridge: Cambridge University Press, 1994), 176–84 (179–80); L. Dirven, "Aspects of Hatrene Religion: A Note on the Statues of Kings and Nobles from Hatra," in *The Variety of Local Religious Life in the Near East in the Hellenistic and Roman Periods* (ed. T. Kaizer; Leiden: Brill, 2008), 209–46 (245).

attempt to remind YHWH of the people of Israel: "Sucht man in der atl Kultsprache nach einer entsprechend allgemeinen Formel für die Bedeutung, die der Kultus für Israel hatte, so könnte man sagen, dass er Israel bei Jahweh ins Gedächtnis bringt."[45] This is the case in Num 10:10, for instance, towards the end of the passage giving the instructions for the manufacture of the two silver trumpets:

> Also on your days of rejoicing, at your appointed festivals and at the beginnings of your months, you shall blow the trumpets over your burnt offerings and over your sacrifices of well-being; they shall serve as a reminder (לזכרון) before your God: I am YHWH.

In the previous verse the same trumpets are to be sounded when the Israelites go to war, "so that you may be remembered (נזכרתם) before YHWH your God and be saved from your enemies." Other examples of a זכרן are the gemstones on Aaron's breastplate and the two stones on the ephod in Exod 28.[46] The stones on the shoulder pieces of the ephod, engraved with the names of the sons of Israel, are "stones of remembrance" (אבני זכרן) and "Aaron shall bear their names before YHWH on his two shoulders for remembrance (לזכרן)" (Exod 28:12; 39:7). Likewise, the twelve stones on the breastplate are each engraved with one of the names of the sons of Israel and they are to be "a continual (תמיד) remembrance (זכרן) before YHWH" (Exod 28:29). The engraved stones underline the high priest's cultic role as the representative of the entire people. As the only person able to enter the Holy of Holies, he brings the people of Israel to YHWH's attention by physically bringing a reminder of their existence into YHWH's presence.[47]

The relationship between remembrance and material objects has been described in helpful terms by the archaeologist Andrew Jones. Jones uses

45. G. von Rad, *Theologie des Alten Testaments*. Band 1, *Die Theologie der geschichtlichen Überlieferungen Israels* (Munich: Kaiser, 1957), 241. For an English translation, see G. von Rad, *Old Testament Theology*. Vol. 1, *The Theology of Israel's Historical Traditions* (trans. D. M. G. Stalker; Edinburgh: Oliver & Boyd, 1963), 243.

46. The exact character of the *ḥošen*, breastplate or breastpouch, is debated. See O. Keel, "Die Brusttasche des Hohenpriesters als Element priesterschriftlicher Theologie," in *Das Manna fällt auch heute noch: Beiträge zur Geschichte und Theologie des Alten, Ersten Testament. Festschrift für Erich Zenger* (ed. F. L. Hossfeld and L. Schwienhorst-Schönberger; Freiburg: Herder, 2004), 379–91. See also J. Milgrom, *Leviticus 1–16* (AB 3; New York: Doubleday, 1991), 501–13, on the priestly vestments.

47. Keel, "Brusttasche," 384. See F. H. Gorman Jr., *The Ideology of Ritual: Space, Time and Status in the Priestly Theology* (JSOTSup 91; Sheffield: Sheffield Academic, 1990).

the sign theory developed by C. S. Peirce to describe the relationship between material objects and memory. Material objects function as what Peirce calls "indexical signs" of past actions or events rather than mere external banks or deposits of memory.[48] The index "is a sign which refers to the object it denotes by being really affected by that object."[49] Thus, a rash is an indexical sign or index of measles, a weathervane is an index of the wind's direction and smoke is an index of fire.[50] The index does not equal what it signifies, but points to it. The material object serves as an index of the past and therefore it helps to invoke memory: "As material indices objects have the capacity to elicit remembrance. Remembrance is a process distributed between people and objects, and the process of evocation indexed by objects allows people to remember."[51]

In Jones's terminology the silver trumpets and the engraved stones index the Israelites: they point to them and thus help YHWH to remember them. Similarly, the dedicatory inscriptions from Mount Gerizim index their donors and remind YHWH of their gift and their worship. Just as the dedicatory inscription is placed in the wall surrounding the inner sanctuary in the immediate proximity of the deity, so is the worshipper by means of a proxy brought to the deity's attention and is therefore granted good remembrance "before the god in this place." The request of the worshipper to be remembered favourably by the deity is effected by the materiality of the dedicatory inscription.[52] The inscription's physical presence in the temple, in the place where the deity is thought to be, brings about the remembrance asked for in the text.

So far we have looked at dedicatory inscriptions as examples of what one could call "vertical communication": that is, communication with the

48. A. Jones, *Memory and Material Culture* (Cambridge: Cambridge University Press, 2007), 22–26; C. S. Peirce, *The Collected Papers of Charles Sanders Peirce* (ed. C. Hartshorne and P. Weiss; Cambridge, Mass.: Harvard University Press, 1960). Jones developed his theory partly as a critique of the psychologist M. Donald's concept of external symbolic storage, but see Donald's response in "Material Culture and Cognition: Concluding Thoughts," in *Cognition and Material Culture: The Archaeology of Symbolic Storage* (ed. C. Renfrew and C. Scarre; Cambridge: McDonald Institute for Archaeological Research, 1998), 181–87 (184).

49. J. Buchler, *The Philosophical Writings of Peirce* (New York: Dover, 1955), 102.

50. R. A. Rappaport, *Ritual and Religion in the Making of Humanity* (Cambridge: Cambridge University Press, 1999), 54–55; Jones, *Memory and Material Culture*, 23.

51. Jones, *Memory and Material Culture*, 26.

52. Cf. K. Dijkstra, *Life and Loyalty: A Study in the Socio-Religious Culture of Syria and Mesopotamia in the Graeco-Roman Period Based on Epigraphical Evidence* (Leiden: Brill, 1995), 289.

divine. But as has often been noted, there is also a powerful social component to giving gifts to the gods: that is, a form of "horizontal communication." By giving a gift to YHWH and having a memento of the gift put up in public—in the sanctuary, where other worshippers would pass by and see the inscription—the donor would gain prestige for himself and his family. This has been pointed out by, among others, Walter Burkert, who writes of the common custom in ancient Greek religion of putting gifts to the gods on display in the sanctuary: "With *anathémata*, giving to the gods is not so much giving away as setting up a monument of one's own action, thus perpetuating a claim to special relations with higher powers."[53]

However, the horizontal aspect of the practice of giving gifts to the gods should not be overemphasized at the expense of the vertical aspect. Votive objects and texts have often been interpreted as nothing but attempts by individuals to glorify themselves, but this, I believe, is missing the point of the practice. Although other humans witness the gift, this does not erase the importance of the divine recipient.[54] The donor of the dedicatory inscription is not the only one who is honoured when the inscription is put on display in the sanctuary. Ton Derks draws attention to another and generally more overlooked kind of prestige generated by votive practice, namely that which befalls the deity. The amount and lavishness of gifts given to a god testifies to his powers and portrays him as a responsive and potent patron.[55] A sanctuary laden with gifts serves as a recommendation for future worshippers: "a deity receiving many costly offerings is not only powerful, but apparently also lends a willing ear to people's needs."[56]

One could say, however, that votive practice as a form of gift-giving has multiple social goals: forming a lasting and beneficent social relation with the deity in the vertical plane while generating social prestige for the donor on the horizontal level.[57] The fact that votive practice produces

53. W. Burkert, "Offerings in Perspective: Surrender, Distribution, Exchange," in *Gifts to the Gods*: *Proceedings of the Uppsala Symposium 1985* (ed. T. Linders and L. Nordquist; Uppsala: Academia Ubsaliensis, 1987), 43–50 (49).

54. Cf. Dirven, "Aspects of Hatrene Religion," 232 with references; Satlow, "Giving for a Return," 91, 102.

55. T. Derks, *Gods, Temples and Ritual Practices: The Transformation of Religious Ideas and Values in Roman Gaul* (Amsterdam Archaeological Studies 2; Amsterdam: Amsterdam University Press, 1998), 217. Cf. T. Linders, "Gods, Gifts, Society," in Linders and Nordquist, eds., *Gifts to the Gods*, 115–22 (118).

56. Derks, *Gods, Temples and Ritual Practices*, 234.

57. The practice of giving gifts to the gods belongs to the mode of religion which Stanley K. Stowers has named "the religion of everyday social exchange." In this

social capital on both levels does not reduce the importance of either aspect of communication.

This leads us to a different use of Peirce's sign theory: the anthropologist Roy A. Rappaport uses Peirce's definition of indices and symbols to describe the two kinds of messages which are inherent to ritual actions.[58] According to Rappaport, a ritual consists of canonical messages and self-referential messages. The self-referential messages say something about the current state of the ritual participants, whereas the canonical messages are the liturgical order or worldview encoded in the ritual.[59] Rappaport likens the canonical messages to Peirce's symbols: the canonical messages relate to their content the same way a symbol relates to that which it signifies. The relationship between the two is purely arbitrary and is established only by law or convention. Self-referential messages, on the other hand, relate to their content the way an index relates to its object. As described above, this is a relationship in which the index is directly affected by or connected with its object.[60]

During the performance of a ritual, the ritual participant becomes an index of the abstract content of the canonical message. In the case of symbols it is usually the sign which is immaterial and the object that is material, as is the case in the relationship between the sign/word "table" and an actual table. In ritual, however, this relationship is inverted: the sign or index (the ritual participant) is material whereas the signified (the canonical message) is immaterial.[61]

According to Rappaport it is the combination of the canonical and self-referential messages which makes the ritual situation so unique. The

mode of religion, religious practices and ritual actions are social actions directed towards gods and other supernatural beings who are perceived as person-like agents and interested parties in a system of reciprocal exchange. See Stanley K. Stowers, "The Religion of Plant and Animal Offerings Versus the Religion of Meanings, Essences, and Textual Mysteries," in *Ancient Mediterranean Sacrifice: Images, Acts, Meanings* [ed. J. W. Knust and Z. Varhelyi; Oxford: Oxford University Press, 2011]), 35–56. Cf. Robert N. McCauley and E. Thomas Lawson's description of ritual acts as ordinary actions that manipulate entities (and situations) in a world entertained within a conceptual scheme that includes culturally postulated super-human agents (*Rethinking Religion: Connecting Cognition and Culture* [Cambridge: Cambridge University Press, 1990], 5–8).

58. Rappaport, *Ritual and Religion*. See also A. K. de H. Gudme, "How Should We Read Hebrew Bible Ritual Texts? A Ritualistic Reading of the Law of the Nazirite (Num 6:1–21)," *SJOT* 23 (2009): 64–84.

59. Rappaport, *Ritual and Religion*, 50–52.

60. Ibid., 4.

61. Ibid., 54–58.

self-referential messages add to the symbolically encoded canonical messages something which the canonical messages cannot express on their own. Likewise the self-referential messages are dependent on the canonical messages in order to be interpreted and understood. The abstract content of the canonical messages are realized when they are given a bodily sign in ritual.[62]

By participating in a ritual the ritual actor indicates (to himself and to anyone present) an acceptance of the world-view which is encoded in the ritual. An outward indication of acceptance, however, does not necessarily equal personal belief; it is possible for a person to disagree with the canonical message in a given ritual and still perform the ritual.[63] Thus while taking part in a ritual does not bring about acceptance of the ritual's worldview, any actions against the ritual order will be perceived as transgression because the ritual participant has seemingly submitted himself to the ritual order by participating in the ritual. Participation in a ritual does not guarantee that the ritual participant will behave in a certain way, but it does create a convention of how the ritual participant ought to behave.[64]

As long as a certain ritual is in use, the performance of this ritual creates and maintains conventions representative of the worldview of the ritual system to which the particular ritual belongs. To Rappaport this is the *metaperformativity* of ritual. Ritual is merely *performative* when it performs a conventional act—such as transforming a couple from an unmarried to a married state or a youth from child to adult—but ritual is *metaperformative* when at the same time it establishes and supports the conventions which are the basis of the conventional act.[65] If a certain ritual ceases to be performed it will no longer be able to generate the *metaperformativity* that keeps its worldview alive; this ritual's canonical messages will simply be forgotten and die out.[66]

Now, let us return to the dedicatory inscriptions from Mount Gerizim. It was argued above that the dedicatory inscription serves as a proxy for its donor as soon as it is put in place in the wall in the sanctuary.[67] The

62. Ibid., 31, 58.
63. Ibid., 119–20.
64. Ibid., 123.
65. Ibid., 278–80.
66. Ibid., 278.
67. Cf. Postgate, "Text and Figure in Ancient Mesopotamia," 179–80, and Renfrew, *Archaeology of Cult*, 23. See also K. Radner, *Die Macht des Namens: Altorientalische Strategien zur Selbsterhaltung* (Wiesbaden: Harrasowitz, 2005), 43–66, for a list of votive objects in Mesopotamian sanctuaries inscribed with the names of their donors.

inscription represents its donor and, according to Jones' use of Peirce's sign theory, it serves as an index of the donor and thus reminds the deity of his worshipper. If we follow Rappaport's use of Peirce, then the dedicatory inscription is still a proxy for its donor and as such the inscription becomes the self-referential message of the gift-giving ritual. In place of the worshipper himself, the inscription becomes an eternal presence in the sanctuary, an eternal index pointing to the canonical message of the ritual and a perpetual display of submission to the ritual's world-view. As a self-referential message the inscription would help to maintain the convention that it is good, meritorious and worthwhile to give gifts to YHWH, the god who listens and remembers. Through the metaperformativity of ritual the durability and tangibility of the dedicatory inscription helps to uphold the worldview of the ritual of giving gifts to YHWH. Long after the actual sacrifice or donation had been made, the dedicatory inscription stands as a testimony to ritual participation and acceptance of the worldview of Yahwistic worship. This works as a recommendation for other worshippers visiting the sanctuary to join in and follow the convention of giving gifts to YHWH. The metaperformativity of ritual functions as a self-sustainable engine: participation in the ritual reproduces and maintains the conventions inherent in the canonical messages which in turn inspire further participation.

To sum up, two directions of communication have been discussed above: communication with the divine on a vertical axis and communication with the surrounding society on a horizontal axis. To begin with the latter, the practice of giving gifts to the gods generates prestige for the donor on a horizontal level. Furthermore, the dedicatory inscription which serves as a proxy for the worshipper becomes the self-referential message of the ritual of gift-giving and thereby helps to maintain and re-create the worldview inherent in this ritual. Thus the dedicatory inscription becomes part of the perpetual-motion machine that is ritual's metaperformativity.

On the vertical axis, the dedicatory inscriptions communicate with the divine on a level that supersedes the mere textual level of the written message. By virtue of an inscription's physical presence before the deity, the inscription serves as an index which points to the votary and reminds the deity of his worshipper. In this way, the materiality of the dedicatory inscription brings about the good remembrance requested in the text and realizes the lasting relationship with the deity intended by the gift.

The Hermeneutics of Mesopotamian Extispicy: Theory vs. Practice

Nils P. Heeßel

Divination played an important role in Babylonian and Assyrian society.[1] In a world governed by divine powers whose decisions directly affected human life as well as determining their physical well-being, length of life and social status, reading the divine will and aligning one's actions with it was crucial for leading a full life. Thus it comes as no surprise that the means to beseech, address, contact and communicate with the gods have a prominent role in the surviving cuneiform texts.[2] Extispicy stands out among these means to interact with the divine sphere, as it enabled humankind to obtain a direct answer of the gods to a question about the outcome of a specific event, which has already begun in the present but whose end is in doubt. Extispicy thus represents real, two-way communication between humankind and the gods, not merely the one-sided contact like prayers and benedictions on the one hand or unprovoked signs

1. For general introductions to Mesopotamian divination, see S. M. Maul, "Omina und Orakel: A. Mesopotamien," in *Reallexikon der Assyriologie und Vorderasiatischen Archäologie*, vol. 10 (ed. D. O. Edzard; Berlin: de Gruyter, 2003–2005), 45–88, and F. Rochberg-Halton, *The Heavenly Writing: Divination, Horoscopy, and Astronomy in Mesopotamian Culture* (Cambridge: Cambridge University Press, 2005). U. Koch-Westenholz, *Babylonian Liver Omens: The Chapters* Manzāzu, Padānu *and* Pān Tākalti *of the Babylonian Extispicy Series Mainly from Aššurbanipal's Library* (Carsten Niebuhr Institute Publications 25; Copenhagen: Museum Tusculanum, 2000), 9–70, and N. P. Heeßel, *Divinatorische Texte II: Opferschau-Omina* (Keilschrifttexte aus Assur literarischen Inhalts 5; Wiesbaden: Harrassowitz, 2012), 1–15, offer overviews of extispicy in particular.

2. Of course we must be careful to avoid a hermeneutic circle. As an example: because we have many divinatory texts among the literary cuneiform texts we assume that divination played a crucial role in Mesopotamia, and because divination was so important in Mesopotamia many divinatory texts are to be expected among the literary texts. However, external evidence from letters, historical inscriptions, and administrative documents supports the conception of the prime importance of divination in general, and extispicy in particular, for Mesopotamian societies; see Maul, "Omina," 48–51, 75–76.

sent by the gods on the other. The possibility of receiving a divine reply to urgent questions explains the popularity of extispicy for commoners and kings alike. Not only would the desired answer reassure the people involved that they were acting in accordance with the divine will, for the king such a means of communication with the gods also offered the possibility of using the legitimizing power of a divine decision to shift the burden of responsibility for a human decision.

These divine messages, however, were not given in a clear, easily understandable way, but were embedded in the physical world. They remained, therefore, open to interpretation. In extispicy, the gods wrote their answers to human questions into the entrails of the sacrificial animal, especially the liver, which is accordingly called "the tablet of the gods." Over more than a millennium and a half, extispicy interpretation developed into a sophisticated system which produced an abundance of theoretical texts detailing ever greater interpretative intricacies. At the same time, the written reports of extispicies actually performed exhibit a remarkable conceptual stability.[3] The following contribution examines the different interpretative methods detailed in the theoretical texts and in the reports in order to assess how much the intellectual effort spent on the theoretical framework of extispical interpretation actually affected the practical way of interpreting extispicies in the first millennium B.C.E.

Extispicy in Mesopotamia

In an extispicy ritual a query was formulated and presented to the gods, after which specialists read the answer from the intestines of the sacrificial animal. The basis for this was the idea that the gods wrote their answer into the entrails of the sacrificial animal immediately before the slaughtering, under the aegis of Šamaš and Adad who were specifically connected with extispicy. The extispicy ritual was elaborate, starting at the end of one day and continuing over the course of the night, during which the *bārû*, "diviner," as the ritual specialist, had to recite prayers and to arrange several ritual settings.[4] At sunrise, the diviner slaughtered

3. I. Starr, "Extispicy Reports from the Old Babylonian and Sargonid Periods," in *Essays on the Ancient Near East in Memory of Jacob Joel Finkelstein* (ed. M. de Jong Ellis; Hamden, Conn.: Archon, 1977), 201–8.

4. For the process of the extispicy ritual, see P. Steinkeller, "Of Stars and Men: The Conceptual and Mythological Setup of Babylonian Extispicy," in *Biblical and Oriental Essays in Memory of William L. Moran* (ed. A. Gianto; BibOr 48; Rome: Pontifical Biblical Institute, 2005), 11–47, and J. C. Fincke, "Ist die mesopotamische Opferschau ein nächtliches Ritual?," *BiOr* 66 (2009): 520–77.

the sacrificial animal, took out the entrails and started the inspection.[5] By a careful examination of the lungs, intestines, heart, kidneys, bladder, pancreas, spleen and, above all, the liver of the sacrificial animal—which was most often a ram or lamb—the diviner was able to "read" the answer of the gods.[6] Not everyone, however, was qualified to become a diviner in Babylonia. According to Babylonian tradition, the gods Šamaš and Adad revealed the knowledge of extispicy to Enmeduranki, an antediluvian king of Sippar, who then taught citizens of different Mesopotamian cities.[7] According to the self-presentation of the scholars, only descendants of this king were qualified to become diviners and, among them, only those who were both physically and mentally without flaw. In reality, this was probably handled differently, with a father training his son in the profession and sharing his knowledge with "his son whom he loves." The knowledge of extispicy, in any event, was available only to a small group of scholars in possession of the exclusive prerogative of interpretation, who guarded the dissemination of this knowledge. A range of texts called explicitly *niṣirti bārûti*, "secret of extispicy," illustrates how jealously the diviners protected the knowledge of extispicy.[8] The exclusivity of the written knowledge is regularly stressed in extispicy compendia: "these are extraneous omens which not every diviner knows. The diviner as a father will preserve them for his favourite son, swear him and teach him."[9] Letters also indicate that people could not

5. For the sequence of entrails observed, see R. K. G. Temple, "An Anatomical Verification of the Reading of a Term in Extispicy," *JCS* 34 (1982): 19–27.

6. Ewes were used as sacrificial animals only very rarely. For the inspection of sacrificial birds, see J. Nougayrol, "'Oiseau' ou oiseau?," *RA* 61 (1967): 23–38. The Babylonian phraseology often uses words referring to writing to describe the interpretation of the animal's entrails; the liver, for example, is described as the "tablet of the gods."

7. W. G. Lambert, "The Qualifications of Babylonian Diviners," in *Festschrift für Rykle Borger zu seinem 65. Geburtstag am 24. Mai 1994:* tikip santakki mala bašmu... (ed. S. Maul; CM 10; Groningen: Styx, 1998), 141–58.

8. For these texts, see U. S. Koch, *Secrets of Extispicy: The Chapter Multābiltu of the Babylonian Extispicy Series and Niṣirti bārûti Texts Mainly from Aššurbanipal's Library* (AOAT 326; Münster: Ugarit-Verlag, 2005), 58–61. The so-called secrecy remark, comprehensively treated by A. Lenzi, *Secrecy and the Gods: Secret Knowledge in Ancient Mesopotamia and Biblical Israel* (SAAS 19; Helsinki: Helsinki University Press, 2008), was used by scholars of all fields for different texts, the connecting element of which is often hard to discern, and was not peculiar to extispicy texts.

9. VAT 9934 vi 61–63: *an-nu-tu*$_4$ BAR.MEŠ *šá* ^{l}]^{ú}ḪAL *mam-ma la* Z[U-*ú*] [^{lú}ḪAL AD *ana*] DUMU-*šú ša i-ra*[*m-mu i-na-aṣ-ṣa-ru*] «*ú*»-*tam-mu-ú ú-šáḫ-ḫa-za*. See Heeßel, *Divinatorische Texte II*, 42, 51, and Koch, *Secrets*, 544.

merely attempt to learn divinatory knowledge or use it for unsanctioned purposes.[10]

Extispicy compendia comprise a large part of the religious, divinatory, literary and scientific texts handed down over the centuries from the first half of the second millennium B.C.E. (the Old Babylonian period) onwards. These constitute what A. L. Oppenheim appropriately called the "stream of tradition."[11] In the compendia, omens concerning specific parts of the liver or the lung or concerning one of the other organs were gathered together. In the second half of the second millennium, when the compendia were standardized and started to become serialized, new types of compendia began to appear addressing the hermeneutic principles of extispicy: explaining difficult signs or illuminating the way towards a more sophisticated interpretation of extispical signs. Part of these texts were serialized in the series *multābiltu* and incorporated as the tenth and last chapter into the *bārûtu*-series, which comprised ten chapters with 100 tablets on almost all aspects of extispicy. In addition to texts collected in the *multābiltu*-series, a great number of different texts, with and without specific titles, contain rules of interpretation for difficult omens, the "stipulated term," and the "joker" signs *nipḫu* and *pitruštu*.[12]

10. For a letter denouncing someone who bought a scholar as a slave and had him teach his son, see SAA 16 65, with comment in M. Luukko and G. Van Buylaere, *The Political Correspondence of Esarhaddon* (SAA 16; Helsinki: Helsinki University Press, 2002), xxxv–xxxvi; S. Parpola, "A Man Without a Scribe," in Ana šadî Labnāni lū allik*: Beiträge zu altorientalischen und mittelmeerischen Kulturen: Festschrift für Wolfgang Röllig* (ed. B. Pongratz-Leisten et al.; AOAT 247: Neukirchen–Vluyn: Neukirchener Verlag, 1997), 321; B. Pongratz-Leisten, *Herrschaftswissen in Mesopotamien: Formen der Kommunikation zwischen Gott und König im 2. und 1. Jahrtausend v. Chr* (SAAS 10; Helsinki: Neo-Assyrian Text Corpus Project, 1999), 298. For the case of a conspirator against the Assyrian king trying to make a diviner drunk in order to persuade him to perform extispicies regarding the success of the rebellion, see M. Nissinen, *References to Prophecy in Neo-Assyrian Sources* (SAAS 7; Helsinki: Neo-Assyrian Text Corpus Project, 1998), 107–53; compare E. Frahm, "Hochverrat in Assur," in *Assur-Forschungen: Arbeiten aus der Forschungsstelle "Edition literarischer Keilschrifttexte aus Assur" der Heidelberger Akademie der Wissenschaften* (ed. S. M. Maul and N. P. Heeßel; Wiesbaden: Harrassowitz, 2010), 89–137, here 121, nn. 110, 132.

11. A. L. Oppenheim, *Ancient Mesopotamia: Portrait of a Dead Civilization* (rev. ed.; Chicago: University of Chicago Press, 1996), 13.

12. These texts have been edited together with the *multābiltu* series in Koch, *Secrets*.

Rules and Conventions of Interpretation

The hermeneutics of extispicy concern the question of how a sign—a single observation on the liver, lung, or another part of the entrails—was considered to be favourable or unfavourable and how multiple different signs were interpreted and weighted to reach a final answer to the original query, in the form of "yes" or "no." Any deviation of the normal, healthy part of the entrails under inspection was evaluated according to the way it affected the normal features of the given organ and according to its exact location, size, extension, direction, colour, general texture and any other possible alteration.

That the liver is the most important organ for extispicy is no coincidence, since diet and living conditions as well as diseases alter the appearance of the liver so that every liver is unique. It exhibits a richly structured surface with anatomical parts including grooves and elevations, the gall bladder and the portal vein, all the alterations of which are meticulously observed during extispicy. The Akkadian designations of these parts refer to the different areas of interpretation of the observed signs and also had symbolic value. Thus a groove with the name "presence" refers to the presence of the gods in this extispicy (whether or not the extispical query was answered by the gods), while the umbilical fissure named "palace gate" refers to events and income of the palace; the groove "path" refers to campaigns and expeditions and the area called "throne dais" to the king's private life, his court and the stability of the dynasty. For example, the appearance of a marking which looked like a corn (a lymph node or a nodule resulting from paratyphoid fever) at the top of the groove "presence" was seen as a sign that the gods requested some benediction from the ruling prince which, if given, would grant him long life.[13] Such an ominous sign is noted in the extispicy compendia as the connection of an observation and its corresponding interpretation, a protasis–apodosis relationship: "If a corn lies at the top of the 'presence': A request of the gods to the prince, the days of the price will be long."[14] The apodoses were linked with the protases on the basis of principles including association of ideas, contrast or

13. R. Leiderer, *Anatomie der Schafsleber im babylonischen Leberorakel: Eine makroskopisch-analytische Studie* (Munich: Zuckschwerdt, 1990), 27, sees the *erištu* mark as a lymph node; according to J.-W. Meyer, *Untersuchungen zu den Tonlebermodellen aus dem Alten Orient* (AOAT 39; Neukirchen–Vluyn: Neukirchener Verlag, 1987), 77, it represents a nodule resulting from paratyphoid fever.

14. The protasis and apodosis are connected here by the homophony of the word *erištu*(*m*), which designates a corn as well as a request.

paronomasia.[15] The omen just cited is a nice example of the latter. Yet an important issue that suggests itself at this point has not yet been sufficiently resolved, namely, why the observation should be connected with an often lengthy apodosis, if—as we shall see below—the question of whether the sign is favourable or unfavourable is the only thing that ultimately mattered. This problem has been discussed but not yet convincingly explained.[16]

In addition to anatomical markings on the liver's surface, additional markings appearing as a result of diseases, worms, parasites or the like could also be observed. These irregular markings, called "fortuitous marks" by Jean Nougayrol, may be "holes," "notches," weapon-shaped or foot-shaped protrusions of flesh, "crosses," "corns" (discussed above) and others besides.[17] Their exact position, orientation, colour and texture were all interpreted; some signs could not only add one positive or negative value to the overall result of the extispicy, but could change the whole outcome. In this category belong, in particular, the "joker" signs *pitruštu* and *niphu*. In this manner Babylonian diviners added layer upon layer of interpretation, with each layer judged for its effect on the preceding layers of interpretation. In the following subsections these different layers of interpretation will be presented in more detail.

Simple Binary Differentiation

Many descriptions of the appearance of a part of the liver or lung are based on binary differentiation. This is particularly evident in the distinction of the light or dark appearance of a part of an organ; this does not refer to colour but, according to Ulla Jeyes, describes "the bright, light reflecting, bouncy look of a healthy organ" on the one hand, and the

15. I. Starr, *The Rituals of the Diviner* (Bibliotheca Mesopotamica 12; Malibu, Calif.: Undena, 1983), 9–12.

16. For different explanations, see Oppenheim, *Ancient Mesopotamia*, 214; J. Nougayrol, "Trente ans de recherches sur la divination babylonienne (1935–1965)," in *La Divination en Mésopotamie ancienne, et dans les Régions voisines, XIVe RAI (Strasbourg, 2–6 juillet 1965)* (Paris: Presses Universitaires de France, 1966), 5–19, here 13–14; Starr, *Rituals*, 12–14.

17. J. Nougayrol, "Textes hépatoscopiques d'époque ancienne conservés au musée du Louvre (II)," *RA* 40 (1945–46): 59–97, here 70, lists *kakku* ("weapon"-mark), *šēpu* ("foot"-mark), *šīlum* ("hole"), *piṭrum* ("notch") as "fortuitous" marks, citing Rm. 130, for which see now Koch, *Secrets*, 381–91, text 58.

Multābiltu tablet 2/3, entry 44 (Koch, *Secrets*, 114), cited by U. Jeyes, *Old Babylonian Extispicy: Omen Texts in the British Museum* (Istanbul: Nederlands Historisch-Archaeologisch Instituut te Istanbul, 1989), 81, lists ^{giš}TUKUL GÌR BÙR DU8 KAM-*tu4* BAR-*tu4* *kak-su-ú* KAR-*tu4* *ni-ip-ḫ[u]* "weapon-mark, foot-mark, hole, notch, corn, cross, arrow-head, hidden part and *niphu*."

"dull flabby look of unhealthy meat" on the other.[18] The light appearance of a part of the liver is considered favourable, the dark unfavourable.

Another example of such a pair is the distinction of "curved" (*kapāṣu*) and "flat" (*naparqudu*). These observations appear regularly with specific organs and certain parts of the sacrificial sheep, such as the breast-bone and the lung or the "dyeing vat" and the "finger" of the liver. Since "curved" is consistently seen as a favourable sign and "flat" as an unfavourable one, it may be assumed that this verbal pair is used especially with curved, round organs, with "curved" describing the normal state and "flat" describing the deviation.[19]

These simple binary differentiations correspond to the most fundamental, axiomatic beliefs of Babylonian society: normal is superior to abnormal, light to dark, firm to weak, etc.[20] The first tablet of the chapter *multābiltu* of the *bārûtu*-series makes these basic assumptions explicit, listing the pairs and citing an omen for each as an example:

> Length (means) success (as in:) If the "presence" is long and reaches the "path": The prince will have success on the campaign.
> Excessive growth (means) fame (as in:) If there is one rib too many on the right side of the rib-cage: My army will win fame.
> Width (means) excellence (as in:) If the top of the right vertebra is as wide as a fetlock: Weapon of Sargon, the king's army will be strong and have no rival.[21]

Additional Binary Differentiation: Right and Left

Another basic rule of interpretation is binary differentiation between right and left. Any alteration of the normal appearance of a part of the liver could be further differentiated depending whether it appeared on the right or left side. The right side corresponded to the client of the extispicy, the left to his adversary, as is sometimes made explicit in extispicy texts: "The right median area pertains to me, the left to the enemy."[22] So the right side was favourable for the client, while the left side was favourable for the enemy and therefore unfavourable for the client. For example:

18. Jeyes, *Extispicy*, 154.

19. For the interpretation of the verbal pair *kapāṣu–naparqudu* ("being curved"–"lying flat"), see Starr, *Rituals*, 22–24. Starr discusses this pattern in connection with left and right, but the paradigm also holds true in general, as may be deduced from omens such as: "If the breast-bone is completely curved: The prince will enjoy shares of booty wherever he goes. If the breast-bone lies completely flat: The enemy will defeat me in a single battle." See Heeßel, *Opferschau-Omina*, no. 1 i 18–19.

20. On this point, see Starr, *Rituals*, 15–16.

21. Cited from Koch, *Secrets*, 90–92 (text 2, entry 1, 5 and 9).

22. This appears again in *multābiltu* tablet 2/3, entry 44 (ibid., 114).

> If the right side of the path "stands up": The gods will come to the aid of my army.
> If the left side of the path "stands up": The gods will come to the aid of the enemy army.[23]

However, when combined with a "fortuitous" mark which was considered to have a negative value, this basic rule is modified:

> If a hole is placed on the right side of the "Strength": Defeat of the army.
> If a hole is placed on the left side of the "Strength": Defeat of the enemy army.[24]

A hole on the right side is unfavourable for the client of the extispicy; a hole on the left side is favourable for him, as the hole in itself is a negative sign. Such a negative sign on the right side, which pertains to the client, means something unfavourable to him; placed on the left side it points to something unfavourable to his adversary. Thus, a negative sign on the left, negative side is considered a favourable omen for the client, as two negative signs cancel each other and become positive: a negative sign that befalls the adversary is favourable for the client.[25]

Subdivision of Parts of the Liver or Lungs and the Zones of the Liver
The different anatomical parts of the liver or the lungs may be divided again, most often into "top," "middle," and "base." The location or direction of any given deviation or fortuitous mark may therefore be described in a more exact way. By combing the top, middle, and base with the left side, centre, and right side of a given feature, nine fields were created on and around a given part of the liver, with each field having its own positive or negative value.[26] For the groove "presence," one of the most important parts of the liver, this may be summarized as follows:[27]

23. VAT 9934 i 67–68, edited by Heeßel, *Opferschau-Omina*, 44, no. 1 i 67–68. See the commentary in Koch-Westenholz, *Babylonian Liver Omens*, 238, 42/63–64 and further duplicates cited there.

24. Koch-Westenholz, *Babylonian Liver Omens*, 325, 59/107–8.

25. Compare, for example, Koch-Westenholz, *Babylonian Liver Omens*, 339, 62/87–88: "If the right 'Door Jamb of the Palace Gate' is notched: Escape of a slave. If the left 'Door Jamb of the Palace Gate' is notched: The slave who runs away will return." In the last omen the negative left side and the negative notch offset each other, akin to the mathematical rule in which the multiplication of two negative numbers results in a positive number.

26. For the sub-divisions of the parts of the liver and the lungs as well as their pathological alterations, see generally Meyer, *Tonlebermodellen*, 56–177, and Koch-Westenholz, *Babylonian Liver Omens*, 46–70.

27. For the values of the subdivisions, see Meyer, *Tonlebermodellen*, 94, and Koch-Westenholz, *Babylonian Liver Omens*, 53.

Left	the Presence	Right	
–	+	+	Base
+	+	–	Middle
–	+	+	Top

For example, a hole situated on the left side of the base of the "presence" was a favourable sign, as the two negative connotations—the hole itself and its location on the left side of the base of the "presence"—cancelled each other.[28] The same hole appearing on the right side of the base or on the left middle part of the "presence" led to an unfavourable sign.

Subdivision of this kind, however, did not stop with the subdivision of the parts of the liver and the lungs. As illustrated by so-called orientation tablets and also by a Neo-Babylonian liver model, the whole surface of the liver was further divided into small squares, or zones. Each of these was designated "right" or "left," which indicated how this zone affected the interpretation of a marking placed therein. As noted by Ulla Jeyes, this refinement, although clearly aimed at clarifying the problem of the exact location of signs, created new risks of misinterpretation, as the more subsections there were, the higher was the chance that a marking might be situated directly on a borderline.[29]

Double-encoded Markings and More Sophisticated Differentiation

Not only does the right/left-dichotomy become more and more sophisticated on an interpretative level through the subdivision of the surfaces of liver and lung, the deviations and markings appearing in these zones may also be variably assessed. While "fortuitous marks" like "holes," "notches," and "crosses" bear a certain negative or positive value in general, this could be modified by additional observations like size, colour, texture, and the like. A "corn" (*erištu*) mark, for example, is generally a positive sign, but if it is of unusual size, either very small or very big, it is considered negative; a pustule (*ziḫḫu*) is favourable if it is soft, but unfavourable if it is hard.[30] However, not all observations are considered to have a value which in itself changes the interpretation. Certain colour

28. Koch-Westenholz, *Babylonian Liver Omens*, 108, omen 36: "If a hole lies in the left base of the 'presence': Fall of the evil and the e[nemy]."

29. U. Jeyes, "Divination as a Science in Ancient Mesopotamia," *JEOL* 32 (1991–92): 23–41, here 35.

30. Koch-Westenholz, *Babylonian Liver Omens*, 48. For the interpretation of this, called *ziḫḫu* in Akkadian, as the larva of *taenia hydatigena*, see Leiderer, *Anatomie*. However, R. Biggs, "*Qutnu*, *maṣraḫu* and Related Terms in Extispicy," *RA* 63 (1969): 159–67, here 163 n. 1, interprets it as "cysts which occur in the liver and lungs of sheep in hyatid disease."

changes, like red or black, are considered to have negative value but reinforce a negative outcome rather than changing it:

> If a pustule lies in the normal place of the "Well-Being": Defeat of the army.
> If a pustule lies in the normal place of the "Well-Being" and it is red: Defeat of the army. Wailing will come to the land of the prince.[31]

Here, the fact that the pustule is red does not change a negative omen, but leads to an extension of the apodosis.[32] That colour can change an omen is also indicated by other examples:

> If a hole lies in the normal position of the "Well-Being": Someone who is ill in a man's household will get worse and die.
> If a hole lies in the normal position of the "Well-Being" and its centre is white: Someone who is ill in a man's household will get worse but will recover.[33]

Special Signs: niphu *and* pitruštu

To complicate things even further, some signs were considered so powerful that they affected the interpretation of the whole extispicy. As these signs, called *nipḫu* and *pitruštu* in Akkadian, had the force to change the result of an extispicy into the opposite, they are sometimes characterized as "joker signs."[34] The interpretation of these signs plays a major role in the chapter *multābiltu* of the *bārûtu*-series and the *niṣirti bārûti* texts, allowing us to discern their interpretative value clearly. The texts are explicit about the joker effect of the signs; compare, for example, the note on a list:

> *Nipḫu* and *pitruštu*, such as could be present in your extispicy, are listed. Should in your favourable extispicy one ominous feature among these (listed here) occur for you, this extispicy is not favourable.[35]

However, there are certain differences between the two signs. The appearance of a single *nipḫu* has the "joker" effect: "If you perform an extispicy and in a favourable extispicy there is one *nipḫu* it is unfavourable, in an unfavourable extispicy it is favourable."[36] Two *nipḫu* signs in

31. Koch-Westenholz, *Babylonian Liver Omens*, 348, 64/49–50. Note that "defeat of the army" is missed out in the translation of 64/50.

32. Similar observations can be made on quite a number of texts; compare, for example, A 8 (Heeßel, *Opferschau-Omina*, no. 37) rev. 40–43.

33. Koch-Westenholz, *Babylonian Liver Omens*, 349, 64/58–59 and duplicates.

34. For *nipḫu* and *pitruštu*, see Koch, *Secrets*, 10–21.

35. Koch, *Secrets*, 125, 3/123.

36. Ibid., 129, 3/157, and 140, 4/A 19′.

an extispicy had no effect, but three or more *nipḫu* signs reinstated the joker effect. A *pitruštu*, on the other hand, had the power to decide the final outcome of an extispicy: one *pitruštu*-sign in an extispicy was considered positive but still had to be checked and could turn the outcome upside-down; two generally led to a favourable result and more than two to an unfavourable one. The combination of *nipḫu* and *pitruštu* signs led to unequivocal results.[37]

In addition, there existed special *nipḫu*-signs called "seven weapons, five holes, three notches." The appearance of these signs—either seven weapons, five holes or three notches—overruled all other signs. These special *nipḫu* signs were interpreted differently than the normal *nipḫu* signs, as they were considered to have a joker effect no matter whether they appeared once or twice.

The Time Component

A very important aspect of any extispicy is the time component. This applies not only to the observance of auspicious days for performing the extispicy ritual, but especially to the limited time period for which an extispicy result was considered valid.[38] This "stipulated term" (*adannu*) seldom exceeded a year and was most often only four to eight months. This means that extispicy results were not considered to reveal everlasting, unchangeable predictions about the future but to inform the inquirer regarding the outcome of developments which already have begun in the present. The "stipulated term," according to extispicy compendia, was calculated with a specific formula based on the *uddazallû*, the "constant correction," and the appearance of specific marks on the *processes caudatus* of the liver, called the "finger" in Akkadian.[39]

37. Ibid., 20.

38. Hemerological texts detail exactly which days are auspicious or inauspicious for the performing of an extispicy. Jeyes, "Divination as a Science," 30–32; A. Livingstone, "The Case of the Hemerologies: Official Cult, Learned Formulation and Popular Practice," in *Official Cult and Popular Religion in the Ancient Near East* (ed. E. Matsushima; Heidelberg: Winter, 1993), 97–113, here 109–10; A. Livingstone, "New Dimensions in the Study of Assyrian Religion," in *Assyria 1995: Proceedings of the 10th Anniversary Symposium of the Neo-Assyrian Text Corpus Project Helsinki, September 7–11, 1995* (ed. S. Parpola and R. M. Whiting; Helsinki: Helsinki University Press, 1997), 165–77, here 174 and fig. 4; and Pongratz-Leisten, *Herrschaftswissen*, 172–75, on the basis of dated Neo-Assyrian extispicy reports, have shown that these auspicious days were generally observed.

39. N. P. Heeßel, "The Calculation of the Stipulated Term in Extispicy," in *Divination and Interpretation of Signs in the Ancient World* (ed. A. Annus; Oriental Institute Seminars 6; Chicago: Oriental Institute of the University of Chicago, 2010), 163–75.

The Practical Side: Interpreting Extispicies in Reports

Apart from the many extispicy compendia collecting observations of special parts of the liver, the lung or other parts of the entrails, mostly following the omen structure of protasis and apodosis and partly collected in the large series *bārûtu*, there are also texts reflecting the practical side of the extispicy ritual, such as reports and queries. Extispicy reports, attested from the early second millennium until the middle of the first millennium, state the question laid before the gods and detail the results of a specific extispicy.[40] They are crucial to understanding the way extispicies were carried out in practice.

While the hermeneutics of Old Babylonian extispicy reports have been the object of several studies, the extispicy reports from the time of Assurbanipal have not been studied in detail for their relationship to the extispicy compendia of that time.[41]

Unfortunately, only a few of the known extispicy reports from Nineveh are completely preserved such that they can be analyzed in detail. Here, three reports are studied for the way the observations are expounded to achieve a result. The reports are not cited in their entirety, but only in those parts containing the documentation of the extispical observations.

Report 1 (K 159; PRT 105; SAA 4 280)

This is an extispicy concerning the question whether Nabû-bēl-šumāti from the Sea Lands (in the south of Babylonia) will join the war against

40. The extispicy queries, only documented in Neo-Assyrian times, differ from the reports in that they follow distinct formulas and emphasize not the result of the extispicy but the query. In particular they seek to eliminate misunderstanding and ritual failure by including a lengthy formula where each sentence starts with the word *ezib*, "disregard (that)," which aims at ruling out specific mishaps and other problems posing a threat to the ritual from the start. See for this I. Starr, *Queries to the Sungod: Divination and Politics in Sargonid Assyria* (SAA 4; Helsinki: Helsinki University Press, 1990), xiii–xxviii, and J. Aro, "Remarks on the Practice of Extispicy in the Time of Esarhaddon and Assurbanipal," in *La Divination en Mésopotamie ancienne, et dans les Régions voisines, XIVe RAI (Strasbourg, 2–6 juillet 1965)* (Paris: Presses Universitaires de France 1966), 109–17.

41. I. Starr, "In Search of Principles of Prognostication in Extispicy," *HUCA* 45 (1974): 17–23, and *Rituals*, 110–19; and T. Richter, "Untersuchungen zum Opferschauwesen III: Drei übersehene Opferschauprotokolle aus altbabylonischer Zeit," in *Munuscula Mesopotamica: Festschrift für Johannes Renger* (ed. B. Böck, E. Cancik-Kirschbaum and T. Richter; AOAT 267; Münster: Ugarit-Verlag, 1999), 399–414, here 399. The extispicy reports from the time of Assurbanipal were first edited by E. G. Klauber, *Politisch-religiöse Texte aus der Sargonidenzeit* (Leipzig: Pfeiffer, 1913). A new edition was published by I. Starr as SAA 4, and Aro, "Remarks," has analyzed the similarities and differences of the reports and queries.

Assyria and is dated to January 4, 651; the extispicy was performed by *Aššur-daᵓᵓin-šarru* and *Dannaia*:

1. If the "presence" is there. If there are two "paths," the left path is located above the right "path":
2. The enemy's weapons will prevail over the prince's weapons.
3. If the "strength" is not there: It is a *nipḫu*-sign.
4. If there is a hole in the right side of the "presence": Fall of the army.
5. Secondly, "presence" means shrine and dais.
6. If the left of the gall bladder is attached: Your expedition force is the slayer of the enemy.
7. The "finger" and "increment" are sound.
8. If the back of the lung is smashed on the right side: Defeat,
9. change of mood of my army.
10. The upper part is elevated.
11. The "outside" rides upon the "cap." The base of the middle "finger" of the lung is "loose."[42]
12. The "breast-bone" is thick. The coils of the colon are 14 in number.
13. The heart of the ram is sound.

---

14. The "paths" are two, the left "path" is located above the right "path."
15. The "strength" is not there. There is a hole in the right side of the "presence."
16. The back of the lung is smashed on the right side.
17. The "outside" rides upon the "cap."
18. There are five unfavourable omens in the extispicy.
19. There are no favourable omens.
20. It (= the extispicy) is unfavourable.

This report is a fine example of the way in which the extispicy result was presented in the Neo-Assyrian period: first, the observations made in the inspection of specific parts of the entrails of the sacrificial sheep are described. A deviation from the normal is described in omen format, that is, with an apodosis attached to the observation. After a division mark, the unfavourable omens are listed and counted and the outcome of the extispicy is stated.

However, it is surprising to find the explicit statement in line 19 that "There are no favourable omens," even though line 6 contains one such favourable sign (made clear by attached apodosis "Your expedition force is the slayer of the enemy"). Has this omen been simply overlooked or, if not, on what theoretical assumptions is it disregarded? Furthermore, it is noticeable that in line 3 the apodosis notes a *nipḫu*-sign, which is simply

42. The conventional translation of the verb *uššuru*, written with the logogram BAR.

counted as an unfavourable omen in the list in line 15. It is not regarded as the "joker" sign in this report as it is in the theoretical extispicy compendia.

Report 2 (K 4; PRT 109; SAA 4 282)
This is an extispicy concerning the question whether Šamaš-šumu-ukīn, king of Babylon and treacherous brother of Aššurbanipal, is fleeing to Elam; it is dated to July 15, 651 and was performed by *Dāri-šarru* and *Dannaia*:

1. [If the base of the "presence"] is sunken. The "path" is there.
2. [If...] is there. The left of the gall bladder is attached.
3. [If in the t]op of the left surface of the "finger" a "weapon-mark" is placed and
4. it faces [the top] of the "finger": Successful attack of the enemy.
5. [If abo]ve the "increment" a "weapon-mark" is placed and it rises from left
6. to right: My army will consume the spoil of the enemy.
7. If the "mass" rides upon the left of the gall bladder: The mass of the enemy's army (will march) against my country.
8. If the upper part is elevated.
9. If the "outside" rides upon the "cap."
10. If in the left side of the lung there is a "foot-mark." The top of the breastbone is notched.
11. If the coils of the colon are 14 in number. The heart of the ram is sound.

---

12. If the base of the "presence" is sunken. In the top of the left surface of the "finger"
13. a "weapon-mark" is placed and it faces the top of the "finger."
14. If the "mass" rides upon the left of the gall bladder.
15. If in the left side of the lung there is a "foot-mark." The top of the breastbone is notched.
16. If there is a hole in the wide part of the left side of the "finger" at the side of the middle surface of the "finger."
17. There are five unfavourable omens in the extispicy.

It is noticeable that some careless counting has been done in this extispicy report. In line 10′ (not cited), four negative omens are counted instead of the five omens noted here in line 17. In fact, there are six unfavourable omens in the extispicy, because lines 8 and 15 each contain two. The omen in line 8, clearly negative, is not listed in the list of unfavourable omens, and the omen listed there in line 16 does not appear in the proper report.[43] This last-mentioned omen, at least, might be

43. On this point, see Starr, *Queries*, 265, in the commentary to lines 12–17.

explained as an additional observation, as sometimes another diviner would add omens overlooked in the first examination.[44]

Report 3 (K 102; PRT 106; SAA 4 317)

This is an extispicy concerning the well-being of Aššurbanipal, dated to February 26, 651 and performed by *Marduk-šumu-uṣur*, *Dāri-šarru* and *Sîn-šarru-ibni*:

1. If the "presence" is there. There are two "paths" and they lie separately:
2. Change of mood, change of mood. The campaign you have planned
3. will fail but you will go on another. In council the plan of kings
4. will fail but they will conceive others.
5. If you perform the extispicy for the practice of medicine: The physician shall not
6. touch the patient, the diviner shall not make a prediction,
7. a deceitful *nipḫu*.
8. If a bifurcation in its middle points to the gall bladder. If the "well being" is like the cuneiform sign ḪA: Deprivation.
9. If the "path" on the left of the gall bladder and the "base of the throne" are there. The "increment" is sound.
10. If the "mass" rides upon the left of the gall bladder: The mass of the enemy's army (will march) against my country.
11. If the upper part extends beyond the surface of the right lung. The coils of the colon are 16 in number
12. and they are of equal height.
13. If the base of the middle "finger" of the lung is "loose." If the top of the breastbone is notched in the centre and its left side lies flat:
14. abandonment of a city. For warfare: Downfall of a well-known person.
15. If the vertebrae are visible: a *nanmurtu*-occurrence.

---

16. There are five unfavourable omens.

This report leaves out the explicit list of unfavourable omens and merely counts them in line 16. Among these five unfavourable omens are two whose value is interesting: the omen with the long, detailed apodosis cited in lines 1–7 is said to be a "deceitful *nipḫu*" (*nipḫu tasrirru*), which, akin to the *nipḫu* sign in report 1 (SAA 4 280) line 3, is simply counted as one negative sign without any "joker" effect. Also notable is that the "*nanmurtu*-occurrence" in line 15 is also considered a negative

44. See SAA 4 308 5′–7′: "When Dannaya checked his extispicy with him, they added two unfavourable omens."

sign, in contrast to the theoretical texts where it is seen as a sign for an indecisive feature.[45]

Hermeneutic Principles of the Neo-Assyrian Extispicy Reports

As was long ago noted, the extispicy reports from seventh-century Nineveh are compendia-orientated.[46] While normal observations and those without consequence for the result are simply stated, the observations relevant for the result of the extispicy are often cited as omens, that is, complete with protasis and apodosis. It can be shown that these omens, thus stated, are identical with the omens collected in the extispicy series *bārûtu* and that basic hermeneutic principles govern the compendia and reports alike. Contrary to earlier reports, therefore, this practice of citing omens from the compendia indicates that the reports from Nineveh are connected both to the extispicy compendia in general and to the series *bārûtu* in particular.

Furthermore, the earlier suggestion about the way diviners achieved an overall result from different observations is confirmed, namely, that the majority of favourable or unfavourable signs is decisive. The reports explicitly state the number of negative signs in the extispicy, leading to a negative result. As has been demonstrated already by Starr, the simple counting of favourable and unfavourable signs is made explicit in a passage in one of the tablets of the *multābiltu* chapter of the series *bārûtu*:

> When you perform an extispicy and its good signs are many, its bad signs are few: That extispicy is favourable.
> When you perform an extispicy and its bad signs are many, its good signs are few: That extispicy is unfavourable.[47]

It is interesting to note that the first of these two observations is explicitly cited in one report—unfortunately in a broken passage which does not allow an interpretation of the reasons for this citation.[48] That such a citation is not an exception is illustrated by another fragmentarily preserved citation from the chapter *multābiltu* in the reports.[49]

45. The exact interpretation of *nanmurtu* is still a matter of debate, see T. Richter, "Untersuchungen zum Opferschauwesen I: Überlegungen zur Rekonstruktion der altbabylonischen *bārûtum*-Serie," *Or* 62 (1993): 121–24.

46. Aro, "Remarks," 110.

47. Cited from *multābiltu* tablet 2/3; see Koch, *Secrets*, 127–28 no. 3, omens 145–46.

48. SAA 4 288 rev. 5′–6′.

49. SAA 4 315 rev. 1′. The phrasing of this line ("[in a favour]able and in an unfavour[able extispicy it is favourable/unfavourable]") is typical for tablet 2/3 of the chapter *multābiltu*; see Koch, *Secrets*, no. 3, lines 157, 159, 173, 175 and 177.

Starr has also tried to show that the appearance of an unchanged, sound part of the liver was considered a positive sign both in the extispicy reports and the compendia.[50] He concluded that "all the protases where the organ is described as present (i.e. *išû*, *šakin*, *ibašši*) result in a favourable apodosis."[51] While this principle certainly applies to the theoretical compendia, Thomas Richter noticed in an Old Babylonian extispicy report a deviation from this rule: there the normal, healthy organs were simply ignored when calculating the extispicy result.[52] That this is not an isolated case is indicated by the same phenomenon in the extispicy reports from the time of Aššurbanipal. Healthy, unchanged parts of the liver are not considered in the extispicy result, as may be seen from SAA 4 280 above, where it is stated explicitly that there are five unfavourable and no favourable omens in the extispicy. In addition to the one favourable omen not counted, however, there are four organs that appear normal, namely the "presence," the "finger," the "increment" and the heart. Were these observations all considered favourable, five favourable omens would counter-balance the five unfavourable ones. While in SAA 4 282 and SAA 4 317 the number of normal organs does not equal the number of unfavourable omens, other reports corroborate this result including, for example, SAA 4 296, whose scribe again recorded five unfavourable omens and five organs appearing normal.[53] This disregarding of the appearance of normal organs or parts of the liver and lung in the reports is not only a marked difference to the extispicy compendia but might also be connected to the fact that the reports most often note unfavourable extispicy results. Of the 37 cases where the outcome of the extispicy can be ascertained within the reports from Nineveh, 28 are negative and only seven positive; two are indecisive. If the normal, unchanged appearance of parts of the entrails is not seen as a positive sign, as it is in the compendia, but disregarded, it is not surprising that the majority of extispicy cases are negative. However, it may be premature to draw wide-ranging conclusions from this observation, as we do not know whether or not the extispicy reports found in Nineveh

50. Starr, "In Search of Principles."

51. Ibid., 22.

52. Richter, "Untersuchungen zum Opferschauwesen III," 408 and 414.

53. The scribes of SAA 4 282 and SAA 4 317 listed five unfavourable omens, while SAA 4 282 contained three remarks on sound organs, and SAA 4 317 two. It is interesting to note that in some Neo-Assyrian extispicy reports a missing organ is not counted as an unfavourable omen, as it is in the compendia. In SAA 4 306, a missing "strength" (line 3) is not cited with an apodosis and also not mentioned in the list of the unfavourable omens.

represent the complete textual material nor whether the written reports contained all the extispicies performed. In other words, we know nothing about the motivation for writing these reports. The fact that the queries are formulated straightforwardly, with no negative phrasing, might indicate that negative extispicy results were not expected to appear in greater quantity than usual.[54]

Another noticeable deviation between the reports and the compendia is in the interpretation of the so-called joker-sign, *nipḫu*. Whereas in the compendia this sign leads to a re-interpretation of the whole extispicy, in the reports it is considered to be only one negative sign, as can be deduced from SAA 4 280 and SAA 4 317.[55] Unfortunately, there is as yet no evidence of two or more *nipḫu*-signs in the preserved reports; this would allow us to evaluate whether or not these signs were interpreted differently in the reports than in the compendia.

Theory vs. Practice: Similarities and Differences Between the Extispicy Compendia and Reports

This short overview has demonstrated that the same primary hermeneutic methods were used in the extispicy compendia and in the reports from the first millennium. The fact that observations relevant for the result of the extispicy are often cited as omens, that is, with protasis and apodosis, clearly illustrates the connection between the reports and the compendia. Furthermore, the hermeneutic values of the observed signs are generally the same in both text genres.

However, there are also considerable differences between the reports and the compendia. Most importantly, the appearance of a normal, unchanged, healthy organ or part of it is considered to be a favourable sign in the compendia, while the reports ignore these signs in their calculation of the extispicy result. As these signs occur frequently in extispicies and are often recorded in extispicy reports, their different interpretation affects the outcome of extispicy queries to a considerable extent. Furthermore, as detailed above, the evaluation of a *nipḫu* sign in an extispicy differs between compendia and reports; while it is considered

54. The phrasing of the query is essential for the practical result of an extispicy. By changing the phrasing from "will he recover?" to "will he die?" or from "will he be loyal?" to "will he be treacherous?" an answer "unfavourable" (or simply: "no!") gets very different practical results.

55. This can also be seen in SAA 4 320 4′.

to make the extispicy result unreliable in the compendia, it is counted as one negative sign in the reports.[56]

While the extispicy compendia display a tendency to develop increasingly refined interpretative methods, the reports appear to work on a much less sophisticated level. The more advanced layers of interpretative knowledge, which make up such a substantial part of the extispicy compendia, are rarely mentioned in the extispicy reports. The writers of the reports, by contrast, seem to be more interested in checking certain organs or parts of organs for the appearance of characteristic signs. As has been already noted some time ago, certain regularly observed parts of the liver or the lungs were only searched for two conditions, such as the middle "finger" of the lung which is said to be either "loose" or "bound."[57] The diviners, we can assume, were expecting such binary observations in these specific parts and actively looked for them, dutifully noting them when compiling the reports. The hermeneutic effort in such a predilection is rather limited; here, interpreting an ominous observation has more to do with simple handicraft than with scholarly aspirations to the subtleties of the secret art of extispical hermeneutics.

From this short overview it has become apparent that there are clear connections between the compendia and the reports, and that the intellectual effort visible in the theoretical framework of extispical interpretation did affect the practical way of interpreting extispicies in the first millennium. By the nature of things, the sophisticated and very specific interpretative problems discussed in the compendia appear rarely in the reports. At the same time, however, the extispicy reports reveal a tendency to limit the interpretative range by deliberately searching for specific conditions of certain regularly observed parts of the liver or the lungs. Here, the reports demonstrate that there was more to the practical way of obtaining an extispicy result than the knowledge laid down in the compendia: a learned diviner had not only to master the written knowledge collected in extispicy texts, but also to be initiated into the art and the craft of performing an extispicy ritual and interpreting the ominous

56. Of course, more differences between the reports and the compendia may be identified, including, for example, the role of the heart in the extispicy: its observation plays a marginal role in the extispicy compendia in general and no role at all in the *bārûtu*-series, while it is mentioned regularly in the reports. Such differences, however, do not concern the general hermeneutic paradigms, only the question of which organs were observed in extispicy.

57. Starr, *Ritual*, xlvii, notes, regarding the middle "finger" of the lung, that "In the Sargonid reports, this part is commonly, if not exclusively, said to be either 'loose' or 'bound.'" See Starr, "Extispicy Reports," 204–5, for further examples.

signs found in the inspection of the sacrificial animal's entrails. This educational knowledge of the diviner was, at least in most cases, transmitted orally from father to son and does not appear in the extispicy texts.[58] Therefore, it remains a "secret of extispicy" as much to us as it was to them.

58. Lambert, "Qualification," 142–48.

The Curious Case of Failed Revelation in *Ludlul Bēl Nēmeqi*: A New Suggestion for the Poem's Scholarly Purpose

Alan Lenzi

Revelation was generally an elite undertaking in ancient Mesopotamia. Gods typically communicated with only a few humans in society—diviners, exorcists, dream-interpreters and the like—and these professionals were responsible for transmitting and interpreting the divine communications they received to others, who were dependent on the experts for divine knowledge.[1] But what happened when the individuals

1. Common individuals could receive revelations from the gods via visions, prophetic messages, dreams and other signs, but even in these cases an expert was usually required to interpret such revelations and take appropriate ritual actions, if necessary (see *Ludlul* I 51–54, cited later in this study). For an example of (apparent) non-specialists receiving visionary or prophetic revelations, see the intriguing situation discussed in M. Nissinen, *References to Prophecy in Neo-Assyrian Sources* (SAAS 7; Helsinki: The Neo-Assyrian Text Corpus Project, 1998), 108–53. In a series of three letters a certain Nabu-reḫtu-uṣur delivers a prophecy he received, describes a vision he had and reports to the king that a "slave girl" was prophesying against him in Harran (though Nissinen believes that this latter prophecy was a politically motivated fabrication). The Mari letters also contain several examples of non-specialists having revelatory dreams; see, for example, the report of Shimatum, the daughter of King Zimri-Lim (J.-M. Durand, *Archives Épistolaires de Mari I/1* [ARM 26; Paris: Recherche sur les Civilisations, 1988], no. 239), and the report of a certain Timlu (no. 240), an otherwise unknown young woman. (For a general discussion of dreams in the Mari documents and a proposed *Sitz im Leben* that would have included a specialist's assistance, see A. Zgoll, *Traum und Welterleben im antiken Mesopotamien: Traumtheorie und Traumpraxis im 3.–1. Jahrtausend v. Chr. als Horizont einer Kulturgeschichte des Träumens* [AOAT 333; Münster: Ugarit-Verlag, 2006], 157–88; 169 for the *Sitz im Leben*.) The so-called Assyrian Dream Book existed to interpret the ominous dreams of non-specialist individuals such as the king, his court and probably others. See A. L. Oppenheim, *The Interpretation of Dreams in the Ancient Near East, with a Translation of an Assyrian Dream Book* (TAPS 46/2; Philadelphia: American Philosophical Society, 1956) for an edition. Finally, the ritual corpus of the exorcist assumes that people encounter ill-boding signs in their daily life and need releasing from the impending evil via namburbi-rituals. See

normally responsible for identifying and interpreting revelatory signs failed? What happened when those charged with performing the divinely revealed rituals to mediate between troubled humans and the divine realm were frustrated by uncooperative gods? What happened when individuals trusted the divinatory and ritual experts and the experts simply could not live up to people's expectations? And perhaps most importantly, what happened when, after the failed attempts of the experts, people resolved their problems outside the normal ritual means? What did the experts have to say for themselves to the people—and to themselves—in such a case? *Ludlul bēl nēmeqi* offers an invaluable perspective on this situation.

Ludlul bēl nēmeqi, "I will praise the lord of wisdom," is a 480-line poem written in Standard Babylonian Akkadian during the late second millennium B.C.E.[2] In the course of four tablets of equal length, *Ludlul* presents a first-person, retrospective account of the suffering and deliverance of a man named Shubshi-meshre-Shakkan. His story may be summarized briefly as follows: Marduk gets angry at Shubshi-meshre-Shakkan and subjects him to tremendous suffering in the form of social alienation (Tablet I) and physical affliction (Tablet II). Eventually, Marduk has mercy on Shubshi-meshre-Shakkan and restores his physical well-being (Tablet III) and social repute (Tablet IV). Despite his nearly unbearable suffering, the speaker never repudiates Marduk. In fact, quite to the contrary, he praises the deity throughout.

S. Maul, *Zukunftsbewältigung: Eine Untersuchung altorientalischen Denkens anhand der babylonisch-assyrischen Löserituale (Namburbi)* (Baghdader Forschungen 18; Mainz: Philipp von Zabern, 1994) for a study of namburbi-rituals with numerous examples. Clearly, therefore, non-specialists could receive revelation. Yet the documentation that we have at our disposal indicates that such revelations usually needed the assistance of specialists to be understood and acted upon. (Of course, this is not all that surprising, since our sources are mostly official documents from the institutional spheres in which the specialists worked.)

2. All of the known sources for the poem, however, are from first-millennium sites. For a survey of the introductory issues surrounding the poem and its textual basis, see my previous statement in the introduction to A. Annus and A. Lenzi, *Ludlul bēl nēmeqi: The Standard Babylonian Poem of the Righteous Sufferer* (SAACT 7; Helsinki: Neo-Assyrian Text Corpus Project, 2010), ix–lvi; henceforth SAACT 7. The (eclectic) text of the poem as reconstructed in this handbook edition (see pp. 15–30 for the transliteration) will be the basis for all citations of the poem unless otherwise noted. The few variations I use here represent my own preferred reading that was not selected for the text of the collaborative edition. I follow the MS sigla of the SAACT 7 edition. The preserved text of each of the 54 textual exemplars of *Ludlul* is available in transliteration at http://oracc.museum.upenn.edu/cams/ludlul/corpus.

Although Shubshi-meshre-Shakkan is the narrator of his own story, the first-person voice in *Ludlul* is a literary device that masks the identity of the poem's author.[3] Setting his learned vocabulary and sophisticated poetics alongside what we know about the authorship of other Standard Babylonian literary compositions, it is quite likely that this anonymous author was a scholar (*ummânu*). More precisely, the author probably was an exorcist (*āšipu*), an important specialist among the corps of Mesopotamian ritual and divinatory experts.[4] The exorcists were in charge of expelling demons, placating angry gods, and turning away the harmful effects of evil omens via a divinely revealed corpus of ritual material.[5]

Given that the poem opens with a hymn (I 1–40) lauding Marduk's wrath and mercy (I 1–28, 33–34) as well as his sovereignty and inscrutability (I 29–32, 35–36) and ends with an entire tablet (IV) dominated by praise (see especially IV 69–83 and 120), the poem is, on the one hand, very clearly doxological and hortatory in character. Marduk, the lord of wisdom and sovereign god, the poem asserts, may inflict evil upon whom he will, but he also brings deliverance in due time. As the sufferer says, "he who struck me, Marduk, restored me" (IV 10–11).[6] The one who hears *Ludlul*, the poem preaches, ought to learn from its words and join the protagonist in praise of Marduk (see I 39 and III line p).[7]

Given its preoccupation with human suffering at the hand of a deity, the poem is, on the other hand, also thematically coupled to the issue of theodicy. Why does the deity inflict suffering upon people and what is their proper response to such suffering? The poem's answer, bluntly

3. On the issues of authorship and the first-person voice in the poem, see SAACT 7, xvi–xix, xxviii–xxx.

4. See P.-A. Beaulieu, "The Social and Intellectual Setting of Babylonian Wisdom Literature," in *Wisdom Literature in Mesopotamia and Israel* (ed. R. J. Clifford; SBLSS 36; Atlanta: SBL, 2007), 3–19 (9); W. G. Lambert, "A Catalogue of Texts and Authors," *JCS* 16 (1962): 59–77; A. Lenzi, *Secrecy and the Gods: Secret Knowledge in Ancient Mesopotamia and Biblical Israel* (SAAS 19; Helsinki: The Neo-Assyrian Text Corpus Project, 2008), 119–20; and K. van der Toorn, *Scribal Culture and the Making of the Hebrew Bible* (Cambridge, Mass.: Harvard University Press, 2007), 42–49.

5. For a brief introduction to the five most important ritual/divinatory experts (exorcists, diviners, physicians, lamentation singers and astrologers) in late second- and early first-millennium Babylonia and Assyria and the divinely revealed and secret character of their ritual corpora, see Lenzi, *Secrecy and the Gods*, 68–103.

6. The Akkadian text: [*ša*] *imḫaṣanni / Marduk ušaqqi rēšī*.

7. See also IV 69–83, where people praise Marduk after seeing the deliverance he brought to Shubshi-meshre-Shakkan. These people are introduced to exemplify the audience's proper response to the events recounted in the poem.

stated, is that Marduk does as he wants. People must accept his sovereignty (I 15–16, 35–36), know that he responds to their entreaty (I 39) and wait patiently for his inevitable display of mercy (III 51–54). Although this is the poem's fundamental understanding of suffering, to its credit it presents this rather pat answer in a manner that takes into account human emotional and existential reactions. Lamentation and even religious doubt may be voiced in the course of one's troubles; but suffering will end, and praise for the deity is the appropriate expression of one's gratitude.

In what follows I develop the idea that these two intertwined literary themes—Marduk's divine sovereignty and human resignation to endure divinely sanctioned suffering—combine to support a previously unrecognized rhetorical purpose for *Ludlul bēl nēmeqi*, serving the interests of the official ritual experts among whom this poem seems to have originated. Namely, *Ludlul* accounts for the occasional failure of the experts' ritual and divinatory apparatus and provides both a literary salve—hope—to mollify the attendant emotional and existential toll such failure may have taken upon the ritual participants (the experts' clients) and an ideological tool—damage control—to avert any potential professional consequences thence from their clients or among their own ranks.[8]

This suggestion, it should be noted, does not necessarily imply any impugning of the ancient author's intentions or integrity. At the same time, however, the author should not be insulated from criticism. The author, perhaps acting on behalf of the ritual experts more broadly, may have been acting in good faith, but maybe not. We will probably never know. In any case, it is likely that the person(s) responsible for this text was doing what needed to be done to uphold the divinely sanctioned divinatory and ritual order, of which the ritual experts were the primary custodians (and among its greatest beneficiaries).

The suggested purpose of *Ludlul* is realized through several interlacing rhetorical and thematic elements. First, it is realized in the poem's theologically expedient appeal to Marduk's inscrutable, sovereign prerogatives in all matters, both human and divine, essentially denying the experts any control over their professional failures. Second, it is realized

8. For a survey of ritual failure in cuneiform sources from Mesopotamia, including comments on *Ludlul*, see C. Ambos, "Types of Ritual Failure and Mistakes in Ritual Cuneiform Sources," in *When Rituals Go Wrong: Mistakes, Failure, and the Dynamics of Ritual* (ed. U. Hüsken; Numen Book Series: Studies in the History of Religions 115; Leiden: Brill, 2007), 25–47, especially 28–30. Ambos makes very clear that the experts' ritual failure in *Ludlul* is due to Marduk's prerogative to do as he pleases. (I wish to express my gratitude to Dr. Ambos for sending me a digital offprint of his article.)

in the poem's condoning (via example) of the ritual client's emotional reaction to the experts' failure, thereby allowing a vent for potentially explosive frustrations and devastating doubts with regard to the competence of the experts. And third, it is realized through the incorporation of the sufferer's personal revelation, that is, dreams initiated by Marduk himself, into the ideology of the official ritual system. The form and content of the dreams offer hope to the sufferer but also revalorize the very system that had initially failed him.

According to *Ludlul*, when the official diagnostic and therapeutic rituals do not work one may lament and even question the *status quo*; however, ultimately, the poem exhorts, one must resign oneself to the divine prerogative, which trumps the experts' efforts, while holding firmly to the expectation that the deity will, eventually and in his own way, reveal his plan for deliverance.[9] The following presents a reading of the poem in light of this suggestion.[10] The epilogue offers reflections on the book of Job from the perspective of this new reading of *Ludlul*.

Marduk's Sovereignty

Ludlul's opening hymn sets the tone for the remainder of the poem.[11] Set apart from the narrative beginning in I 41 by its hortatory tone, the hymn

9. The idea for this suggestion came from the questions Bruce Lincoln asks in the fourth thesis of his "Theses on Method" (*Method & Theory in the Study of Religion* 8 [1996]: 225–27), which reads as follows: "The same destabilizing and irreverent questions one might ask of any speech act ought be posed of religious discourse. The first of these is 'Who speaks here?,' i.e., what person, group, or institution is responsible for a text, whatever its putative or apparent author. Beyond that, 'To what audience? In what immediate and broader context? Through what system of mediations? With what interests?' And further, 'Of what would the speaker(s) persuade the audience? What are the consequences if this project of persuasion should happen to succeed? Who wins what, and how much? Who, conversely, loses?'"

10. Just to be clear, it is not my intention to claim that the following interpretation is the only way to read this poem. There are many other aspects of the poem that this interpretation does not highlight. For example, since the poem was probably written by a scholar and was certainly intended for other scholars (along with others, presumably, including non-scholars and scribal students), its sophisticated language and learned scribal plays (see, e.g., the twelve gates in IV 39–50) are probably intended to demonstrate the author's scribal virtuosity.

11. For a reading of the poem that gives special attention to the opening hymn's influence on the interpretation of the whole, see R. Albertz, "*Ludlul bēl nēmeqi*—eine Lehrdichtung zur Ausbreitung und Vertiefung der persönlichen Marduk-frömmigkeit," in *Geschichte und Theologie: Studien zur Exegese des Alten Testaments und zur Religionsgeschichte Israels* (Berlin: de Gruyter, 2003), 85–105.

contains Shubshi-meshre-Shakkan's present response to his past suffering. As the hymn is dominated by praise for Marduk's contrasting moods of anger and mercy, vividly exemplified here in its opening ten lines, the hymn makes perfectly clear that Shubshi-meshre-Shakkan's response to his suffering—and thus the audience's proper response—is doxological:

1. *ludlul bēl nēmeqi ilu muš*[*tālum*][12]
2. *eziz mūši muppašir urri*
3. *Marduk bēl nēmeqi ilu muštālum*
4. *eziz mūši muppašir urri*
5. *ša kīma ūmi meḫê namû uggassu*
6. *u kî mānit šērēti zâqšu ṭābu*
7. *uzzuššu lā maḫār abūbu rūbšu*
8. *mussaḫḫir karassu kabattašu târat*
9. *ša nakbat qātīšu lā inaššû šamāʾū*
10. *rittuš rabbat*[13] *ukaššu mīta*

1. I will praise the lord of wisdom, the cir[cumspect] god,
2. Angry at night (but) relenting at daybreak.[14]
3. Marduk, the lord of wisdom, the circumspect god,
4. Angry at night (but) relenting at daybreak.
5. Whose fury, like a violent storm, is a wasteland,
6. But whose blowing, like a breeze of the morning hours, is pleasant.
7. (Who) in his anger is irresistible, his fury a flood,
8. (But) his mind turns back, his mood relents.
9. The brunt of whose hand the heavens cannot bear,
10. (But) whose palm is (so) gentle it rescues[15] the dying.

The emotional contrast developed throughout the opening hymn—rather severe mood swings that would probably warrant medication today—is not proof of Marduk's capricious character. Rather, Marduk's quickly changing disposition is attributed in I 29–36 to his sovereign and inscrutable prerogatives as the unrivalled high god of the pantheon:

29. *bēlum mimma libbi ilī ibarri*
30. *manām*[*a ina il*]*ī alaktašu ul īde*
31. *Marduk* [*mi*]*mma libbi ilī ibarri*

12. Brackets in the transliteration and translation indicate restored text.

13. *Rabbat* follows MSS AA from Nineveh (*rab-bat*) and *ff* from Nimrud (*ra*[*b-ba*]*t*). SAACT 7, 15 follows the late Babylonian MSS gg and ii, both of which read *rab-ba-a-ti*.

14. Parentheses in the translation indicate words supplied for meaning.

15. This translation derives the verb from CAD's *kâšu* B, "to help," rather than *kâšu* A, "to delay" (CAD K, 295), as did W. G. Lambert, *Babylonian Wisdom Literature* (repr. with corrections; Winona Lake: Eisenbrauns, 1996), 344; henceforth *BWL*.

32. *ilu ayyumma ul ilammad ṭēššu*
33. *ana kî kabtat qāssu libbaš rēmēnî*
34. *ana kî gaṣṣu kakkūšu kabattašu mušneššat*
35. *ša lā libbīšu mannu miḫiṣtašu lišapšiḫ*
36. *ela kabtatīšu ayyu lišālil qāssu*

29. The Lord, he sees everything in the heart of the gods,
30. (But) no on[e among the god]s knows his way.
31. Marduk, he sees [eve]rything in the heart of the gods,
32. (But) no god can learn his counsel.
33. As heavy as is his hand, his heart is merciful.
34. As murderous as are his weapons, his intention is life-sustaining.
35. Without his consent, who could assuage his striking?
36. Apart from his intention, who could stay his hand?

In this most explicit statement of Marduk's inscrutable sovereignty the poem asserts that no one can plumb the depths of Marduk's counsel, not even the other gods. And no one can alter his disciplinary decisions unless the high god himself gives his personal consent (I 35–36).

Taken as a whole, the hymn presents Marduk as powerful, inscrutable, and without peer; he does as he wishes. Sometimes he is angry, but he is also forgiving and tender. No one can discern his reasoning and no one can overrule his punishments. Cynicism and bitterness have no place in this hymnic confession. Rather, as the sufferer confidently asserts in I 37–40, Marduk's ultimate intention towards humanity is benevolent; one need only be patient.

Reflections on divine sovereignty do not arise explicitly in the poem again.[16] But IV 73–74 are generally relevant to the discussion since they form a kind of conceptual *inclusio* with the statements in I 35–36:[17]

73. *ša lā Marduk mannu mītūtašu uballiṭ*
74. *ela Zarpānītu ištartu ayyītu iqīša napšassu*

73. Without Marduk, who would have revived (him) from his deathly condition?
74. If not for Zarpanitu, which goddess would have given (him) his life?

Where I 35–36 is concerned with punishment, IV 73–74 centres on deliverance (and includes Marduk's spouse). In both cases it is Marduk (and his spouse, in IV 74) who acts decisively and effectively. This

16. One could say, however, that Tablets III and IV are the sufferer's coming to terms with Marduk's sovereignty. See especially IV 1–4 and IV 37–88.

17. Note also the clear parallel in the opening words of each pair of lines: *ša lā* (I 35; IV 73) and *ela* (I 36; IV 74).

conceptual framing of the poem is significant for understanding the failure of divinatory and ritual experts to help the sufferer, a theme that the poem brings up in several structurally significant places.

Professional Ritual Failure and Human Response

To understand the failure of the ritual specialists in relation to Shubshi-meshre-Shakkan's suffering one must first understand his situation from the theological perspective presented by the poem in I 41–46, the lines immediately following the opening hymn (I 1–40):

41. *iš*[*tu*] *ūmi Bēl* (or, *bēlum*)[18] *īninanni*
42. *u qarradu Marduk isbusu* [*it*]*tīya*
43. *iddânni ilī šadâšu īli*
44. *ipparku ištarī ibēš aḫītum*
45. [*i*]*slit* [*š*]*ēd dumqi ša idīya*
46. *iprud lamassī-ma šanâm-ma iše*ʾ[*e*]

41. Fr[om] the day Bel (var., the Lord) punished me,
42. And the hero Marduk was angry [wi]th me,
43. My god abandoned me, he disappeared.[19]
44. My goddess left, she departed from (my) side.
45. [The protect]tive spirit (*šēdu*) of good fortune who (was) at my side [spl]it off,
46. My divine guardian (*lammasu*) became terrified[20] and was seeking out another.

18. I am following MS *ff* (from Nimrud) here, which has ^{d}EN. MS *m* (from Sultantepe) has *be-lum*, "the Lord." This reading is better, I think, than the Sippar MS gg (followed by SAACT 7, 16, but see my translation on p. 32), which has *be-lí*, "my lord" (tentatively, the final vowel in this late MS is taken as the first common singular pronominal suffix). Aside from this line in MS gg, Marduk is not referred to as the sufferer's lord (i.e. *bēlu* does not appear with a pronominal suffix that refers back to the sufferer) explicitly until III 15, where Marduk's personal lordship over the sufferer is announced to him in a dream (*bēlka*, "your lord"), and then again in III 51, where the sufferer seems to accept Marduk's lordship over him personally (*ša bēlīya libbašu*, "the heart of my lord"). The sufferer emphatically affirms Marduk's lordship over him at the beginning of Tablet IV, where the first four lines begin with *bēlī*, "my lord." In other words, the best readings of I 41 cohere with the idea that Marduk is not recognized explicitly as the sufferer's lord until the announcement of the sufferer's imminent, Marduk-initiated deliverance.

19. Lit. "he went up his mountain."

20. Based on a few parallels and tenuous comparative Semitic data (in 1960 without the benefit of the CAD P volume), Lambert derives *iprud* from a root that he believes means "to flee, to leave," and translates the verb in line 46 as "has taken to flight," *BWL*, 33, 283–84, followed apparently by B. R. Foster, *Before the Muses: An*

Marduk's anger lay at the root of Shubshi-meshre-Shakkan's troubles. The first consequence of this anger was the abandonment of the protagonist's protective deities. The opening hymn affirms Marduk's ability and prerogative to command personal gods and protective spirits to leave or to return to their wards (I 15–16). In I 43–44 Marduk exercises that prerogative against the sufferer. The divine abandonment changed the sufferer's entire disposition (I 47–48) and had catastrophic effects for him both socially, as described in I 50, 55ff., and physically, as depicted in II 49ff. Of particular interest for our purposes here, however, is how the divine anger and attendant abandonment negatively affected the sufferer's ability to assess and to take action against his problems via the usual divinatory and ritual techniques employed by experts, especially the diviner, the exorcist and the dream interpreter, all of whom worked together for their clients' well-being. As we shall see, Marduk's anger trumped the revealed means for discerning the appropriate actions to help the troubled man.

The ritual experts are first mentioned in I 49, 51–54, at the very start of Shubshi-meshre-Shakkan's problems:

49. *iššaknānim-ma idāt piritti*
...
51. *dalḫā têrētūya nuppuḫū uddakam*
52. *itti bārî u šāʾili alaktī ul parsat*
53. *ina pî sūqi lemun egirrûya*
54. *attīl-ma ina šat mūši šuttī pardat*

49. Portents of terror[21] were established for me.
...
51. My omens were confused, equivocal[22] every day,

Anthology of Akkadian Literature (3d ed.; Bethesda, Md.: CDL, 2005), 396, who renders it "retreated"). Although this sense provides a nice parallel with the verb in line 45, the text here and the parallels Lambert adduces are probably better understood by the well-attested Akkadian verb *parādu*, "to be fearful, disturbed, restless, upset" (see CAD P, 141, 143). The root to which Lambert appeals only seems to occur in the N stem in Akkadian, "to separate oneself," is attested only during the Neo-Babylonian era, and almost certainly entered the language under West Semitic influence (see *CDA*, 264). CAD P, 144 emends Lambert's root away.

21. As omen results were sometimes considered secret (*pirištu*), this line may be making an ironic word-play (omens were *piritti* instead of *pirišti*). On the secrecy surrounding extispicy and its results, see Lenzi, *Secrecy and the Gods*, 27–66.

22. I understand *nuppuḫū* (a third masculine plural predicative for the expected third feminine plural form) to be a denominative from *nipḫu*, which sometimes has the sense of "unclear, false omen result." See W. von Soden, "Weisheitstexte in akkadischer Sprache, 1. Der leidende Gerechte," in *Texte aus der Umwelt des Alten*

52. My oracle was not decided[23] by diviner and dream interpreter.
53. What I overheard in the street (portended) evil (for me),[24]
54. (When) I lay down at night, my dream was terrifying.

Shubshi-meshre-Shakkan had experienced terrifying omens (I 49), but when he consulted the divinatory experts (here, the diviner and dream interpreter) they could not clearly diagnose his problem.[25] The determination of the kind of evil afflicting the sufferer would have allowed the experts to prescribe the appropriate apotropaic or therapeutic ritual to dispel it. Unclear omens left them with complete uncertainty and thus without actionable information (I 51–52). The description in I 53–54 leaves the reader with the impression that the homeless sufferer (see I 50) was hounded night and day by what he perceived to be evil. This framing of the ritual experts' failure in I 51–52 by Shubshi-meshre-Shakkan's perception of ubiquitous evil omens in I 49 and 53–54 highlights how the sufferer's experiences with the ritual experts had only exacerbated his dilemma. He had problems, but those best suited to help could offer him no clear answers. As Shubshi-meshre-Shakkan would later learn and then express in the opening hymn (I 35–36), until Marduk changed his mind and relented from his anger, no one, including the ritual experts, could avert the consequences of his anger. But where else could the sufferer turn for help in his time of need if not to the experts?

Given his situation and powerlessness, the sufferer understandably has only one thing to do: give vent to his emotions through lamentation. In I 55–114, therefore, the sufferer laments the events that transpired in the wake of Marduk's anger, the protective spirits' abandonment and the ritual experts' inconclusive diagnoses. From his recounting of it, his entire social world fell apart around him bit by bit.

Near the end of Tablet I the sufferer takes matters into his own hands and attempts to initiate communication with the gods since they were not

Testaments III/1 (ed. O. Kaiser; Gütersloh: Gütersloh Verlagshaus Gerd Mohn, 1990), 110–35 (117)—henceforth *TUAT* III/1.

23. For this understanding, see I. T. Abusch, "*Alaktu* and *Halakhah*: Oracular Decision, Divine Revelation," *HTR* 80 (1987): 15–42 (29–30).

24. Lit. "according to the mouth of the street, my *egirrû* was evil." On this unprovoked form of divination (cledonomancy), see the recent discussion in S. A. L. Butler, *Mesopotamian Conceptions of Dreams and Dream Rituals* (AOAT 258; Münster: Ugarit-Verlag, 1998), 151–57. Given the parallelism between I 53–54 and the attestations of *egirrû* in other contexts dealing with dreams (cited by Butler, 155–57), it is unclear why Butler understands *egirrû* in *Ludlul* I 53 to represent the "ordinary" (as she puts it) sense of the word: "reputation" (151).

25. More details about their methods are mentioned at II 6–7, discussed below.

"speaking" to him. Despite somewhat opaque similes and metaphors (they seem to imply a long-standing, emotion-laden struggle), it is clear that his attempts at prayer were to no avail:

115. *kīma nabli muštaḫmiṭi emât taslītu*
116. *kīma ṣāltu puḫpuḫḫu supûya*
117. *ušṭīb šaptīya kî daʾīmu ašṭā*
118. *ṭābtiš ātammu napraku nāpalûya*

115. (My) prayer became as an ever-burning flame,
116. My prayer (was) a brawl, like a quarrel.[26]
117. I sweetened my lips, (but) they[27] were as obscure[28] as darkness,[29]
118. I would speak sharply,[30] (but) my conversation (was) an obstacle.

Even with these setbacks, the first tablet of the poem ends with the sufferer holding out hope for the future (I 119–120).

But Shubshi-meshre-Shakkan's hopes were dashed. With the passing of time (II 1) his misfortune only increased (II 3), besetting him on every side (II 2 and II 10–11). Situated between these two assessments of his continuing problems (II 2–3, 10–11) lies a passage that reprises the sufferer's divine abandonment (II 4–5) and the ritual experts' diagnostic and therapeutic failure (II 6–9) in terms similar to I 43–46, 51–52 (discussed above):

26. The use of language from the semantic domain of fire in relation to quarrelling is paralleled in lines 36–37 of the composition Lambert entitled "Counsels of Wisdom": *ina pān ṣāltim-ma puṭur ē-takpud / lū ṣāltakā-ma napiḫta bulli*, "When confronted with a dispute, go your way; pay no attention to it. Should it be a dispute of your own, extinguish the flame!" (*BWL*, 100–101, translation following Lambert).

27. That is, the sufferer's lips, which function here as a metonymy for his speech.

28. Lit. "hard, obdurate," and thus "difficult (to understand)"; see III 90 (according to the line numbering of SAACT 7) and A. R. George and F. N. H. Al-Rawi, "Tablets from the Sippar Library: VII. Three Wisdom Texts," *Iraq* 60 (1998): 187–206 (201).

29. For the philological reasoning to reject "spear" as the meaning of *daʾīmu* here and to posit a new, homonymous word meaning "darkness" from the root *daʾāmu*, "to be dark," see George and Al-Rawi, "Three Wisdom Texts," 201. See now also *CDA*, 53, s.v. *daʾīmu* I, "gloom."

30. Lit. "like salt," which I have assumed is in contrast to the clearly positive *ušṭīb* in the previous line. If *ušṭīb* conveys making one's speech acceptable, ingratiating and thus "sweetened," then the saltiness of the speech in this line could mean speech that is stern, harsh or sharp. Of course, one might also consider that the salt simile is supposed to convey a positive idea: the sufferer's prayers were seasoned to please but failed. In any case, the result is the same: the sufferer's petitions were not effective.

4. *ila alsī-ma*[31] *ul iddina pānīšu*
5. *usalli ištarī ul ušaqqâ*[32] *rēšīša*
6. *bārû ina bīri arkat ul iprus*[33]
7. *ina maššakki šāʾilu ul ušāpi dīnī*
8. *zaqīqu abāl-ma ul upatti uznī*
9. *āšipu ina kikkiṭṭê kimilti ul ipṭur*

4. I called to (my) god, but he did not pay attention to me.
5. I implored my goddess, but she did not lift her head to me.
6. The diviner could not determine the situation with divination.
7. The dream interpreter could not clarify[34] my case with incense.
8. I prayed to the dream god,[35] but he did not reveal anything to me.[36]

31. As Mayer notes, the verb *šasû*, "to call to," was commonly used in prayers, including several dingir-šà-dib-ba-prayers not published in W. G. Lambert's edition; see W. Mayer, *Untersuchungen zur Formensprache der babylonischen "Gebetsbeschwörungen"* (Studia Pohl: Series Maior 5; Rome: Pontifical Biblical Institute, 1976), 129; for Lambert's edition, see n. 37. *Sullû*, "to beseech, to pray to," in line 2, on the other hand, is less common in actual prayers, occurring according to Mayer only in the Great Ishtar Prayer (Mayer's Ishtar 2; see *Untersuchungen zur Formensprache*, 131).

32. For this reading, see the comments by Lambert, *BWL*, 288.

33. The idiom *(w)arkat parāsu* is often used in contexts of divinatory inquiry. See CAD P, 174.

34. Lit. "make manifest," see line II 110.

35. For the meaning of *zaqīqu*/*ziqīqu*, including its use as the name of a dream god/spirit, see Butler, *Dreams and Dream Rituals*, 78–83 and a nuanced proposal in Zgoll, *Traum und Welterleben im antiken Mesopotamien*, 299–307. Butler discusses the possibility that the *zaqīqu* mentioned in *Ludlul* II 8 designates a human ritual functionary rather than a spirit or a deity. Given the presence of ritual specialists in the adjacent lines (II 6–7 and 9) and other texts that seem to support the existence of such a functionary, this is a plausible understanding of our line (and Butler's preference [81]). Against this interpretation, however, is the fact that the verb *baʾālu*, "to pray to, to beseech," is almost exclusively used with reference to deities. The one exception has a human king as the object of the verb, but ritual functionaries are never attested with it (see CAD B, 2). We know from the opening of the Assyrian Dream Book that at least one incantation was directed to a being called *Ziqīqu* (see Butler, *Dreams and Dream Rituals*, 321–24 for the text). We also have a prayer to Sin (the moon god) in which a supplicant mentions the use of Anzagar, another dream deity, as an intermediary between the high god and the supplicant, so dream gods were invoked or used at times by people. As for the context of *Ludlul* II, the sufferer describes calling out to his personal deities in II 4–5, but, as mentioned above, this probably would have required the assistance of a ritual specialist. The same kind of explanation could apply to II 8: the sufferer mentions the deity/spirit he called upon (Zaqiqu), which implies some ritual activity involving a specialist. In light of all of this, and without dismissing the possibility that there was a ritual functionary called a *zaqīqu* attested elsewhere, it seems likely that a non-human,

9. The exorcist did not release the divine anger (against me) with rituals.

Because Shubshi-meshre-Shakkan believed his personal deities to have abandoned him (I 43–44), he needed to find a way to appease them (II 4–5) and thus renew their protection and enjoy the prosperity that they could bring him. He probably would have employed the dingir-šà-dib-ba-prayers in consultation with an exorcist for this purpose.[37] But as he recounts it, these were of no avail (II 9).[38] In II 6–7 the sufferer again turned to the divinatory specialists (see I 52), hoping they might discover an omen that would clarify his situation. The diviner would have used extispicy to obtain an omen for his client, reading the will of the gods from the sheep's liver, the tablet of the gods.[39] The dream interpreter presumably would have used the incense mentioned here to produce the smoke required for a libanomancy, thereby obtaining an omen from the gods.[40] Unfortunately for our protagonist, the experts failed once again;

non-obvious being is meant in *Ludlul* II 8 (see likewise Zgoll, *Traum und Welterleben im antiken Mesopotamien*, 326).

36. Lit. "he did not open my ear."

37. See W. G. Lambert, "Dingir.šà.dib.ba incantations," *JNES* 33 (1974): 267–322, for a provisional edition of texts belonging to this kind of exorcistic incantation. Margaret Jaques at the University of Zurich is publishing a fuller edition and study, including both the prayers and their rituals. KAR 44, obv. 4 (and duplicates) lists dingir-šà-dib-ba-prayers as part of the curriculum of the exorcist. See M. J. Geller, "Incipits and Rubrics," in *Wisdom, Gods, and Literature: Studies in Assyriology in Honour of W. G. Lambert* (ed. A. R. George and I. L. Finkel; Winona Lake, Ind.: Eisenbrauns, 2000), 225–58, for the most recent edition. A person might also have used an ér-šà-ḫun-gá-lament to turn away divine anger, administered by a *kalû*, "lamentation-singer." For these texts, see S. Maul, *"Herzberuhigungsklagen": Die sumerisch-akkadischen Erschahunga-Gebete* (Wiesbaden: Harrassowitz, 1988).

38. *Kimiltu*, the word used in II 9 for anger, is used exclusively for divine anger against humans. See CAD K, 372–73.

39. See P. Steinkeller, "Of Stars and Men: The Conceptual and Mythological Setup of Babylonian Extispicy," in *Biblical and Oriental Essays in Memory of William L. Moran* (ed. A. Gianto; BibOr 48; Pontifical Biblical Institute, 2005), 11–47 (14).

40. For dream interpreters in ancient Mesopotamia generally, see S. B. Noegel, "Dreams and Dream Interpreters in Mesopotamia and in the Hebrew Bible (Old Testament)," in *Dreams: A Reader on Religious, Cultural, and Psychological Dimensions of Dreaming* (ed. K. Bulkeley; Hampshire: Palgrave-St. Martin's, 2001), 45–71, and more recently Zgoll, *Traum und Welterleben im antiken Mesopotamien*, 401–37. The commentary to *Ludlul*, preserved only in MS G, offers the following explanation of II 7: *maššakku surqinnu* (a by-form of *surqēnu*) *ša šāʾili*, "incense (means) offering of the dream interpreter" (see SAACT 7, 19). For the view that

neither could shed light on the sufferer's problem. Finally, there is the sufferer's effort mentioned in II 8. In one reading of this line, Shubshi-meshre-Shakkan sought the help of a minor dream deity, perhaps invoked as an intermediary between the sufferer and a higher god, to discover the cause of the sufferer's problems. The results of the god's activity might then have been manifested to the sufferer via a revelatory dream; this is unclear.[41] If this were the case, a ritual specialist would have likely been needed, perhaps a dream interpreter or an exorcist to perform the ritual.[42] In another reading of the line, the *zaqīqu* is not a deity but a human ritual functionary (see n. 35) employed to help the sufferer alleviate his problems. In either case, here again the sufferer's attempts to utilize the official ritual apparatus of the experts yielded nothing.

Shubshi-meshre-Shakkan's response to ritual failure in Tablet II is two-fold. First, he complains that he is being unfairly treated by the gods: he feels as though he is being treated like an impious clod even though he knows himself to be quite the opposite (II 12–22, 23–32). This religious crisis leads Shubshi-meshre-Shakkan to question, in perhaps

this line refers to libanomancy, see Oppenheim, *The Interpretation of Dreams in the Ancient Near East*, 222. On libanomancy generally, see I. L. Finkel, "A New Piece of Libanomancy," *AfO* 29–30 (1983–84): 50–55. For a broader discussion of *maššakku* in relation to the dream interpreter, see Butler, *Dreams and Dream Rituals*, 229–30, and Zgoll, *Traum und Welterleben im antiken Mesopotamien*, 325–26. Butler mentions the possibility that the incense was used in aleuromancy (divination via the scattering of flour) or that the incense smoke was inhaled by the dream interpreter to induce a vision. The latter possibility is also discussed by Zgoll (326).

41. In one understanding of the prayer to Sin mentioned in n. 35 the supplicant sends Anzagar to Sin in order to gain forgiveness for his sins, which were the cause of his personal deities' anger. As this prayer is a šu-íl-lá, an exorcist would have been present to guide the supplicant through the ritual-prayer. See A. Lenzi, ed., *Reading Akkadian Prayers and Hymns: An Introduction* (ANEM 3; Atlanta: SBL, 2011), 396. For a different understanding of this prayer, utilized as a parallel to the dream experience in *Ludlul* III 40–45, see B. Pongratz-Leisten, "From Ritual to Text to Intertext: A New Look on the Dreams in *Ludlul Bēl Nēmeqi*," in *In the Second Degree: Paratextual Literature in Ancient Near Eastern and Ancient Mediterranean Culture and Its Reflections in Medieval Literature* (ed. P. Alexander, A. Lange and R. Pillinger; Leiden: Brill, 2010), 139–57 (153–54).

42. The ritual failure mentioned here in II 8 is particularly interesting since the sufferer will eventually have three dreams at the start of Tablet III that effectively announce his deliverance. So why is this dream-related activity ineffectual here in Tablet II? The answer is simple: Marduk does as he pleases, and he is not pleased to use dreams just yet. When it is time, he will initiate a series of effective, salvific dreams; until then, no expert can force his hand.

the starkest terms in all of Akkadian literature, humanity's ability to discern the divine will accurately (II 33–38).[43] Coming as it does between two accounts in Tablet II of the ritual experts' inability to do their jobs (II 6–9 and II 108–113, see below), this statement in II 33–38 should be read as calling the entire divinatory and exorcistic ritual apparatus into question.[44] The contradiction between religious expectation and actual experience also leads Shubshi-meshre-Shakkan to reflect on the vacillating and unstable character of human existence in light of the divine decrees that order it (II 39–47). As much as the protagonist of the poem vents his emotions and angst in these lines, his existential and philosophical musings and rants provide no reprieve from his trouble (II 48). Thus Shubshi-meshre-Shakkan turns again in II 49ff. to lamentation, his second response to ritual failure. In this long lament he enumerates a wide array of physically debilitating maladies that leave him on the very brink of death (II 114–115).

Toward the conclusion of this second lament Shubshi-meshre-Shakkan once more drags up the failure of the ritual experts to help him (II 108–113):

108. *sakikkîya išḫuṭu mašmaššu*
109. *u têrētīya bārû ūtešši*
110. *ul ušāpi āšipu šikin murṣīya*
111. *u adanna siliʾtīya bārû ul iddin*
112. *ul irūṣa ilu qātī iṣbat*
113. *ul irēmanni ištarī idaya ul illik*

108. The exorcist was scared by (?) my symptoms.
{{Or: 108. My symptoms "removed" (lit. stripped away) the exorcist.}}[45]

43. Given the fact that Marduk's inscrutability is already praised in I 29–33 in the opening hymn, the sufferer's angst described here must be read within the past unfolding of Shubshi-meshre-Shakkan's suffering. The opening hymn represents the later, post-trauma setting during which the poem is recited, that is, after Shubshi-meshre-Shakkan had been delivered and gained insight into the events that befell him.

44. See SAACT 7, xxi, and K. van der Toorn, "Theodicy in Akkadian Literature," in *Theodicy in the World of the Bible: The Goodness of God and the Problem of Evil* (ed. A. Laato and J. C. de Moor; Leiden: Brill, 2003), 57–89 (80).

45. As is often the case in *Ludlul*, this line presents philological difficulties. In this translation the exorcist is taken as the subject of the verb *išḫuṭu* and the verb is rendered as a by-form of the root *šaḫātu*, "to fear, to become afraid." Others have taken it in a similar manner: "shied away from" by CAD Š/1, 87, "recoiled from" by Foster, *Before the Muses*, 401, and "scheute" by von Soden, *TUAT* III/1, 126 n. 108a, who notes that the verb should be understood as having a singular subject despite the final vowel. In contrast to these translations, Lambert (*BWL*, 45) made

109. And the diviner became confused by my omens.
110. The exorcist did not clarify[46] the nature of my illness.[47]
111. And the diviner did not give the duration[48] for my sickness.
112. (My) god did not rush in to help, he did not take my hand,
113. My goddess did not have mercy on me, she did not come to my side.

This final instance of the experts' failure completes the pattern of broken communication between the divine and human realms (I 51–52, 115–118; II 4–9). Inability to communicate effectively with or receive revelation from the divine realm occurs near the start and conclusion of the sufferer's complaints and laments in both Tablets I and II, and divine abandonment is close by in three of these four places. Just as his life was surrounded by evil in the narrative's reality, his laments are surrounded by ineffectual professional ritual and divinatory experts in the narrative's literary presentation. No one could help him but the lord of wisdom, whose anger (and inscrutable plan for his suffering) would have to run its course before deliverance could occur.[49]

the symptoms the subject and translated the line with "my complaints have exposed the incantation priest," apparently taking the verb from *šaḫāṭu*, "to strip, to tear away, to flay" (CAD Š/1, 92). This understanding has the advantage of accounting for the final vowel on the verb (since the subject is plural), but this rendering would be the only attestation of a metaphorical use of the verb *šaḫāṭu*. This may not be a significant argument against the derivation, since *Ludlul* likes to use words in unusual ways (see SAACT 7, xxvi–xxviii). Moreover, the metaphorical meaning would be ironic, adding some literary depth to the line, since the same word is often used when some kind of evil or disease is removed from one's body (see CAD Š/1, 94). The alternate translation therefore is possible. On either understanding, the sufferer is left without help.

46. Lit. "make manifest," see II 7.

47. See CAD Š/2, 437 for further references to *šikin murṣīya*. A Neo-Assyrian letter attests an interesting situation in which specialists could not determine the nature of Esarhaddon's illness; see LAS 246 and the commentary in S. Parpola, *Letters from Assyrian Scholars to the Kings Esarhaddon and Assurbanipal*. Part 2, *Commentary and Appendices* (AOAT 5; Neukirchen–Vluyn: Neukirchener Verlag, 1983), 237. Clearly, the situation in *Ludlul*, as I will discuss below, is neither unrealistic nor unique.

48. See II 1 for its use of *adannu*.

49. See likewise the conclusion of Ambos's discussion of *Ludlul* in his general treatment of ritual failure. He writes, "Ritual could never work against the will of the gods or even force the gods to an action desired by the ritual's human participants. As long as Šubši-mešrê-Šakkan was exposed to Marduk's wrath and abandoned by his own protective deities, all the said efforts [of the experts] were doomed to failure" ("Types of Ritual Failure and Mistakes," 30).

Before advancing to the account of Shubshi-meshre-Shakkan's deliverance in Tablet III, we should consider the fact that the ritual and divinatory failures described several times in *Ludlul* I and II are not unique to the poem. Evil signs, equivocal or confused omens, troubling dreams, and inability of ritual experts to help are all lamented in various Akkadian and Sumerian texts.[50] Due to its remarkably similar language to that in *Ludlul*, the bilingual ér-šà-ḫun-gá 4R 22, no. 2, lines 6′–19′, directed to Marduk, is worth citing at length as an example of such texts.[51]

6′. ù ma-mú-da-ta bu-bu-luḫ-e in-na-mar
7′. *u ina šutti gitallutum šakiššu*
8′. azu-e máš-a-ta si nu-mu-ni-íb-sá-e
9′. *bārû ina bīri ul ušteššeršu*
10′. ensi-e še-e-ta i-bí-a nu-mu-un-na-an-bad-dè
11′. *šāʾilu ina muššakka*[52] *ul ipettēšu*
12′. [ám]-gig-ga-bi-šè ^{túg}ám-lá-a-ta nu-sed-dè
13′. *[an]a maruštīšu ina ṣindi ul inâḫ*
14′. [šim-mú-e] ka-kug-ga-aš nu-mu-ni-íb-te-en-t[e]-en
15′. *āšipu ina š[ipt]i ul upaššaḫšu*
16′. gu_4-gim kar-mud-d[a]-[...] e-da-šub
17′. *kīma alpi [ina] idiptīšu nadī-ma*
18′. udu-gim murgu-ba e-[d]a-lù-lù
19′. *kīma immeri i[na tabāš]t[ā]nīšu*[53] *bullul-ma*

50. For an instance of such motifs in another wisdom composition, see J. Nougayrol, "Choix de textes littéraires: 162. (Juste) suffrant (R.S. 25.460)," *Ugaritica* 5 (1968): 265–73, with a plate on 435, no. 162 (267: 1′–8′ with a translation on 268). For attestations in incantation-prayers, see Mayer, *Untersuchungen zur Formensprache*, 103–6. See also Abusch, "*Alaktu* and *Halakhah*," 28, who cites a relevant therapeutic text (*BAM* 316 iii 12′–16′), and Ambos, "Types of Ritual Failure and Mistakes," 30, who cites several relevant lines from Sumerian laments (for which see M. E. Cohen, *The Canonical Lamentations of Ancient Mesopotamia* [2 vols.; Potomac, Md.: Capital Decisions, 1988], 1.123.14; 1.124.35ff. and 1.277.b+100, with translations at 136–37 and 294). Even the diagnostic handbook used by exorcists occasionally admits that a diagnosis is simply not possible. For examples, see N. P. Heeßel, *Babylonisch-assyrische Diagnostik* (AOAT 43; Münster: Ugarit-Verlag, 2000), 74 with n. 29, where he cites SA.GIG 16/74′ (p. 178), 22/3 (p. 251), and 27/13 (p. 297), each of which read: *āšipu* (*ana bulliṭīšu*) *qība lā išakkan*, "the exorcist should not give (for his recovery) a diagnosis."

51. For the text, see Maul, *"Herzberuhigungsklagen,"* 332.

52. Muššakka is used here for the expected muššakki (see ibid., 333).

53. *Tabāštānu* is a very rare word, occurring only in a few bilinguals and in *Ludlul* II 107 among monolingual texts. OB Lu A 225 (also OB Lu D 138 and OB Lu Frag. I 5) attest the equivalency lú mur_7.ba.ná.a = *ša ina tabāštānīšu bullulu*, "the

6′–7′.	And in (his) dream(s) constant anxiety is inflicted on him.
8′–9′.	The diviner could not give him the correct decision with divination.
10′–11′.	The dream interpreter could not reveal (anything) to him through libanomancy.[54]
12′–13′.	He could not get relief [fo]r his affliction via medicine.[55]
14′–15′.	The exorcist could not relieve him with an inca[ntation].
16′–17′.	He is laid up (i.e., sick)[56] like an ox [in] his "wind."[57]
18′–19′.	He is sullied like a sheep b[y][58] his (own) [excrem]ent.[59]

Although this and other texts demonstrate that the complaint about ritual and divinatory failure in *Ludlul* is not unique, *Ludlul* is unique in the frequency with which this motif comes up and in the highly developed lamentation and religious doubt that are expressed in conjunction with the protagonist's undiagnosed, untreatable suffering. This particular feature of *Ludlul* deserves a more prominent place in any attempt to understand the poem's broader purpose.

one sullied by (lit. coated, smeared with) his (own) excrement." See CAD T, 24. The *Ludlul* commentary (MS G) explains the term with *zû šīnātum*, "feces, urine" (see SAACT 7, 22). See also the commentary to LBAT 1577 iv 13, cited by CAD T, 24.

54. Akkadian, lit. "with incense." The Sumerian adds another, more general term for smoke, i-bí-a (= Akkadian *ina qutri*), "with smoke."

55. Lit. "with a bandage." See *Ludlul* III 44–45.

56. *Nadû* (= Sumerian šub) sometimes has the sense of "laid up, ill" in the stative. See *CDA*, 230 and CAD N/1, 92; the latter provides examples.

57. "Wind" seems to be some kind of cattle illness. See CAD I/J, 9. The word is rarely attested as a disease.

58. Lit. "coated with."

59. These last two lines resonate with *Ludlul* II 106–107, which occur just before the experts' failure is mentioned near the end of Tablet II:

106. *ina rubṣīya abīt kî alpi*
107. *ubtallil kî immeri ina tabāštānīya*
106. I spent the night in my (own) filth like an ox,
107. I wallowed in my own excrement like a sheep.

Although one can interpret the imagery in these lines in various ways (e.g. as an indication of the sufferer's utter misery), it seems to me that one could (also?) view these lines as an indication that the chasm between human knowledge about the causes of suffering (e.g. sin) and the knowledge of the gods is as wide as that between the ways of civilized humans (the proper way to act) and ignorant animals (the way the sufferer feels he is acting). For ignorance of sin being likened to animal behaviour elsewhere in Akkadian religious literature, see, e.g., Section II, lines 3–4 and 12–13 in the dingir-šà-dib-ba's edited by Lambert ("Dingir.šà.dib.ba Incantations," 284–85).

Deliverance Through Dreaming

Although opening with a brief recapitulation of his suffering (III 1–8), Tablet III mainly centres on Shubshi-meshre-Shakkan's deliverance and recovery. Given the poem's grounding of the sufferer's problems in Marduk's anger and its assertion in I 35–36 that apart from his consent, no one, including the divinatory and ritual experts, could turn back his discipline, the only possible agent who could have initiated deliverance for the sufferer was Marduk. He brings this deliverance to the sufferer by way of three unusual dreams.

So-called message dreams were the only accepted form of direct, personal revelation in ancient Mesopotamia that was believed to be divinely initiated and could occur without any kind of professional presence or assistance.[60] According to Butler, "[t]he main criterion of a Mesopotamian message dream is that a figure (usually divine) gives an unequivocal message to a dreamer."[61] Since Marduk needed to be the one to initiate the sufferer's deliverance, the message dream was the best medium of revelation for the poem to use; it was perfectly suited to the

60. Of course there was professional assistance available, as even I 52 and II 7 shows. Such assistance may have been typical, though apparently not required. One could suggest that prophecy and visions were forms of revelation that did not require specialist assistance, but such revelations were generally not personal; rather, they were received by individuals (acting as a deity's messenger) in order to deliver them to others. On message dreams, see Butler, *Dreams and Dream Rituals*, 15–18, who builds on Oppenheim's work (*Interpretation of Dreams in the Ancient Near East*, 186–206) and refines the category with its constituent elements. Zgoll has proposed a completely new classificatory scheme based on a thorough review of the relevant data in the second chapter of her book *Traum und Welterleben im antiken Mesopotamien* (pp. 55–257, but see especially 87–95 [critique of old schemes] and 237–40 [summary of her new scheme]). Her scheme is based on the predominance of two kinds of dream content: images and speech. There are image-dreams (*Bildträume*), speech-dreams (*Redeträume*), and some dreams that combine these two kinds of content. The location of the addressee clarifies the classificatory situation of dreams in the latter, mixed group. That is, if speech in a dream addresses someone within the dream, the speech is considered intrarelational. If speech is directed to someone outside the dream, the speech is extrarelational. Intrarelational speech remains within the world of the dream. Zgoll therefore categorizes this sub-group with image-dreams. The resulting scheme is as follows: 1. intrarelational image-dreams; 1a. image-dreams entirely comprised of images; 1b. image-dreams comprised of both images and intrarelational speech; 2. extrarelational speech-dreams; 2a. speech-dreams entirely comprised of speech; 2b. speech dreams comprised of both extra-relational speech and images (238). As pointed out in n. 63, Zgoll's system is helpful for understanding the dreams in *Ludlul* by grouping them with similar examples.

61. Butler, *Dreams and Dream Rituals*, 18.

author's theological needs. Furthermore, because dreams are private and impossible to verify objectively—especially when the dreamer is a literary character—the author of *Ludlul* could shape the sufferer's experience of the dream—the dream's content—to suit his purposes. Finally, although one revelatory dream might easily be overlooked or dismissed, a series of similar dreams with explicit claims about their divine origin was undeniably and emphatically portentous.[62] In other words, including a series of dreams in the poem gave the author of *Ludlul* an opportunity to use, in a highly artificial, tendentious and emphatic manner, an acceptable medium of revelation that could occur outside of the official ritual system:[63]

9. *ištânu eṭlu atir šikit*[*ta*]
10. *minâta šurruḫ lubušta udd*[*u*]*š*
11. *aššu ina munatti šiddūšu gatta zu*[*mm*]*û*
12. *melammê ḫalip labiš pulḫ*[*at*]*i*
13. [*īr*]*ubam-ma ittaziz e*[*lī*]*ya*
14. [*āmur*]*šu-ma iḫḫamû šīrūya*
15. [*iqbī*]*-ma bēl*[*k*]*a*[64] *išpura*[*nni*]

62. On the issue of multiple dreams as a sign of authentic revelation, see Oppenheim, *Interpretation of Dreams in the Ancient Near East*, 208, and Zgoll, *Traum und Welterleben im antiken Mesopotamien*, 365.

63. Oppenheim has already noted the artificiality of the dreams. Although each of the three dreams in *Ludlul*, taken individually, is an example of what he identifies as message dreams, the series of three, more typical of what he calls symbolic dreams (208), defy his categorization (see likewise, Butler, *Dreams and Dream Rituals*, 16, and Noegel, "Dreams and Dream Interpreters," 48; contrast Zgoll, whose classificatory scheme would place these dreams with others from the group "image-dreams comprised of both images and intrarelational speech" [*Traum und Welterleben im antiken Mesopotamien*, 241]; see n. 60 above). The dreams in *Ludlul*, Oppenheim opines, "seem to be the product of a somewhat learned imagination guided by literary aspirations, and show the influence of individual artistic creativeness" (*Interpretation of Dreams in the Ancient Near East*, 217). Toward the end of his comments about the dreams in *Ludlul* he states that "[n]o reference…is made to the several dream-apparitions, which thus remain unconnected with the story. They are apparently not used functionally but only for stylistic reasons" (217). Contrary to Oppenheim's opinion in this matter, this study suggests the inclusion of dream-figures was a very important rhetorical element to achieving the purpose of the poem. Pongratz-Leisten, although offering a different interpretation than this study, agrees that the dreams and dream figures have an important function in the meaning of the poem ("From Ritual to Text to Intertext," 146).

64. The reading *be-el-*[*k*]*a*, though differing in the placement of the brackets, follows von Soden, *TUAT* III/1, 127 n. 15a. Collation with the photo of MS *t*, the only exemplar that preserves this part of the line, indicates that this reading is more likely than Lambert's *be-el-*[*t*]*u*, "lady," though the latter is not impossible.

…[65]

21. *aš*[*n*]*ī-ma šunata* [*anaṭṭal*]
22. *ina šutti aṭṭulu* [*mūšitīya*]
23. *ištânu ramku* […]
24. *bī*[*nu*] *mu*[*l*]*lilu tamiḫ ri*[*ttuššu*]
25. *Laluralimma āšib Nippur*
26. *ana ubbubīka išpuran*[*ni*]
27. *mê našû elīya it*[*buk*]
28. *šipat balāṭi iddâ umaššiʾ z*[*umrī*]
29. *ašluš-ma šuttu ana*[*ṭṭal*]
30. *ina sutti aṭṭulu mūšit*[*īya*]
31. *ištēt ardatu*[66] *banû zī*[*mūša*]
32. *nišiš la*[*bš*]*ati*[67] *iliš maš*[*lat*]
33. *šarrat nišī* […]
34. *īrubam-ma itta*[*šba ina idīya*][68]
35. *qibâ*[69] *aḫulapī* […]
36. *lā tapallaḫ iqbâ uša*[…]
37. *u ina mimma*[70] *šutta iṭṭul* […]
38. *iqbī-ma aḫulapī*[71] *magal šūnuḫ-ma*
39. *ayyumma ša ina šāt mūši ibrû bī*[*ra*]

65. Only one sign is preserved in III 16. The next four lines are fragmentary and thus hard to follow with any certainty (III 17–20). There is mention of a king, the sufferer speaking perhaps, and someone being silent and being heard. Until duplicates are found for these lines we are left with only speculations about their meaning.

66. The logogram is preserved as KI.SIKIL.

67. The final vowel on this third person feminine singular predicative construction is superfluous.

68. Amar Annus suggested this restoration, based on line 13: two verbs (preterite-*ma* perfect) followed by preposition + first common singular suffix (the apparatus in SAACT 7, 24 at III 34 is incorrect). Lambert's reading of MS q, namely, x […] x *ma-a* […], at the end of his III 33 (see *BWL*, 50, but note that Lambert's III 33 is SAACT 7's III 34) is best taken with the previous line (see SAACT 7, 24 at III 33) and therefore does not affect this suggested restoration.

69. Variant in MS ee: *iqbâ*, "she ordered." I prefer to read the imperative with the sufferer as the speaker rather than the finite verb with the female dream-figure as the speaker. Since the sufferer seems to speak in III 17 during the first dream, it seems reasonable that he would here, too. (Speaking in dreams is more common than has been previously recognized; see Butler, *Dreams and Dream Rituals*, 17–18.) Also, the imperative in III 34 produces an element of movement in the second dream: the sufferer's request in III 34 can be granted in III 37 (*iqbī-ma*).

70. The opening several words follow MSS ee (*ù ina mim-ma*) and q (*ù i-na mim-ma*) rather than MS *p* (*me-mu-u*), as does the text of SAACT 7, 24.

71. The final vowel, attested in two Assyrian MSS (G and *p*), may not be a first common singular pronominal suffix. A variant in MS q shows the word clearly without it: *a-ḫu-lap*.

40. *ina šutti Ur-Nintinugga* [...]
41. *eṭlu ṭarru āpir agâšu*
42. *mašmaššum-ma nāši lē*ʾ[*um*]
43. *Marduk-ma išpuran*[*ni*]
44. *ana Šubši-mešrê-Šakkan ubilla ṣi*[*mda*]
45. *ina qātīšu ellūti ubilla ṣi*[*mda*]
46. *ana muttabbilīya qātuššu ipq*[*id*]

9. (There was) a singular man,[72] extraordinary[73] in fo[rm],
10. Magnificent in physique, clothed in new gar[ment]s.[74]
11. Because (I was just) waking up,[75] his stature[76] la[cke]d form,
12. He was clad in radiance, clothed in a[w]e.
13. [He en]tered and stood [over m]e.
14. (When) [I saw] him, [my] flesh was paralyzed.
15. [He said], "[You]r lord sent [me]."

...

21. [I saw] a dream a sec[on]d time.
22. In the dream I saw [at night],[77]
23. (There was) a singular purifier...
24. He was holding in [his ha]nd a pur[if]ying t[ama]risk rod.
25. "Laluralimma,[78] resident of Nippur,
26. Has sent m[e] to purify you."
27. He po[ured] the water that he was carrying over me.
28. He pronounced[79] the incantation of life (and) rubbed [my bod]y.
29. I s[aw] a dream for a third time.
30. In the dream that I saw at ni[ght],
31. (There was) a sin[gul]ar young woman, [whose feat]ures were beautiful,
32. Cl[oth]ed like a human, (but) eq[ual] to a god.
33. A queen of peoples...

72. *Ištânu* here and in III 23 and *ištēt* in III 31 may mean that only one figure appeared at a time rather than conveying a sense of the uniqueness of each figure (see CAD I/J, 278), as Foster's translation suggests (*Before the Muses*, 402). The context, however, does support the latter rendering. "Singular" in my translation is an attempt to capture something of both meanings.

73. *Atir* can convey extraordinary quality or size. For the latter, see the figure in Gudea's dream discussed by Oppenheim, *Interpretation of Dreams in the Ancient Near East*, 189.

74. Lit. "he was renewed with regard to the garment."

75. Lit. "because in the moment of waking."

76. Lit. "his sides, edges." As von Soden notes, "the mere shadowy outline caused the dreadful appearance" (author's translation), *TUAT* III/1, 127 n. 11a.

77. Lit. "my night." For the pronominal suffix on this noun in the context of dreaming, see CAD M/2, 271.

78. For other references to this name, see Lambert, *BWL*, 296.

79. Lit. "threw," a verb typically used with incantations.

34. She entered and sat [down beside me].
35. "Speak my deliverance…"
36. "Do not fear," she said, "I will…"
37. "And whatever he saw in a dream…"[80]
38. She spoke my deliverance, "He is utterly exhausted,[81]
39. "Whoever (may be) the one who saw a vis[ion] in the night."
40. In the dream, Ur-Nintinugga[82]…,[83]
41. A bearded man, wearing his crown,
42. An exorcist, carrying a writing-[board].
43. "Marduk sent m[e].
44. "I brought (this) band[age] to Shubshi-meshre-Shakkan,
45. "From his (i.e. Marduk's) pure hands I brought a band[age]."
46. He entr[usted] (me) into the[84] hands of my ministrant.

In the lines following the dreams the sufferer awakens, accepts his deliverance, and then begins a litany that runs from III 61 to the end of Tablet III in which he describes how Marduk actively reversed all of the physical maladies mentioned in Tablet II.[85] Tablet IV is largely concerned with praising Marduk for deliverance and the sufferer's reintegration into society. Clearly, the dreams are the turning point in Shubshi-meshre-Shakkan's fortune.

Although several obscurities remain in III 9–46, enough can be understood about the dreams to suggest that their literary function offers the final conceptual element to understanding the poem's broader ideological purpose.

An important initial point to raise about these dreams is that although the poem has prepared us for Marduk's display of mercy, the actual actions attributed to the god to implement that mercy are atypical. The use of divine representatives appearing in dreams to perform ritual actions is not at all the usual manner in which gods effected healing in the broad scheme of the Mesopotamian ritual system. Rather, as already mentioned, the gods normally worked through human divinatory and ritual experts, and these experts performed rituals on people in waking life. From a very broad corpus of texts we know that the experts' rituals frequently employed prayers to the gods, included divinely empowered

80. This line is unclear, as is the similar one at III 39. On the latter, see Foster, *Before the Muses*, 403 n. 1 for a suggestion.

81. Alternatively, "She said, 'Enough! He is utterly exhausted!'"

82. See Lambert, *BWL*, 296 for other references to this name, which means "servant of the lady (i.e., goddess), who makes the dead alive" (see O. Edzard, "Nin-tin-uga, Nin-tila-uga," *RLA* 9 [1998–2000]: 506).

83. Perhaps the final verb here should be "appeared" or "entered."

84. Lit. "his."

85. Marduk is the subject of nearly all of the verbs in III 61-line j.

incantations against malevolent forces, and exhibited a rich mythology in which the gods cooperate with the specialists to reveal signs or effect change for human clients like Shubshi-meshre-Shakkan. Moreover, there are good reasons to believe that from the late second millennium on many ritual experts (i.e. exorcists, diviners, lament-singers, physicians and astrologers)[86] recognized the divine origins of their crafts and traced their professional ancestries back through the *apkallu*s to Ea, Marduk's father.[87] The intermediation of these ritual experts was therefore the accepted and, perhaps more importantly, divinely authorized channel for bringing divine assistance to the people.

Why therefore are dreams and dream-figures used by Marduk in *Ludlul* III rather than allowing the divinely sanctioned human experts to do their work in waking life? The answer is at least two-fold. The first part of the answer to this question lies in the previous section of this study. The experts mentioned earlier in the poem had repeatedly failed to do their job. The divinatory and ritual system in their hands had not helped the sufferer. Others were needed, and the dream figures fit the bill.

As *Ludlul*'s opening hymn makes clear, the reason for the human experts' failure was divine, inscrutable sovereignty. Without Marduk's cooperation the experts were powerless (I 35–36). This was a tenable answer for ritual failure within the official ritual system; the poem could have left matters there.[88] But it doesn't. Why? The answer to this question forms the second part of the answer to why dream figures rather than human experts are used to effect the sufferer's deliverance.

The poem does not stop its theological exploration of ritual failure with the assertion of divine sovereignty because sometimes people actually recovered from their suffering outside the normal channels of assistance, that is, despite the (failed) attempts of the ritual experts.[89] On the one hand, such a possibility could offer hope to the suffering patient. On the other, such cases could have been perceived as a threat to the experts and their ritual system (even as it demonstrated Marduk's

86. To the best of my knowledge there is no evidence for dream interpreters in this matter.

87. See Lenzi, *Secrecy and the Gods*, 67–134.

88. Despite the critical presentation of ritual experts in Tablets I and II, I do not agree with Pongratz-Leisten's assessment that *Ludlul* is anti-institutional ("From Ritual to Text to Intertext," 147, 150). As will be shown below, it is quite the opposite.

89. This is presumably also why the poem does not simply have Marduk lift his uncooperative attitude and allow the human ritual experts finally to diagnose and treat the sufferer successfully: there was another agenda at work.

sovereignty in matters of mercy—also lauded in the opening hymn). I suggest that the poem's use of dreams in *Ludlul* III accounted for the possibility of healing outside of the normal ritual channels, and its manner of presenting rituals in the dreams helped shape the potential reactions to such healing from both the ones healed as well as the human ritual experts excluded from the process. In more general terms, the author utilized a common revelatory means in an unusual manner to address an anomalous situation in order to incorporate the anomaly into the accepted ritual system. Since gods do not normally perform rituals, the author utilized the dream figures as Marduk's ritual agents.[90] Who then are these dream figures, and how does their presence advance the agenda of the poem?

The male figure in the first dream and the female figure in the third, as far as we can tell from the preserved text, do not perform any ritual functions. Based on their descriptions and namelessness/lack of association (contrast the other two figures), they are probably lower-level divine beings. The male figure has extraordinary features (III 9b–10a) and the poem attributes a radiance (*melammû*) and an awe (*pulḫatu*) to him that are typical of divine beings (III 12). As for the female figure, the first half of III 32 may describe her garb anthropomorphically, *nišiš labšati*, "she was clothed as a human," but its second half explicitly identifies her as a being from the divine realm, *iliš mašlat*, "she was equal to a deity." Moreover, she utters words in III 36 often found in the mouth of divine beings, especially goddesses speaking to humans, *lā tapallaḫ*, "fear not!"[91] Although there is no way to be sure, I am inclined tentatively to identify these two low-level divine figures with the sufferer's personal deities.[92] Since Marduk has the power to expel and call back the personal

90. Note Lambert's comment in his edition of the poem: "A god may appear in a dream, but gods themselves did not perform ritual curing. This was the task of priests, and they did not normally practice their rites in other people's sleep. So the writer resorts to a succession of none too convincing dreams as a means of bringing the necessary priests to the sick man's bedside" (*BWL*, 24). As suggested above, casting two of the dream-figures as ritual experts was a very important rhetorical element to achieving the purpose of the poem.

91. See the references provided in CAD P, 40.

92. The fragmentary description of the female figure in III 33 as "a queen of peoples" (*šarrat nišī*) remains difficult for this identification, but we do not yet know how this line concluded. The queen (Zarpanitu?) may have been the person who sent the female figure; she is, after all, the only figure of the four in the dreams without a sender. And this would prepare the reader for Zarpanitu's role in Tablet IV (see lines 26, 50, 76, and 104). Pongratz-Leisten proposes to identify the female figure as Ishtar ("From Ritual to Text to Intertext," 151). Zgoll sees an ascending hierarchy

gods (I 15–16) and he has already sent these deities away (I 43–44), it seems reasonable to assume, in a kind of reversal of the logic in I 41–44, that he would compel their return when his anger subsided so the sufferer could recover from his woes. (The woes enumerated in Tablets I and II followed directly upon the divine abandonment described in lines I 43–46, so it seems logical to think the healing would require the return of the personal gods.[93]) If this identification is correct, the poem's use of a dream to signal the return of personal gods is unusual. A supporting reason for understanding these two figures as returning personal gods comes from the ritual actions attributed to the second and fourth figures in the dreams, the purification priest from Laluralimma and the exorcist named Ur-Nintinugga.

These two named figures and their significance were presumably known to the author and the assumed audience, but we have very little to go on beyond what is described in the text.[94] Both appear to be humans and both were likely from Nippur, a city well-known for its physicians and their prowess in the healing arts. According to the text Laluralimma sent a representative who appears in the second dream as a *ramku* or purification priest. In the latter half of the third dream Ur-Nintinugga appears, claiming to be the representative of Marduk. If the sufferer's personal gods were angry, this purification-priest and Ur-Nintinugga, the exorcist, would need to perform some kind of appeasement ritual on

among the senders of the (four, according to her) dreams, culminating with Marduk (*Traum und Welterleben im antiken Mesopotamien*, 285). I share the view that Ur-Nintunugga's mention of Marduk as his sender in III 43 is climactic. But my tentative restoration and understanding of the first dream's sender (i.e. "your lord" in III 15 is Marduk; see nn. 18 and 64 above) preclude the idea of an ascending hierarchy among the senders of the dreams.

93. After Tablet II, personal gods are not mentioned again in the poem until IV 115 and 117, and these are probably not to be identified with the sufferer's personal gods. IV 40 mentions the return of the divine guardian, but where, if not in the first and third dream, is the return of the personal gods? William Moran suggested the idea that Marduk becomes the sufferer's personal god in an essay entitled "The Babylonian Job," in *The Most Magic Words: Essays on Babylonian and Biblical Literature* (ed. R. S. Hendel; CBQMS 35; Washington, D.C.: Catholic Biblical Association of America, 2002), 182–200. But this is not tenable: although there is no doubt that *Ludlul* was written to exalt and proclaim Marduk's divinity and sovereignty, it is doubtful in light of the newly recovered lines near the end of the poem (IV 115 and 117) that Marduk can be viewed as becoming the personal god of the sufferer and by his example the personal god of the poem's audience. Certainly, the sufferer enters into a close relationship to his lord, Marduk, by the end of the poem, but this need not be understood in terms of personal religion.

94. See nn. 78 and 82 above.

behalf of the sufferer to quell the personal gods' anger. But they do not. Rather, they both perform therapeutic ritual acts, suggesting thereby that the divine anger and abandonment were already past.[95] The first purifies Shubshi-meshre-Shakkan, speaks an incantation over him, and performs a therapeutic ritual. Ur-Nintinugga applies a (medicated?) bandage from Marduk. The most significant feature to recognize for our purposes here is that both of these figures are presented as if they were exorcists; that is, they are presented as if they are from among the very experts in the human ritual system that had failed the sufferer.[96]

The dreams display Marduk's sovereign power to show mercy when and as he sees fit, offering hope to the sufferer who had slipped through the cracks of the official divinatory and ritual system. Yet the means by which the dream-figures achieve the sufferer's healing belong to the professional sphere of the ritual experts. Thus even when Marduk acted independently of the divinely sanctioned human ritual experts, he maintained the authority and integrity of the official ritual system the human experts oversaw.[97] This would have quelled the sufferer's concerns about the competence of the divinatory and ritual experts and the general effectiveness of the divinely sanctioned ritual system. Moreover, Tablet IV describes the sufferer entering Marduk's temple complex and celebrating his recovery there (IV 37–60, 67). Thus the poem brings the sufferer back into the ambit of the temple institution, an important social locus for contact with ritual experts and thereby affirms again the normal means and agents of ritual healing.

The above reading has assumed that the lamentation and doubt that may have arisen due to ritual failure would have done so among ritual participants and not the ritual specialists themselves. *Ludlul* would have assured the ritual participants that there was hope even when the experts failed. This hope, although extraordinary when it came, should not be understood as undermining the normal ritual system, as it indicates that even in an extraordinary circumstance of divine intervention the official system would be employed. Yet we actually do not know to what degree non-scribes would have known (or understood) *Ludlul*. The one group

95. For the two-track healing process in which divine appeasement worked along with therapeutic means, see Heeßel, *Babylonisch-assyrische Diagnostik*, 82, 95.

96. See likewise Pongratz-Leisten, "From Ritual to Text to Intertext," 152.

97. Interestingly, even the position of the dreams in the larger structure of the poem may support this point about the official ritual system. While identifying parallels to *Ludlul* in the incantation literature, Lambert observes that "[a]t the point where, if *Ludlul* were an incantation, the prescriptions for the ritual would be found, the dreams occur in which the ritual is performed and an incantation priest presents himself," even if—quite extraordinarily—in a dream (*BWL*, 27).

that we are certain would have known and understood the poem was the master scribes, whom we have called *ummânū*, "scholars," and identified as comprising a significant group among Mesopotamian ritual experts. We might entertain for a moment therefore the idea that the sufferer's situation in the poem also spoke to ritual experts or experts in training, since students copied the poem in their curriculum.[98]

Mesopotamian scholarship circumscribed a very exclusive group with extremely strong ideological notions about their value and importance to the king, society and cultural tradition broadly considered.[99] As with any group, a crack in its ideological foundation would need to be patched carefully to guarantee the perpetuation of the group's social position and cultural significance. *Ludlul* would have effectively achieved this purpose with regard to ritual failure by assuring scholars that the ritual system did indeed work even in extraordinary cases. Their occasional failures or frustrations were not due to their incompetence or the inadequacy (or falsehood) of their ritual system, the poem assured. Rather, in his sovereignty Marduk, the lord of their crafts—all of which were designated *nēmeqi*, "wisdom"[100]— simply trumped their ritual actions. Without his cooperation their hands were tied. It might have been some consolation, however, that when Marduk did act without their involvement he did so, the poem reassures its audience, in a way that would do them proud.[101]

Epilogue

Since the present volume contains a number of essays on biblical literature, in lieu of a redundant conclusion I offer a few brief reflections on

98. Seven tablets have been identified as exercise tablets among the fifty-four recognized manuscripts of the poem (two Assyrian, MSS $s^{1,2}$, and five Babylonian, MSS hh, mm, oo, ss, tt). See SAACT 7, xli–xlvi. According to Gesche, *Ludlul* was studied in the second, more advanced stage of scribal training in first-millennium Babylonia. See P. D. Gesche, *Schulunterricht in Babylonien im ersten Jahrtausend v. Chr.* (AOAT 275; Münster: Ugarit-Verlag, 2001), 173, 183. It seems unlikely that *Ludlul* would have been copied in the schools if it were in fact an anti-institutional document (see n. 88 above).

99. See, e.g., Lenzi, *Secrecy and the Gods*, 67–122, 136–49.

100. See Beaulieu, "The Setting of Babylonian Wisdom Literature," 12, and SAACT 7, xxxiv–xxxv.

101. Of course, this suggestion does not exclude the possibility that the poem, even if never heard by non-experts, could (also) have had pedagogical value for the ritual experts. It could have taught them how to explain to their clients why some problems were unable to be diagnosed while offering them hope.

the biblical book of Job from one of the perspectives that was essential to the above reading, namely, the identification of an atypical use of a common revelatory medium to accommodate an exceptional situation into the accepted theological system.[102]

As is well known, the book of Job concerns a righteous man who suffers for no other reason than YHWH's decision to permit it.[103] Divine sovereignty, as in *Ludlul*, is ultimately behind Job's prolonged suffering. The book makes no qualms and expresses no cynicism about this, but Job's suffering runs against the grain of a generally accepted idea about righteousness and retribution, an idea that was developed in various ways in numerous biblical texts (e.g. Deuteronomy and its notion of covenantal obedience, Ezek 18 and its emphasis on personal responsibility, 1 and 2 Chronicles and its development of immediate punishment for one's own sins, and the book of Proverbs with its strong ties between fear of YHWH, wise living and well-being). One need only ask Job's friends and the young upstart Elihu to understand that Job's situation was anomalous, especially to a view that understood retributive justice in a rigid and mechanical manner. A righteous man suffering, Job's friends all say in their own ways, could not possibly be truly righteous.

The theological problem at the base of Job's situation is what I will call unmerited disfavour. Unaddressed, this problem could have had potentially significant communal implications, as people became disenchanted with their god. In his attempt to make sense of Job's case (and thus the general theological problem of unmerited disfavor which Job's situation represents), the author of the book appropriated two common means of revelation, a vision of YHWH's heavenly council and a storm theophany, and worked them into his literary treatment at two key places, beginning and end. His deployment of each of these revelatory media is, literarily speaking, rather atypical.

In the opening chapters of the book the author twice presents a view on the heavenly council, a form/location of revelatory experience that is only clearly presented elsewhere in biblical literature in the account of Micaiah's prophetic vision in 1 Kgs 22. Rather than making a prophet have a vision of the heavenly council, the author in Job 1–2 simply pulls back the curtain of the heavens by authorial fiat to reveal to the book's audience that which was typically restricted to prophets (Amos 3:7). They see YHWH in the divine court exercising his sovereignty—doing

102. Full development of these suggestions will have to await a different venue.

103. The protagonist of *Ludlul* hints that sin lies at the root of his suffering (see III 58–61 and IV 45, along with my comments in SAACT 7, xxiii), but we do not get that impression at all from Job's monologues.

whatever he sees fit. It is as if the author is himself a prophet, sharing his visions of the divine throne room with his audience. They learn from the author's "visions" precisely why Job is suffering, knowledge of which they carry with them through the futile cycles of dialogue between Job and his friends. Job, the audience knows after ch. 2, is suffering because YHWH can do as he pleases with his servants. Argument, lamentation and doubt, the book seems to suggest, are acceptable. But the audience knows that these understandable human reactions are merely that: human reactions. The audience may experience Job's pain with him in the text, but they have an advantage over him: they have already seen that divine sovereignty takes precedence over everything, including righteousness and wisdom. YHWH is not strictly bound by a rigid understanding of retributive justice. He is free and humans must learn to embrace that. Experiencing Job's pain in the text allows a vent for frustration and space for religious doubt, all of which are part of the process of accepting what the heavenly vision already made clear: YHWH's supreme sovereignty to act outside of one's expectations.

At the other end of the book, Job (and the part of the audience that may have been resisting with him throughout the text) learns to accept YHWH's sovereignty. In Job 38:1 and 40:6 another form/location of divine revelation, a storm theophany, is employed in an atypical fashion. Usually found with elaborate descriptions of its effect upon the earth in collective and/or cultic-military contexts in biblical literature (see Exod 19:9–20; Judg 5:4–5; Hab 3:3–6; and Ps 18:8–18), the storm theophany in Job is simply called a whirlwind without further description of shaking and quaking, and the whirlwind appears uniquely here to an audience of one, Job, just before he and YHWH engage in a personal conversation. Although YHWH reveals himself in a visual and audible manner, Job never really learns why he is suffering; rather, he learns to accept that YHWH has a plan and is in control, executing his sovereign design as he sees fit. YHWH's sovereignty, the theophanies seem to say, trumps common theological notions and the human desire for knowledge which might bring (much wanted) understanding to miserable situations.

Certain views of retributive justice could not make sense of Job's anomalous situation (which represented various situations in the lives of those in the author's community). Such anomalies could have led to serious breaches in the religious solidarity of the community, so the author of Job, adopting a literary technique similar to the one used by the author of *Ludlul*, utilized common revelatory means in an unusual manner to address the anomaly and to incorporate it into his theological system, Yahwism, in an acceptable way. In so doing he buttressed the community's confidence in YHWH and maintained communal solidarity.

The fact that Job received double in the conclusion to the book (42:7–17)—whether the original ending or a later addition—shows that despite Job's exceptional situation, the general notion that the righteous should be blessed remained a firm conviction, even if the blessing was received in a way some had not envisioned or would not have preferred. Retributive justice, the book exhorts, cannot be applied to lives mechanically, but the righteous, in the end, still receive good things from YHWH's sovereign hand. One need only be patient. Just as was the case with the Mesopotamian ritual expert who wrote *Ludlul*, too much was at risk for the author(s) of the book of Job to allow an anomalous situation to upset the *status quo*.

The Exclusivity of Divine Communication in Ancient Israel: False Prophecy in the Hebrew Bible and the Ancient Near East

Herbert B. Huffmon

This essay addresses something of the special character of prophetic communication in ancient Israel. Prophetic communication by means of auditions, visions and dreams occurred throughout the ancient Near East. Apart from Israel, we are especially informed about such prophecy from the Mari texts of the Old Babylonian period, well before the time of Israel, and from the Neo-Assyrian texts, contemporary with some major periods of Israel's history. There are also scattered sources from other places and times. Fortunately, virtually all of these texts have been brought together in *Prophets and Prophecy in the Ancient Near East.*[1] One major difference among these prophetic traditions is that the Mari and Neo-Assyrian texts report revelations to individual prophets which come from or refer to multiple deities, apparently not restricted to the deity or deities who are honoured in the cult of a particular ancient Near Eastern temple. This phenomenon contrasts with the tradition of Israelite prophets, most of whom are described as having revelations only from Israel's god, YHWH. Indeed, revelations alleged to be from any other deity were apparently regarded by the Yahwistic community as inherently false, even if accompanied by signs and wonders (see Deut 13). Likewise, prophets who disagreed with the revelations of YHWH to an Israelite prophet, such as Jeremiah, might be dismissed as prophesying by Baal (Jer 2:8; 23:13), as prophesying falsely (שקר; Jer 5:31; 6:13; 8:10; 14:14; 23:25, 26) or as proclaiming a false vision (חזון שקר; Jer 14:14). The words of the exclusive deity are understood as consistent

1. M. Nissinen, with C. L. Seow and R. K. Ritner, *Prophets and Prophecy in the Ancient Near East* (SBLWAW 12; Atlanta: SBL, 2003), with references. For correlation with the citations in the present study, see Nissinen, *Prophets and Prophecy*, 221–22 ("Concordances").

words, and these divergent prophets are denounced as reporting their own dreams (Jer 23:25) or as manufacturing prophecies from "the deceit of their own heart" (Jer 23:26). Such prophets are said to not speak YHWH's word truthfully (Jer 23:28) and the text of Jeremiah includes many derogatory comments about prophets who differ from Jeremiah (see, e.g., Jer 2:26; 4:9; 14:13–16; 23:9–40; 27–29). The biblical tradition thereby introduces the concept of "false prophecy," an accusation of intentional divinatory falsehood that does not occur in a similar fashion in the Mari or Neo-Assyrian texts. In these texts prophetic revelations may differ or even conflict with the interests of others, but they are not thereby judged to be from a source that is inherently or intentionally false.[2]

It is notable that the Septuagint uses the term ψευδοπροφήτης, "false prophet," particularly in the book of Jeremiah in reference to prophets who differed from Jeremiah.[3] The use of this term in the Septuagint is a contextual rendering, not a literal rendering of any preserved Hebrew text.[4] The term is used, for example, in Jer 6:13, which refers to those

2. The divinatory examination of dreams, whether message dreams or not, is another matter. ARM 26 142, a letter from a diviner, notes that a dream of Sammetar (presumably the well-known official), a dream not otherwise described, is "an evening watch dream; it was not seen." This result falsifies the dream in the sense that the dream is deemed irrelevant or insignificant. Note the discussion by J.-M. Durand, *Archives Épistolaires de Mari* I/1 (ARM 26; Paris: Recherche sur les Civilisations, 1988), 26, 456–57; see also S. A. L. Butler, *Mesopotamian Conceptions of Dreams and Dream Rituals* (AOAT 258; Münster: Ugarit-Verlag, 1998), 29, 30; A. Zgoll, *Traum und Welterleben im antiken Mesopotamien* (AOAT 333; Münster: Ugarit-Verlag, 2006), 355–56. Sammeter's dream may have been examined with use of snippets of the hair and the garment hem of the intermediary, a practice mentioned in more than a dozen Mari texts; see Durand, *Archives Épistolaires*, 40 n. 180. See also the forthcoming study by E. J. Hamori, "Gender and the Verification of Prophecy at Mari," addressing the unequal frequency of this procedure with female prophets/dreamers, scheduled to appear in *Die Welt des Orients* (reference courtesy of J. Stökl).

3. See the Septuagint of Jer 6:13; 33(26):7, 8, 11, 16; 34(27):9; 35(28):1; 36(29):1, 8, as well as Zech 13:2, all translating נביא. In Jer 20:1 some Septuagint MSS identify the priest, Pashhur, son of Immer (MT), as a ψευδοπροφήτης, in keeping with the MT of Jer 20:6 (נבאת להם בשקר). On the occurrences of ψευδοπροφήτης, see E. Tov, *The Septuagint Translation of Jeremiah and Baruch: A Discussion of an Early Revision of the LXX of Jeremiah 29–52 and Baruch 1:1–3:8* (HSM 8; Missoula, Mont.: Scholars Press, 1976), 71–72, 165, 177 n. 52.

4. Note the interesting practice of the Targum of Jeremiah in dealing with "false" prophets, often translating as "scribes." See the discussion in R. Hayward, *The Targum of Jeremiah, Translated with a Critical Introduction, Apparatus and Notes* (The Aramaic Bible 12; Wilmington, Del.: Glazier, 1987), 32–33.

who strive for excessive gain, whether priest or prophet, thereby acting falsely and concealing the truth. It appears also in Jer 33(26):7, 8, 11, 16, which identify the priests and prophets who opposed Jeremiah as priests and false prophets specifically; in Jer 34(27):9, in which the list of untrustworthy intermediaries of the divine realm includes "your false prophets" (MT, נביאיכם); and in Jer 35(28):1, where it identifies Jeremiah's prophetic antagonist, Hananiah.[5] In Jer 36(29), purportedly a letter sent by Jeremiah to the exiles in Babylonia, v. 1 refers to "the elders of the exile, the priests, and the false prophets," and v. 8 refers to the "false prophets" together with diviners and dreamer as clearly untrustworthy. The Septuagint also has one occurrence of ψευδοπροφήτης apart from the examples in Jeremiah, in Zech 13:2, in which the names of the idols will be obliterated from any remembrance in the renewed land, together with "the false prophets" (MT, הנביאים) and "the unclean spirit." For this Yahwistic community a prophetic word from a deity other than YHWH is considered inherently false, whether it concurs with the judgments of Yahwistic prophets or not.

Nissinen has argued that there is evidence of "false" prophecy in the Neo-Assyrian texts.[6] He notes the stipulation in Esarhaddon's Succession Treaty that mandates reporting to the great crown prince designate, Assurbanipal, "any evil, improper, ugly (*la banītu*) word which is not seemly or good to Assurbanipal…either from the mouth of his enemy or from the mouth of his ally, or from the mouth of his uncles, his cousins, his family,…or from the mouth of your brothers, your sons, your daughters, or from the mouth of a prophet (*raggimu*), an ecstatic (*mahhû*), an inquirer of oracles (*šāʾilu amat ili*), or from the mouth of any human being at all."[7] But this refers to anyone who may disagree with the king's succession policy, as noted in the heading supplied by Parpola and Watanabe for this section, viz., "Obligations to Report Treason." Indeed, anyone who induces or suborns treason shall be put to death, and their name and their seed destroyed, as indicated in a subsequent section (lines 130–146). The actual issue here is not that the

5. Note the identification of Hananiah as a ψευδοπροφήτης also in some MSS of Jer 35(28):5.

6. M. Nissinen, "Falsche Prophetie in neuassyrischer und deuteronomistischer Darstellung," in *Das Deuteronomium und seine Querbeziehungen* (ed. T. Veijola; SFEG 62; Helsinki: Finnische Exegetische Gesellschaft, 1996), 172–95, and *References to Prophecy in Neo-Assyrian Sources* (SAAS 7; Helsinki: The Neo-Assyrian Text Corpus Project, 1998), 107–53, 166–67.

7. SAA 2 6 108–122. See also the edition by K. Watanabe, *Die adê-Vereidigung anlässlich der Thronfolgeregelung Asarhaddons* (Baghdader Mitteilungen Beiheft 3; Berlin: Mann, 1987), 71–73, 148–49, who offers a somewhat different translation.

divine intermediaries are knowingly or intentionally falsifying their revelation, but that their words are contrary to the interests of the king, that is, traitorous words from the perspective of the king. Such "traitorous" words do not seem to fit Nissinen's definition of false prophecy as "prophecy…not transmitted in due order but fabricated for political purposes using the proclaimer of the message…as a decoy."[8] Prophets and diviners may of course be coerced, if only by circumstances, but that is not the same as "fabricated" or intentionally deceitful words.[9]

Nissinen also cites the correspondence relating to the conspiracy of Sasi in the time of Esarhaddon, particularly the letters of Nabu-rehtu-uṣur (SAA 16 59; see also SAA 16 60–61) which mention a slave-girl who gives an oracle from the god Nusku which endorses Sasi as the proper king rather than the line of Sennacherib. But the focus is not whether or not "the word of the god Nusku" (SAA 16 59 r. 4′) was truly or correctly received by the slave-girl intermediary, but that the reported word was contrary to the interests of Esarhaddon. The charge seems to be that they "sinned against [your] father's goodness (*ina libbi ṭābti ša abi*[*ka*]…*īhṭūnī*), and your [father's] and your (own) treaty, as presumably disclosed by the goddess Nikkal (SAA 16 59 4–5; see also SAA 16 60 5–6; 61 4–6). All of this could be confirmed or disputed by a ritual (*dullu*) regarding the slave-girl, even if that process can be manipulated.

Deuteronomy 13:2–5 aptly describes the biblical exclusivist perspective, one which overrides even the experiential "time will tell" rule, of which the deuteronomic tradition is elsewhere rather fond:

8. Nissinen, *References to Prophecy*, 166–67, with reference to SAA 16 59. See also his earlier definition, which emphasizes that both Esarhaddon's Succession Treaty and Deut 13 focus on deception of the suzerain: "Es geht in beiden Fällen um Betrug gegen den Vertragspartner, und zwar gegen die stärkere Partei, der es frei steht, die Vertragsbestimmungen zu diktieren" ("Falsche Prophetie," 180). Note also the discussion by B. Pongratz-Leisten, who cites Nissinen's earlier definition but notes that the deuteronomic focus is on prophecy supportive of any deity other than YHWH and that Esarhaddon stresses any opposition to the Assyrian king or the crown prince (*Herrschaftswissen in Mesopotamien* [SAAS 10; Helsinki: The Neo-Assyrian Text Corpus Project, 1999], 72–73, 88). The Hebrew Bible, however, emphasizes that prophecy from any source other than YHWH is inherently false and can lay no claim on those who exclusively follow YHWH: it is the source which is decisive, not the content.

9. For an apparent instance of the fabrication of technical divination under duress, as noted by Nissinen (*References to Prophecy*, 167), see SAA 10 179. Whatever the intentions of Kudurru, the expert diviner, he could at least plead with the king that he had been coerced.

> If a prophet or a dreamer arises among you and provides you a sign or a wonder and the sign or wonder that he mentioned comes about, saying, "Let us follow after other gods"—whom you have not recognized/known—"and worship them," you should not heed the words of that prophet or that dreamer. For YHWH your god is testing you to find out whether you really love YHWH your god with all your heart and with all your being.
>
> You should follow after YHWH your god, and him you should fear and his commandments you should keep. You should heed his voice, him you should serve, and you should adhere to him.

The Israelite tradition is expressive of the understanding of a YHWH who, like the great king of the international treaties, demands exclusive loyalty. Such loyalty cannot coexist with revelations from any other deity, or even the recognition of signs or wonders associated with any other divine power. In this regard, even experience can be deceptive. Ideology is decisive. Exclusive loyalty does not allow for any alternative. The issue of false prophecy is thus linked to the biblical tradition of exclusive loyalty to YHWH.

If one turns to the question of experiential models for the exclusive relationship between Israel and its god, the obvious model is that of the relationship of a vassal to a great king, especially as articulated in international treaties of the Late Bronze Age and of the Neo-Assyrian period. The same concept occurs also in the more focused succession treaties of Esarhaddon, further copies of which have recently been found at Tayinat, a site which lies along the Orontes River in the Hatay province of modern Turkey and thus is much closer to Israel and Judah than is Assyria.[10] Israel's god is like the great king in that, for example, the great king forbids his vassals to have any relationship with a rival great king. These other kings are admitted to exist and in the political world represent a very accessible alternative, thus heightening the importance of exclusive loyalty. For any great king to be able to remain such he must be able to count on exclusive loyalty from his vassals. This is emphasized in the loyalty oaths. After all, a claim to be a great king without vassals is not very credible.

In connection with this loyalty the vassal is required to speak with the king—or the crown prince in the instance of Esarhaddon's Succession Treaty: "in the truth of your heart (*ina kitti libbika*), give him sound

10. It appears that this text is a virtual duplicate of the previously discovered succession texts of Esarhaddon. See http://www.independent.co.uk/news/science/archaeology/news2700yearold-royal-loyalty-oath-discovered-in-turkey-2107830.html.

advice loyally, and smooth his way in every respect."[11] The vassals are under oath to convey this instruction to "your sons and grandsons, your seed and your seeds seed."[12] The vassal is admonished that "(you shall not) set any other king or any other lord over yourselves, nor swear an oath to any other king or any other lord."[13] The vassal is also under oath to teach these obligations to sons born after the completion of this treaty, so that "in the future and forever Aššur will be your god and Assurbanipal…will be your lord."[14]

Previous classic formulations of the policy of exclusive loyalty occur, for example, in the treaty of the Hittite king, Suppululiuma I with Huqqana of Hayasa:

> Recognize only My Majesty as overlord. And recognize my son whom I, My Majesty, designate. (§2)
>
> Furthermore, benevolently recognize my sons—his brothers—and [my] brothers in brotherhood and comradeship. But beyond that you shall not recognize any other nobleman, whoever he might be, behind the back of My Majesty; Recognize [only] My Majesty and protect My Majesty! (§3)
>
> You, Huqqana, benevolently protect My Majesty, and stand behind only My Majesty. You shall not recognize anyone else beyond that. (§5)
>
> (But) if you, Haqqana, protect only My Majesty and take a stand only behind My Majesty, then these oath gods shall benevolently protect you, and you shall thrive in the hand of My Majesty. (§11; cf. §22)[15]

In terms of texts contemporary with the prophetic corpora from the Mari and the Neo-Assyrian texts, note an interesting example from a Mari text, cited by Georges Dossin in 1938 yet never fully published. The text refers to a king Yasmah-Addu, who is the king of the Yarih group of the Yaminites (not the Yasmah-Addu who ruled briefly at Mari and who was an actual son of the great king, Samsi-Addu). This Yasmah-Addu could claim the exclusive loyalty of his own group but was himself subordinate to the Mari king, Zimri-Lim. In the excerpt cited by Dossin, the men of Yarih declare, "Apart from Yasmah-Addu, the king our lord (*šarrim*

11. SAA 2 6 51–54, 98–99; Watanabe, *Die adê-Vereidigung*, 62, 69, 146–47, 148–49.

12. SAA 2 6 288–297; Watanabe, *Die adê-Vereidigung*, 98–99, 156–57.

13. SAA 2 6 71–72; see also SAA 2 6 129, 152–161, 194–197, etc.; Watanabe, *Die adê-Vereidigung*, 64–65, 74, 77–78, 83–84, 146–47, 150–51, 152–53, etc.

14. SAA 2 6 393–394; Watanabe, *Die adê-Vereidigung*, 109, 162–63.

15. For these texts, see G. Beckman, *Hittite Diplomatic Texts* (2d ed.; SBLWAW 7; Atlanta: Scholars Press, 1999), 27–29.

be-el-ni), we do not know/acknowledge (*ú-ul ni-di*) any other king."[16] ARM 26 347 9–15 provides another example of two-step exclusive affiliation. The kings of Ida-Maraṣ, under the leadership of Haya-sumu, pledge exclusive loyalty to Haya-sumu and his apparent overlord, Zimri-Lim: "Apart from Zimri-Lim and Haya-sumu, lord and father (*be-lum ù a-bu-um*) there is no other; [what]ever Zimri-Lim, our lord (*be-lí-ne*) says, we will do."[17] This indicates that exclusive loyalty could exist at various levels of affiliation. Another Mari letter, this time with a pledge to Zimri-Lim as a regional great king, recounts the negotiations among a group of kings as to whether or not they would take the oath to Zimri-Lim: "Besides Zimri-Lim, our father, our elder brother, and our guide, there is no other king."[18]

In addition to the emphasis on exclusive loyalty, Esarhaddon's Succession Treaty reminds his vassals that loyalty also means full compliance with the explicit words of the great king:

> You shall neither change nor alter (*tennani tušannani*) the word of Esarhaddon, King of Assyria, but serve this very Assurbanipal, the great crown prince designate, whom Esarhaddon, king of Assyria, your lord, has presented to you. (SAA 2 6 57–60)

> You shall protect Assurbanipal, the great crown prince designate, whom Esarhaddon, king of Assyria, has presented and ordered for you, and on behalf of whom he has confirmed and concluded (this) treaty with you; you shall not sin against him, nor bring your hand against him with evil intent, nor revolt or do anything to him which is not good and proper; you shall not oust him from the kingship of Assyria by helping one of his brothers, elder or younger, to seize the throne of Assyria in his stead, nor set any other king or any other lord over yourselves, nor swear an oath to any other king or any other lord. (SAA 2 6 62–72)

> (You are not to) oust him (Assurbanipal) from the kingship of Assyria, nor sw[ear an oa]th to any other king or any other lord. (SAA 2 6 128–129)[19]

16. G. Dossin, "Les archives épistolaires du Palais de Mari," *Syria* 19 (1938): 112; reprinted in *Recueil Georges Dossin*: *Melanges d'Assyriologie (1934–1959)* (Akkadica Supplementum 1; Leuven: Peeters, 1983), 109. For this Yaminite Yasmah-Addu, see ARM 2 53–56 and ARM 23 428–429.

17. Note the discussion by D. Charpin and N. Ziegler, *Florilegium marianum V: Mari et le Proche-Orient à l'époque Amorrite: Essai d'histoire politique* (MNABU 6; Paris: SEPOA, 2003), 209.

18. ARM 26 404 17–18; see W. Heimpel, *Letters to the King of Mari: A New Translation with Historical Introduction, Notes, and Commentary* (Mesopotamian Civilizations 12; Winona Lake, Ind.: Eisenbrauns, 2003), 133–35, 343–46.

19. Cf. Watanabe, *Die adê-Vereidigung*, 63–64, 74, 145–46, 150–51.

The Israelite prophetic tradition illustrates a similar kind of exclusive recognition of Israel's god, YHWH, a stance labelled the "Yahweh-alone" party or movement by Morton Smith in a course of lectures initially presented at Drew University in 1956–57 and subsequently revised as *Palestinian Parties and Politics That Shaped the Old Testament.*[20]

In fact, this aspect of Israel's "monotheism" has been emphasized in recent studies by the Egyptologist Jan Assmann.[21] Assmann concentrates, however, on Israel's later denial of the reality of any other gods, as in Deutero-Isaiah and many other passages. Rather than Assmann's major emphasis on what he labels the Mosaic distinction, that is, between true and false religion, I want to emphasize another dichotomy which Assmann mentions, viz., exclusive vs. non-exclusive loyalty; Assmann emphasizes that "the rise of biblical monotheism…involves the transference of the political institutions of alliance, treaty, and vassaldom from the mundane sphere of politics to the transcendental sphere of religion."[22]

In the model of the demand for exclusive loyalty by the great king, any affiliation with another great king represents fundamental disloyalty. When loyalty is the focus, the issue is not the existence of other kings or, by analogy, other deities, but the matter of exclusive commitment. In terms of Israel's religion, this exclusivist perspective is that of the YHWH-alone party. For this group, communication with the divine realm can only be communication with YHWH.

Prophetic communications in the Mari and the Neo-Assyrian texts, however, indicate that individual prophets in these contexts, whether

20. M. Smith, *Palestinian Parties and Politics That Shaped the Old Testament* (corrected ed.; London: SCM, 1987), 22. For a discussion of biblical and Near Eastern texts emphasizing the exclusive relationship to a great king or to YHWH, see H. B. Huffmon, "The Treaty Background of Hebrew *Yādaᶜ*," *BASOR* 181 (1966): 31–37; H. B. Huffmon and S. B. Parker, "A Further Note on the Treaty Background of Hebrew *Yādaᶜ*," *BASOR* 184 (1966): 36–38.

21. J. Assmann, *The Price of Monotheism* (trans. R. Savage; Stanford, Calif.: Stanford University Press, 2010), and *Of God and Gods: Egypt, Israel, and the Rise of Monotheism* (Madison: University of Wisconsin Press, 2008), developing ideas presented in his *Moses the Egyptian: The Memory of Egypt in Western Monotheism* (London: Harvard University Press, 1997).

22. Assmann, *Of God and the Gods*, 83. Note his continuing comments: "This semantic core of the prophetic and Deuteronomic movements is not so much concerned with the unity of God as it is with the exclusion of other gods as false or forbidden" (ibid., 83–84, cf. 110, 115). The combination of exclusive monotheism and the international treaties was earlier cited by G. E. Mendenhall, "Covenant Forms in Israelite Tradition," *BA* 17 (1968): 50–73; see also G. E. Mendenhall, *Ancient Israel's Faith and History: An Introduction to the Bible in Context* (ed. G. A. Herrion; Louisville, Ky.: Westminster John Knox, 2001), 57–63.

titled or untitled, may convey revelations from more than one deity. This is consistent with the character of the temples with which the prophets and other inspired persons are often associated, as individual ancient Near Eastern temples supported the cults of a number of deities: one deity might be dominant in a given temple but other deities were honoured as well.[23] This situation is especially obvious in many of the well-preserved temples in Egypt, such as the temple of Seti I in Abydos, with its seven entry chapels.

In terms of revelations from a number of gods communicated through a single intermediary, note ARM 26 194, a unique letter dictated by an *āpilum* of Šamaš, presumably to be identified as the letter to Zimri-Lim of Mari written by the special scribe requested by Atamrum, the *āpilum* of Šamaš cited in ARM 26 414.[24] The letter conveys requests from Šamaš on behalf of Šamaš, Adad of Aleppo, Dagan and Nergal, king of Hubšalum, thereby reflecting a kind of networking among the gods and/or intermediaries.[25] ARM 26 196, though it does not specify the intermediary, conveys to Zimri-Lim messages from various gods,

23. See R. Frankena, *Tākultu: De sacrale maaltijd in het assyrische Ritueel, met een overzicht over de in Assur vereerde goden* (Leiden: Brill, 1954). He studies some Neo-Assyrian texts which have Middle-Assyrian antecedents and indicate the presence of a multitude of deities in individual or joint temples. Just in terms of K. 252, the temples with fifteen or more deities participating in the cult include: in Assur, the Aššur temple (41+), the Anu-Adad temple (32) and the Aššur-Adad temple (23); in Nineveh, the é.maš.maš temple of Ištar-Ninlil (22); and in Babylon, the é.sag.íl temple of Marduk (21+); as well as citing fifteen gods who are "in the presence of Marduk" (Frankena, *Tākultu*, 5–13). Note also A. R. George, *Babylonian Topographical Texts* (OLA 40; Leuven: Peeters, 1992), 9–11, 44–55, for the list of more than ninety divine "seats," that is, shrines, and ten "stations" in the text of Tintir II. He comments that "it seems...very probable that this Tablet of *Tintir* is given over entirely to the listing of the shrines of Marduk's temple... Other texts of the genre that list shrines in a single sanctuary are the Shrine List of E-šarra, dealing with *šubtu*'s in the great temple of Aššur, and the shrine list from Uruk, which lists *šubtu*'s in Ištar's temple in that city" (George, *Babylonian Topographical Texts*, 11). For similar phenomena, cf. modern Hindu temples.

24. Nissinen, *Prophets and Prophecy*, 25 n. a; see also J.-M. Durand, "La religion amorrite en Syrie à l'époque des Archives de Mari," in *Mythologie et Religion des Sémites Occidentaux*. Vol. 1, *Ébla, Mari* (ed. G. del Olmo Lete; OLA 162; Leuven: Peeters, 2008), 488–90.

25. The request for Dagan occurs in a context that could be reconstructed as "the request [which [Qi]šti-Dagan, the [*āpi*]*lum* mentioned to you"; see J.-M. Durand *Archives Épistolaires de Mari*, 419 n. g. But the other requests are placed through Shamash. Note also ARM 26 230 6–12, which mentions a dream in which Itur-Mer responds to someone other than the dreamer, saying, "Hear Dagan and Ninhursagga... [He]ar the utterance of [the gods]."

meeting perhaps in a council of the gods; these include a dialogue between Tišpak and Dagan and words also from Yakrub-El, who in turn cites the goddess Ḫanat/ʿAnat.[26] In ARM 26 230 6–7, Itur-Mer answers someone in a dream, speaking for Dagan and Ninhursagga, while ARM 26 207 (ARM 10 4) reports that Queen Šiptu has inquired about signs from a male and a female who had been given something to drink seeking an oracle (or, she gave a male and a female signs to drink). The resultant oracle indicates that the supporting forces for Zimri-Lim, over against the forces of his adversary, Išme-Dagan, are the immensely powerful gods "Dagan, Šamaš, Itur-Mer, and Belet-ekallim, and Addu, lord of (oracular) decision."

In the Neo-Assyrian texts the phenomenon is attested in SAA 9 1 4, in which the prophet(ess?) Bayâ of Arbela, whose gender is unclear, says, "I am Bel… I am Ištar of Arbela… 'I am Nabû'…," referring also to Sin, Šamaš, (the) Sixty Great Gods, and Aššur. SAA 9 3 1–5 is a collection of five oracles: the first three feature revelations of Aššur, followed by a double line; then there are two oracles from Ištar of Arbela, followed by a double blank line, and an assignment of the oracles to "[La-dagil-i]li, a [*ra*]*ggimu* ('proclaimer') [of Arbel]a," apparently the source of all five of the oracles.[27] In another example, SAA 9 9 5, an oracle of Ishtar of Arbela apparently addressed to the queen mother, also makes reference to Ninurta and Šamaš, but does not provide a preserved message from either of these other deities.[28] By contrast, in the internal prophetic tradition of the Hebrew Bible (i.e. prophet vs. prophet, especially those traditions reflecting the YHWH-alone party) we encounter the exclusive character of divine revelation.

To return to Assmann: he states his agreement with Stephen Geller's comment that Israel is a "truly monotheistic" religion "only in the Deuteronomic form [and] that this is as close to monotheism as one could get in antiquity."[29] Assmann argues that:

26. See Durand, *Archives Épistolaires de Mari*, 384–85. For further discussion, see M. S. Smith, *God in Translation: Deities in Cross-Cultural Discourse in the Biblical World* (FAT 57; Tübingen: Mohr Siebeck, 2008), 136–39.

27. Parpola, *Assyrian Prophecies*, lxiii–lxiv. Parpola bases his restoration of the name "La-dagil-ili" on affinities with other texts and the prominence of that prophet elsewhere (SAA 9 1 10, 2 3); see his discussion at ibid., l–li, cvi nn. 265–66.

28. Cf. SAA 9 1 10.

29. Assmann, *Of God and Gods*, 114–15. The quotation of Geller is from the section, "Discussion and Conclusions," in *One God or Many? Concepts of Divinity in the Ancient World* (ed. B. N. Porter; TCBAI 1; Chebeague, Maine: Casco Bay Assyriological Institute, 2000), 324.

> Correspondingly, the "jealousy" of God belongs within the core semantics of monotheism and cannot be split off and isolated without severely distorting the historical phenomenology of biblical monotheism. This semantic core of the prophetic and Deuteronomic movements is not so much concerned with the unity of God as it is with the exclusion of other gods as false or forbidden. Thus, these movements—which came to be subsumed under the rubric "Yahve-alone-movement" following the groundbreaking work of Morton Smith—should instead be called "No-other-Gods-movement" since this, and not the Yahweh-alone-predication, is what sets them apart from all other religious practices inside and outside the Hebrew world. Exclusive (exclusivist) monotheism typically reckons with other gods, that is, with rival claims for power and truth, which it rejects as incompatible with its own truth.[30]

In contrast with the situation in the Mari and Neo-Assyrian prophetic texts, the prophetic texts in the Hebrew Bible do not make anything other than scornful references to other gods. These other gods cannot make any claim on Israel and—if only in that respect—are fraudulent, as argued in 1 Kgs 18. It seems clear that what is of central importance here is exclusive loyalty to YHWH. For the loyal followers who pledge to follow YHWH alone, there is effectively only one god. Other people may follow a multiplicity of deities and some of them, in the polytheistic fashion, might have included YHWH among the gods who could claim their loyalty; denying the very existence (power) of other gods is a secondary step. It was a step that Yahwistic loyalists eventually took, but that is not our concern here. Yahwists were clearly aware that in the world generally the majority of people gave their allegiance to a wide variety of gods.

Communication with the divine realm was affected by the idea of exclusive loyalty, with the YHWH-alone party convinced that genuine divine communication could only emanate from the one deity, YHWH. This led to the perception of differing prophetic revelations as being a matter of "false" or "lying" prophecy. This perspective did not require the other gods to cease existing, but it did suppose that for loyal Yahwists legitimate prophetic communication came from YHWH exclusively. No other gods' communications had power for or over them. The peculiar problems involved in having but one deity who is the exclusive source of oracles is illustrated in various ways in the traditions concerning the pre-exilic prophets.

The prophetic story in 1 Kgs 22 is a case in point, as it illustrates an understanding of the nature of exclusive loyalty. The king of Israel and

30. Assmann, *Of God and Gods*, 115. Apparently, "no other gods" means denying the existence of other gods, differentiated from giving exclusive loyalty to only one deity.

his vassal, the king of Judah, sought divine reassurance of success in their campaign against Ramoth-gilead, so the king of Israel gathered some four hundred prophets, led by Zedekiah ben Kana'anah, who engaged in group ecstasy (מתנבאים). The leader, Zedekiah, voicing "thus says the Lord," gave a clear assurance of YHWH's support of the campaign, seconded by all the prophets (vv. 10–12). The king of Judah, however, sought confirmation from another prophet, so the individual prophet, Micaiah ben Imlah, was approached and was advised to concur (v. 13). Micaiah, however, as a proper "vassal" who will "neither change nor alter the word of (the king)," replied, "As YHWH lives, I will speak whatever YHWH says to me" (v. 14). Nonetheless, Micaiah initially—apparently in a sarcastic manner and without the "thus says the Lord" phrase—concurred with the four hundred. But being adjured by the king(!) to be a dutiful vassal and to "speak to me in the name of YHWH only the truth" (v. 16), Micaiah reported what he saw and heard of the deliberations of YHWH's heavenly council. Micaiah's report did not challenge the integrity of the prophetic group—they were not knowingly deceiving the king in supporting the campaign against Ramoth-gilead, but according to Micaiah the four hundred had been used by YHWH to deceive the king, because YHWH had sent a רוח שקר—"a lying spirit" or "a spirit of deceit/falsehood"—"into the mouth of all these prophets of yours" (vv. 20–23). YHWH was intentionally misleading the king of Israel. Zedekiah protested and Ahab had Micaiah imprisoned; Micaiah is then quoted as saying that if Ahab returns from the battle alive "the word of YHWH was not in me" (v. 28), in keeping with the "time will tell" rule mentioned above. The spirit of deceit is consistent with maintaining the exclusivity of divine communication from YHWH and thereby falsifying the prophecy of Zedekiah and the four hundred prophets.[31]

Also relevant is the tradition of Elisha's duplicitous response to Hazael, Ben-Hadad's emissary; though this is not presented as a direct word of YHWH, YHWH had shown a contrary vision to Elisha, and Elisha's message for the Aramaean king is described as intentionally deceptive on his part (2 Kgs 8:7–10). Elisha did, however, speak "truthfully" to Hazael of his vision from YHWH (2 Kgs 8:11–15). There is also a close parallel to 1 Kgs 22 in the story of the clash between two royal counsellors, Hushai and Ahithophel, in 2 Samuel. David and Hushai agree on a plan to provide deceitful advice to the usurper, Crown Prince

31. Concerning deceptive prophecy see also Jer 29:8–9 and Ezek 14:9 and note the discussion by J. J. M. Roberts, "Does God Lie? Divine Deceit as a Theological Problem in Israelite Prophetic Literature," in *Congress Volume: Jerusalem, 1986* (ed. J. A. Emerton; VTSup 40; Leiden: Brill, 1988), 211–20.

Absalom. David entreats YHWH to render Ahithophel's advice foolish (2 Sam 15:31) and 2 Sam 17:14 confirms that "YHWH had given an order to render the good counsel of Ahithophel useless."

First Kings 13 presents the intriguing story of a "man of god" from Judah who had been sent on a mission to the northern kingdom. As he is returning from his mission an "old prophet" (נביא אחד זקן) residing in Bethel, who had followed after him, confronts him and offers hospitality. The man of God declines on the basis that it would conflict with the word of YHWH that he had received. The old prophet then counters this word of YHWH with contrary words: he tells the man of God that "I also am a prophet like you, and an angel spoke to me, according to the word of YHWH, 'Bring him back with you to your house…'" (v. 18). The man of god accepts this alternative revelation—reportedly obtained through an angel rather than directly from YHWH—in place of his own, direct word from YHWH. The man of God from Judah is subsequently condemned and killed for having set aside his own exclusive divine word in favour of someone else's (indirect) claim. YHWH's exclusive, direct word, the story contends, cannot be overruled by someone else's report of a divine word to the contrary, whether direct or indirect. The breach of loyalty by the man of God, substituting someone else's word for the direct command from his suzerain, YHWH, leads to his death. As noted above, vassals—by extension, prophets—are not to "change or alter the word (of the suzerain)"; this admonition is paralleled by the injunction to omit nothing of the words or commands of YHWH (Jer 26:2) and not to add or subtract anything from YHWH's commands as transmitted by Moses (Deut 4:2; 13:1).

In 1 Kgs 18, the legendary contest between Elijah and the four hundred and fifty prophets of Baal (who would, in proper polytheistic perspective, have more or less coincided with the four hundred prophets of Asherah) contrasts the strenuous yet ineffective attempts by the prophets of Baal to move Baal to action with Elijah's equally impressive and successful attempt to urge YHWH to act.[32] This legend emphasizes YHWH as the exclusive god for Israel. Baal is "real," with a temple and a cultus in Samaria (1 Kgs 16:31–32), but ineffective. Yet even this affirmation of Elijah as YHWH's prophet is mitigated by Elijah's having to scurry away to Mt. Horeb to escape the wrath of Jezebel. According to the tradition in 1 Kgs 19, the YHWH-alone party became the Elijah-alone

32. The two assemblages mentioned in 1 Kgs 18:19, separable but presumably overlapping in members, are subsequently in the MT reduced to the four hundred and fifty prophets of Baal. The four hundred prophets of Asherah/the grove(s) are again separately mentioned in 3 Kgdms 18:22, though not in v. 40.

party at Horeb, which YHWH rejected. The tradition of Elijah's response to the *Realpolitik* of Jezebel—but not King Ahab—in 1 Kgs 18–19 (unrealistically?) presents his opposition as the "Baal-(and Asherah?)-alone" party of Jezebel.[33]

This survey brings us back finally to Jeremiah and the story of the conflict between Jeremiah and Hananiah in Jer 28. Hananiah's announcement that YHWH would shortly restore to Jerusalem the temple furnishings that had been taken off to Babylon and restore Jehoiachin and the exiled Judahites at the same time—a troubling prospect to Zedekiah, perhaps—is countered by a cautionary personal word by Jeremiah, invoking the "too good to be true" rule together with the "time will tell" addendum (vv. 8–9). Jeremiah is then effectively upstaged by Hananiah's breaking of the symbolic bar off the neck of Jeremiah (v. 10), and Jeremiah retreats. But then Jeremiah comes back with his own word from YHWH, replacing the real but symbolic wooden bar with a strictly symbolic iron yoke, together with a divine word that YHWH has endorsed Nebuchadnezzar and has not sent Hananiah (vv. 14–15). From Jeremiah's point of view, Hananiah has deceived himself and thereby become disloyal to YHWH, which—as in the treaty requirement of strict loyalty to the suzerain—will lead to Hananiah's death: "You shall die, because you have spoken falsehood (סרה) concerning YHWH" (v. 16).[34]

In Jer 23 prophets in Samaria are condemned for prophesying by Baal, breaking with the exclusiveness of YHWH (v. 13), while other prophets, Judahites, are condemned (v. 14) for alleged immoral practices such as adultery (or adultery as a euphemism for following other gods, as in Jer 29:23), denoting a broken vow of loyalty to YHWH. An additional argument is then made: some of the alleged prophets are inventing their messages and have never been present in YHWH's secret council (vv. 17–18) and they are presenting their own, manufactured dreams, which are not from YHWH (vv. 25–28). These texts even cast doubt on dreams in general.

With YHWH's demand for exclusive loyalty, the issue of discerning true prophecy and false prophecy came to the fore in Israel. For the YHWH-alone perspective there is only one divine authority with whom the Yahwistic community can communicate, and thus the multiple constituencies and multiple deities conceived elsewhere are not relevant.

33. Note that Morton Smith, *Palestinian Parties*, 25, associates the legends of Elijah and Elisha with the YHWH-alone party and calls attention to "Jezebel's devotion to Baal."

34. Note the NJPS translation of Jer 28:16: "for you have urged disloyalty to the Lord."

False prophecy is accounted for in part as God's intentional deception, parallel to the intentional deception of royal figures such as David in the case of Hushai. One could also allege that a prophet goes through the motions—for example, self-induced ecstasy—but never actually communicates with YHWH, or attack the moral character of non-Yahwistic prophets. Yet the "time will tell" rule for determining when prophecy given in YHWH's name is not true prophecy, which defers judgment from the present moment of the prophecy, is unhelpful for an immediate audience, nor does such a scheme work very well for eschatological prophecies of hope and peace, such as the elimination of "the bow, the sword, and warfare from the land" (Hos 2:20).[35] YHWH's insistence on exclusive loyalty thus leads to a continuing issue of true or false revelation and is part of what Assmann identifies as the price of monotheism, namely, the easy transition of monotheistic/exclusive religion into violence and persecution directed at all those who do not share the exclusive loyalty. Nonetheless, this exclusive loyalty remains a long-honoured component of the major religious communities—Judaism, Christianity and Islam—which derive from the biblical tradition.

35. Huldah's words in 2 Kgs 22:20 would have given (false) reassurance to Josiah, if he heard them, as they did not fit with subsequent events.

(Intuitive) Divination, (Ethical) Demands and Diplomacy in the Ancient Near East*

Jonathan Stökl

Introduction

The usage of divination as part of the *Herrschaftswissen* of ancient Near Eastern kings is a well-established concept.[1] The term *Herrschaftswissen* here refers to divine information that ancient Near Eastern kings were expected to have in order to govern well and which they acquired through the use of diviners. Such diviners took the place of the special scientific advisers and intelligence officers of the modern state.[2] They provided the king and other decision makers with intelligence from the divine sphere. In the scholarly discussion so far, the concept of *Herrschaftswissen* has been focussed on the interior politics of the state and has—with the major exception of warfare—ignored foreign politics. In this essay I will suggest that divination was used in foreign politics as well, focusing on two principal examples. The example from Old Babylonian Aleppo is clear and refers to the interaction of overlord to vassal (or maybe stronger ally to weaker ally); in the biblical example it is not entirely clear whether we should understand the actions of Balaam as divinatory or as magical. I will also draw attention to the ethical dimension of divination: the texts dealt with here are founded on a demand by Adad of Aleppo for asylum to be granted to those who seek it.[3]

* I would like to acknowledge the support of the European Research Council project BABYLON in the writing of this essay.

1. B. Pongratz-Leisten, *Herrschaftswissen in Mesopotamien: Formen der Kommunikation zwischen Gott und König im 2. und 1. Jahrtausend v. Chr* (SAAS 10; Helsinki: The Neo-Assyrian Text Corpus Project, 1999).

2. Ancient courts had access to scholars and secret services as well, P. Dubovský, *Hezekiah and the Assyrian Spies: Reconstruction of the Neo-Assyrian Intelligence Services and its Significance for 2 Kings 18–19* (Rome: Pontifical Biblical Institute, 2006).

3. There are various forms of the name of this deity. Generally, when speaking about West-Semitic forms, such as Adad of Aleppo, the form Adad is used for the second millennium B.C.E. The Akkadian form is Addu, and therefore all quotes in

Before we can approach that subject, however, a number of preliminary points must be discussed. First, one of the main distinguishing factors usually identified between prophecy in the Hebrew Bible and in Mesopotamian texts is the apparent lack of ethical concerns in Mesopotamian texts. By contrast, they are often regarded as so prominent in the biblical text that Israel's prophets have been called founders of ethical monotheism. Martti Nissinen has pointed out that the difference is not quite a strong as usually thought, but even he conceded that most of the Mesopotamian texts are concerned with ritual or royal matters.[4]

Secondly, there is the matter of how and whether to distinguish between prophecy and divination. In the debate among scholars of ancient Near Eastern prophecy and divination a consensus has emerged that prophecy is but one form of intuitive divination.[5] That means that its function is fundamentally similar to other forms of divination. The only difference between technical and intuitive divination is the method by which the divine information is accessed. For technical divination, a technical, that is, learnable skill is required to interpret the message which the deity has conveyed via, for example, a sheep's liver, clouds, stars, and so on. With intuitive divination, the message is essentially clear and does not require further interpretation. If it does, as for example in Nebuchadnezzar's dream in Dan 4, the king can be regarded as similar to a diviner's sheep; he is not the diviner, but the medium by which the deity conveys its message, which then requires a technical diviner—in this case the oneirocritic Daniel—in order to interpret it.[6]

and direct translations from Akkadian will have that form here, even if they refer to the West-Semitic Adad of Aleppo. Otherwise, I will use the form Adad.

4. M. Nissinen, "Prophecy Against the King in Neo-Assyrian Sources," in *"Lasset uns Brücken bauen...": Collected Communications to the XVth Congress of the IOSOT, Cambridge 1995* (ed. K.-D. Schunck and M. Augustin; Frankfurt am Main.: Lang, 1998), 157–70, and "Das kritische Potential in der altorientalischen Prophetie," in *Propheten in Mari, Assyrien und Israel* (ed. M. Köckert and M. Nissinen; FRLANT 201; Göttingen: Vandenhoeck & Ruprecht, 2003), 1–33.

5. M. Nissinen, "Prophecy and Omen Divination: Two Sides of the Same Coin," in *Divination and Interpretation of Signs in the Ancient World* (ed. A. Annus; Oriental Institute Seminar Series 6; Chicago: Chicago University Press, 2010), 341–51; L. L. Grabbe, *Priests, Prophets, Diviners, Sages: A Socio-Historical Study of Religious Specialists in Ancient Israel* (Valley Forge: Trinity Press International, 1995), 150–51; Pongratz-Leisten, *Herrschaftswissen*.

6. For similar views see, e.g., H. M. Barstad, "No Prophets? Recent Developments in Biblical Prophetic Research and Ancient Near Eastern Prophecy," *JSOT* 37 (1993): 39–60 (47–48); E. Cancik-Kirschbaum, "Prophetismus und Divination - ein Blick auf die keilschriftlichen Quellen," in Köckert and Nissinen, eds., *Propheten in Mari*, 33–53; F. H. Cryer, "Der Prophet und der Magier: Bemerkungen anhand einer

Two Texts from Mari

In the following I will use a particular letter from Yarim-Lim, king of Aleppo, to Zimri-Lim, king of Mari, in which Yarim-Lim adduces divine information in arguing why he will not extradite certain refugees to Zimri-Lim.[7] Studies on the biblical right of asylum usually make a stark distinction between asylum in a foreign country and asylum in a sanctuary.[8] While there are differences between the two forms of asylum, they are not entirely separate, as this text indicates. Since asylum in a foreign country can also be divinely authorized, an entire country may act like a temple or city offering asylum in the biblical and Greek worlds.

Almost all Old Babylonian prophetic texts which we possess were found at Mari. This is also true of the diplomatic correspondence between Yarim-Lim and Zimri-Lim, although a number of them were ostensibly written in Aleppo; among these are most of the texts cited in this study. The first two are written by Nūr-Sîn, a Mariote civil servant,

überholten Diskussion," in *Prophetie und geschichtliche Wirklichkeit im alten Israel: Festschrift für Siegfried Herrmann zum 65. Geburtstag* (ed. R. Liwak and S. Wagner; Stuttgart: Kohlhammer, 1991), 79–88; M. deJong Ellis, "Observations on Mesopotamian Oracles and Prophetic Texts: Literary and Historiographic Considerations," *JCS* 41 (1989): 127–86 (144–46); W. Farber, "Witchcraft, Magic, and Divination in Ancient Mesopotamia," in *Civilizations of the Ancient Near East*, vol. 3 (ed. J. M. Sasson et al.; Peabody, Mass.: Hendrickson, 1995), 1895–1909; Grabbe, *Priests*, 150–51; M. Nissinen, "What Is Prophecy? An Ancient Near Eastern Perspective," in *Inspired Speech: Prophecy in the Ancient Near East: Essays in Honour of Herbert B. Huffmon* (ed. J. Kaltner and L. Stulman; JSOTSup 378; London: T&T Clark International, 2004), 17–37 (21); T. W. Overholt, *Channels of Prophecy: The Social Dynamics of Prophetic Activity* (Minneapolis: Fortress, 1989), 140–47; Pongratz-Leisten, *Herrschaftswissen*; J. C. VanderKam, "Prophecy and Apocalyptics in the Ancient Near East," in Sasson et al., eds., *Civilizations of the Ancient Near East*, 3:2083–94 (2083) and K. van der Toorn, "L'oracle de victoire comme expression prophétique au Proche-Orient ancien," *RB* 94 (1987): 63–97 (67–68).

7. For the publication of the relevant Mari texts, see specifically J.-M. Durand, *Florilegium marianum VII: Le culte d'Addu d'Alep et l'affaire d'Alahtum* (MNABU 8; Paris: SEPOA, 2002), and *Florilegium marianum VIII: Le culte des pierres et les monuments commémoratifs en Syrie amorrite* (MNABU 9; Paris: SEPOA, 2005). More generally, see J.-M. Durand, *Archives épistolaires de Mari I* (ARM 26/I; Paris: ERC, 1988); D. Charpin, *Archives épistolaires de Mari II* (ARM 26/II; Paris: ERC, 1988).

8. See most recently C. Dietrich, *Asyl: Vergleichende Untersuchung zu einer Rechtsinstitution im Alten Israel und seiner Umwelt* (BWANT 182; Stuttgart: Kohlhammer, 2008).

perhaps an ambassador, at Aleppo (FM VII 38–39 = SBLWAW 12 1–2).[9] In both texts Nūr-Sîn writes to his king Zimri-Lim in order to report what he has heard. He puts particular emphasis on a message of *āpilum*-prophets which he has received several times: that Zimri-Lim should give the real estate referred to as *Alaḫtum* to the deity Adad of Kallassu. In language which strongly evokes the Neo-Assyrian oracles of Ištar to Esarhaddon, in which she claims to have raised the king on her lap, Adad of Kallassu claims to have raised Zimri-Lim between his thighs, indicating both a close relationship and, perhaps more importantly, protection and oversight of Zimri-Lim's career. In return, Zimri-Lim ought to organize a *zukrum*-ritual for the memory of his deceased ancestors and to hand control over this piece of real estate to Adad of Kallassu.[10]

The similarities between this and Ištar's Neo-Assyrian oracles, the latter spoken in the context of the Neo-Assyrian empire's internal politics and troubled royal succession, may suggest another possibility, namely, that to the deity from Aleppo and therefore also to Yarim-Lim, the kingdom of Mari was not a foreign partner as such; rather, claiming control over Mari, Adad of Kallassu may speak in the terms of internal politics.[11] The problem with this interpretation is that, as the main deity of Aleppo, we would expect Adad to speak these words to Yarim-Lim, king of Aleppo, not to Zimri-Lim, king of the foreign state of Mari.

It is likely that Aleppo's support for Zimri-Lim when (re-)taking the throne at Mari took a military form as well as involving religious and propaganda support. We do not know what price Zimri-Lim had to pay for the military support, but it is clear from these letters that deities from Aleppo demanded adherence to a religious ritual—which Zimri-Lim should presumably have performed in any case—and the donation of property. In a further oracle transmitted in the letter, Adad of Aleppo demands not earthly goods but rather that Zimri-Lim help the orphan and perform his royal role justly; surely this is an ethical demand, even if it is part of standard ancient Near Eastern royal ideology.

In the next letter, FM VII 1, political asylum plays a major role. The text is a report by an ambassador of Zimri-Lim at the court of

9. One part of FM VII 39 is the first Mari prophetic text to be published. See G. Dossin, "Une révélation du dieu Dagan," *RA* 42 (1948): 125–34.

10. For the *zukrum* at Emar, see D. E. Fleming, "The Rituals from Emar: Evolution of an Indigenous Tradition in Second-Millenium Syria," in *New Horizons in the Study of Ancient Syria* (ed. M. W. Chavalas and J. H. Hayes; Bibliotheca Mesopotamica 25; Malibu, Calif.: Undena, 1992), 51–61, and D. E. Fleming, *Time at Emar: The Cultic Calendar and the Rituals from the Diviner's Archive* (MC 11; Winona Lake, Ind.: Eisenbrauns, 2000).

11. SAA 9 2 5 = SBLWAW 12 82.

Yarim-Lim and it contains Yarim-Lim's answer to a request by Zimri-Lim to hand over a local king and vassal of Zimri-Lim who had dared to insult his king by calling him "my brother" rather than "my father." In his response, Yarim-Lim acknowledges that the local king misbehaved. He reports that he has talked to this king and has made him acknowledge Zimri-Lim's higher status, but Yarim-Lim staunchly refuses to hand over the miscreant.

In another letter at a different point in time, Zimri-Lim had written to Yarim-Lim regarding some fugitives, and Dariš-libur, another ambassador of Zimri-Lim, seems to have been rather tenacious in getting the fugitives extradited. In his responses, Yarim-Lim claims that it is not up to him, but that it is a demand by the mighty Adad of Aleppo that refugees cannot be turned over to their pursuers. Dariš-libur contacts Yarim-Lim at least three times over this matter, until he caves into Dariš-libur's demand, unfortunately without naming a reason. Dariš-libur's ambassadorial report to Zimri-Lim starts with the usual short introduction before moving straight to the issue at hand:

> [to] my [lord] speak, [thus (says) Dari]š-libur, your servant:
> [I have he]ard [the tablet which is f]or Yarim-Lim (the one which) my lord sent [t]o me. I have properly presented the plan of my lord [according to wh]at was written on the tablet [before Y]arim-Lim and A[pl]a[ḫ]anda. M[ay] my lord [listen] (to everything) which they answered [regarding] the m[en]. [According to the word of m]y [lord which] I spo[ke to Yari]m-[Lim] [he an]swe[red m]e: "Zimr[i-Lim] has [ex]pelled [his e]nemies. [N]ow, (however), his [dem]ands are dangerous. [Sumu-Epuḫ], my [father] (who) [re]spected go[d][12] [was succ]essful. N[o] (ot[her]) king [confronted him]. When (he saw what Addu) had given [t]o Sam[si-Ad]du [it overpowered] [Su]mu-Epu[ḫ], my father; he did not reach his old age. [Regardi]ng the lan[d…] [which] he (Addu) had given [t]o Samsi-Addu [(Addu) hit (him)] [Ad]du killed him and until n[ow] Addu has no[t been an]gry with me." This is what he answered me.[13] (lines 3–23)

12. Or "the god." The deity referred to is probably a form of Adad, presumably Adad of Aleppo.

13. *[ana bēlī]ya qibīma [umma Dari]š-libur waradkama [ṭuppam ša an]a Yarīm-Līm [an]a ṣ[ē]rīya bēlī ušabila[m] [ešm]ēma ṭēm bēlīya [kima š]a ina ṭuppim šuṭṭuram [maḫar Y]arīm-Līm u A[pl]a[ḫ]ada [urak]kis u ata[ppu]l[šunu] [aššum] a[w]īli bēlī l[išme] [kima ana Yarī]m-[Līm] [awat bēlīy]a adda[bbubu] [kiam i]pul[ann]i Zimr[i-Līm] [n]akri[šu u]šēṣi in[anna] [d]annu [erē]šušuma [Sumu-Epuḫ] [ab]i īl[am ip]laḫma [ḫidānšu] [lu ik]šud m[amma] šarru ša[num ūl imḫuršu] [an]a Šam[ši-Ad]du iddinūš[u ilteqīma] [Su]mu-Epu[ḫ] abi šibu[ssu] ūl iššib [aššu]m mā[t...] [ša a]na Šamši-Addu iddinū [imḫaṣū] [Ad]du ušmissu u adi i[nanna] [l]ibbi Addu elīya ū[l šab]us annitam ipulanni.*

This is the first response. Yarim-Lim answers that he cannot extradite the refugees to Zimri-Lim because he wants to remain true to Adad, so that, unlike his father, he would not die prematurely.[14] This implies that Adad, the national deity, has demanded that refugees be given asylum in Aleppo. And sure enough, in his second response Yarim-Lim is more explicit:

> In his second response he answered me: "Has Zimri-Lim forgotten the command of Addu? Indeed, I fear that Zimri-Lim does not know that in the land of Addu a refugee cannot be extradited! Otherwise, why should he send to me: 'Drive these men out of your land so that they are no longer there!'" His second response.[15] (lines 24–33)

Yarim-Lim reminds Zimri-Lim of the "command of Addu" in a way that suggests that Zimri-Lim should be well aware of it. The most logical time and place for Zimri-Lim to learn about such a general rule or law of Adad would have been the time that he spent in Aleppo preparing for his own campaign to regain his father's throne. Yarim-Lim presumably received requests by Samsi-Addu to extradite Zimri-Lim but protected his former vassal's son and did not extradite him. Thus, Zimri-Lim probably benefited from the same *ṭēm Addu* which he now wants Yarim-Lim to ignore.

This case demonstrates how the distinction between different forms of asylum usually drawn by biblical scholars does not work: temple asylum and asylum in a different country may both be divinely authorized and protected.[16]

ABL 878 8–9, 11 shows that Aleppo was not the only location of such a form of asylum: "For Babylon is the connection between the lands, whosoever enters it, its protection works… Not even a dog which enters is killed." At least in the ideal form, Babylon was understood as a city of asylum as well. The collecting and analyzing of all ancient Near Eastern texts regarding asylum would be a worthwhile task, but this goes far beyond the scope and aim of this study.

14. In this Akkadian text I have normalized the logographic spelling ᵈIŠKUR as Addu, the Mesopotamian form of the deity. For easier understanding, I will continue to use the West-Semitic form, Adad, outside the translations.

15. *ina šanītim napaltišu kiam ipulanni Zimri-Līm ṭēm Addu imtašši adī assur*[*r*]*ēma kima ina māt Addu munnabtu ina qātim lā innaddinu Zimri-Līm ūl īde ma kiamma lišpuram awīlū šunuti ina libba mātika ku*[*šš*]*issunuti lā uššabu šanītum napaltišu*.

16. See, most recently, C. Dietrich, *Asyl*, with further literature.

Back in FM VII 1, Dariš-libur goes on to write that he pestered Yarim-Lim a third time and that suddenly, without indication of a reason, Yarim-Lim has changed his mind and decides to extradite the refugees to Zimri-Lim. Considering that Yarim-Lim had previously cited a general divine command not to extradite prisoners, we must surmise that either Yarim-Lim was quite devout and was genuinely hesitant to break his divine overlord's command or he found it convenient to refer to it when denying Zimri-Lim's wishes, or some combination of the two. I tend to believe Yarim-Lim's respect of Adad, as denying a request so outspokenly in diplomatic literature is quite unusual. Here now Yarim-Lim's third and different answer, again invoking Adad:

> He answered a third time: "If the men [a]re in my land (and) [I] have refused (to hand) them to Zimri-Lim previously, [Z]imri-Lim may be annoyed (with me). [F]rom now until a year, three year[s], [unt]il ten years, should these men return and come [t]o my land and my kingdom, I will hand them over. I will pass them on [t]o Zimri-Li[m]. [I]f I should [n]ot fulfi[l] my obligation to Zim[ri-Lim], [may] Addu, the lord of Aleppo, demand an answer from Yari[m-Lim]." This he answered me.

In the rest of the letter Dariš-libur tells us about some of the letters that Yarim-Lim sent to his vassals to demand that the refugees be handed over. For our current purpose it is quite important, however, to see that Yarim-Lim invokes Adad as guarantor of his promise to Zimri-Lim to hand the refugees over to his authority. This indicates that Yarim-Lim did not simply decide to change his mind and go against the god's demand, but that the god somehow communicated his agreement to the plan. Sadly, Dariš-libur does not transmit any reason as to what moved Yarim-Lim to change his mind, so we cannot be certain about how this occurred.

Let me summarize what we have found so far. Adad of Aleppo and Adad of Kallassu both make demands of Zimri-Lim, even though Zimri-Lim was not the king of their territory. In fact, it seems as if the two deities were involved in some diplomacy with the human king. The language they use, however, is that of royal oracles to a king, reminding the king that the deity raised the king "between their knees." Normally, this language is used for a deity speaking to the king of the territory in which its temple is located.[17]

17. It may go too far to speculate that this indicates that this thought-model of a deity treating a foreign king like the king who controls the deity's "home-land" indicates that the structure of Deutero-Isaiah's referring to Cyrus as "messiah" and "servant" was known over a millennium previously. On the other hand, the similarity is striking.

Further, Adad of Aleppo had clearly demanded that his country be a country of asylum, something that had at one time been a great help to Zimri-Lim.[18] Some years later, when he had regained his father's throne, the very same right to asylum became a problem for him as he wanted to pursue leaders who did not accept his authority. Yarim-Lim initially adhered to Adad's commandment and Zimri-Lim could do little but keep asking—in the end with success. Sadly, we do not have any Old Babylonian archive from Aleppo which could shed further light on the issue from an Allepine perspective. Thus we do not know how Yarim-Lim came to change his mind and whether he received special dispensation from Adad to extradite the refugees.

The structural difference between the two episodes is that in the first, the deities themselves seem to be involved in foreign politics, while in the second, divine commands—presumably received through some form of divination—have a strong impact on the diplomatic communication between an overlord, Yarim-Lim, and his vassal, Zimri-Lim. In both cases, however, divination—whether by prophecy or haruspicy—has an influence on human foreign politics as well as internal politics. It is important to keep in mind, however, that the divinatory oracles are not oracles against the nations as we find them in the Hebrew Bible. These are in an altogether different category, since they are not aimed strictly at foreign policy; rather, their effect is on the internal politics of the state.

Prophecy and Foreign Politics in Judah? Jeremiah and Balaam

Before we turn to the biblical texts themselves, let me point toward another Mariote text which shows prophets' potential for stirring up popular emotions. The text contains the report of an event at far away Babylon. Yarim-Addu, Zimri-Lim's man at the court of Ḫammu-rapi of Babylon, recounts how an *āpilum*–prophet of Marduk stood at the city-gates and kept on shouting to anybody who would listen that Ḫammu-rapi had given large parts of Marduk's temple treasure away in order to make peace with Elam. It is not entirely clear whether this is the same *āpilum*–prophet of Marduk who is involved in another episode recounted in the same letter, in which the *āpilum* stood at the palace-gate and shouted that Ḫammu-rapi had offered refuge to the ailing king Išme-Dagan of Ekallatum.[19] This shows that, far from being active only in temples, ancient Near Eastern prophets also took to the streets if their

18. J. M. Sasson, "The King and I," *JAOS* 118 (1998): 453–70 (454).
19. ARM 26 371 = SBLWAW 12 47.

addressees were located there. In other words, prophets could act in order to stir up popular emotion and could therefore be capable of influencing the general mood.

A biblical character who is portrayed as stirring up popular emotions in this way is Jeremiah, when he strongly attacks the Judean rebellion against Babylon. Equally, the book bearing his name portrays the Babylonians treating him relatively well after the city of Jerusalem had fallen, so much so that it has been suggested that Jeremiah might have been a Babylonian agent.[20]

Here I will focus on the literary portrayal of Jeremiah without claiming anything about the historical Jeremiah. The literary prophet was in favour of Babylon, and a later redactor of the book enhanced this further by going so far as to call Nebuchadnezzar "my servant."[21] But Jeremiah's political position could also have been due to a relatively astute analysis of the power politics of the Near East at the time, without the need for Jeremiah to be a Babylonian agent. Further, Jeremiah's divinatory action took place within Judah and was addressed to Judahites. He may have

20. E.g. N. Sarna, "The Abortive Insurrection in Zedekiah's Day (Jer. 27–29)," *Eretz Israel* 14 (1978): 89*–96*. I do not entirely share R. Carroll's view that the book of Jeremiah does not provide us with any access whatsoever to a historical prophet Jeremiah (R. P. Carroll, *Jeremiah: A Commentary*, vol. 1 [OTL; London: SCM, 1986]). Instead, I think it is likely that there was a prophet called Jeremiah, and that echoes of his life are contained in the book bearing his name; it is merely that our ability to discern historically accurate episodes in the text is extremely limited. Whether literary or not, the character would have to work in the audience's imagination.

21. See, e.g., A. Schenker, "Nebukadnezzars Metamorphose vom Unterjocher zum Gottesknecht in den beiden Jeremia-Rezensionen," *RB* 89 (1982): 498–27; S. Timm, "Wird Nebukadnezar entlastet? Zu 2Kön 18,24–25,21," in *"Sieben Augen auf einem Stein" (Sach 3,9): Studien zur Literatur des Zweiten Tempels: Festschrift für Ina Willi-Plein zum 65. Geburtstag* (ed. F. Hartenstein and M. Pietsch; Neukirchen–Vluyn: Neukirchener Verlag, 2007), 359–89; K. Schmid, "Nebukadnezars Antritt der Weltherrschaft und der Abbruch der Davidsdyanstie," in *Die Textualisierung der Religion* (ed. J. Schaper; FAT 62; Tübingen: Mohr Siebeck, 2009), 150–66; J. Stökl, "The Villain King: Nebuchadnezzar in Jewish Memory in the Persian and Hellenistic Periods," in *Bringing the Past to the Present in the Late Persian and Early Hellenistic Period: Images of Central Figures* (ed. E. Ben Zvi and D. V. Edelman; forthcoming). For the opposite view, see E. Tov, "The Literary History of the Book of Jeremiah in Light of Its Textual History," in *The Greek and Hebrew Bible: Collected Essays on the Septuagint* (ed. E. Tov; VTSup 72; Leiden: Brill, 1999), 363–84, and "A Textual-Exegetical Commentary on Three Chapters in the Septuagint," in *Scripture in Transition: Essays on Septuagint, Hebrew Bible, and Dead Sea Scrolls in Honour of Raija Sollamo* (ed. A. Voitila and J. Jokiranta; JSJSup 126; Leiden: Brill, 2008), 275–90.

been an agent and employed in the foreign politics of the Babylonians, but his prophetic activity was focused entirely on the internal politics of Judah.

None of the Israelite prophets ever pronounce messages which are truly addressed to non-Israelite addressees. Not even the oracles against the nations are addressed to foreign nations; their purpose is to comfort Israel rather than to frighten the foreign nations. The one case of a non-Israelite diviner speaking directly to Israelites is possibly that of Balaam ben Beor in Num 22–24.[22] Balaam is called by Balak to curse the Israelites—not a divinatory activity as such; rather, he is employed as a magician *cum* diviner. He starts by having seven altars prepared where he can slaughter sacrificial animals; he even enters into conversation with Yhwh, who forbids him from cursing the Israelites. In the end he pronounces a divine blessing on the Israelites which is presented as the result of divine inspiration.

As mentioned before, Balaam operates like a combination between a diviner and a magician, and it is in his function as a magician that he is hired to curse the Israelites. However, his character as a diviner comes through in the end when Yhwh takes control and makes him bless the Israelites instead of cursing them. Balaam can therefore be seen as an example of divination in foreign politics. The difference to the Aleppo-Mari example is that Yhwh is not the god of Transjordanian Moab and Midian but the Israelites' god, speaking through a non-Israelite diviner.

Conclusion

While it is common opinion that divination in general and prophecy in particular are mostly concerned with the decision-making process within a country, we have seen that deities can communicate with kings who do not control the country which hosts their main temple. In doing so, they use language of internal politics and familiarity. One possible explanation for this phenomenon is that, as in our example, the country in which

22. It is well known that a Balaam bar Beor also turns up in the inscription from Deir Alla; see E. Blum, "Die Kombination I der Wandinschrift vom Tell Deir ʿAlla: Vorschläge zur Rekonstruktion mit historisch-kritischen Anmerkungen," in *Berührungspunkte: Studien zur Sozial- und Religionsgeschichte Israels und seiner Umwelt. Festschrift für Rainer Albertz zu seinem 65. Geburtstag* (ed. I. Kottsieper, R. Schmitt and J. Wöhrle; AOAT 350; Münster: Ugarit-Verlag, 2008), 573–601; J. A. Hackett, *The Balaam Text from Deir ʿAllā* (HSM 31; Chico, Calif.: Scholars Press, 1984) and É. Puëch, "Balaʿam and Deir ʿAlla," in *The Prestige of the Pagan Prophet Balaam in Judaism, Early Christianity and Islam* (ed. G. H. van Kooten and J. van Ruiten; Themes in Biblical Narrative 11; Leiden: Brill, 2008), 25–47.

the deity "lived"—Aleppo—was controlled by Yarim-Lim, the overlord of the other king Zimri-Lim: one could see the overlord's authority, and with it the deities' authority, extending into the other kingdom even if the relationship between Yarim-Lim and Zimri-Lim was almost one between equals.

It is important also to note in this context that deities could make important ethical demands from "their" kings, which the kings then had to uphold in their dealings with foreign nations, unless the deity gave a special dispensation, as in the case of the Yaminite refugees mentioned in FM VII 8. While prophecy and divination was more commonly used in interior power struggles as a propaganda tool, it was also used as part of a set of tools of peaceful inter-state relationships, an aspect of prophecy that has hitherto been ignored.

Modes of Communication with the Divine in the Hebrew Psalter

Erhard S. Gerstenberger

"Communication" is a wide-ranging concept today just as it was in antiquity.[1] While everyday connotations revolve around the parameters of "personal dialogue," "interactive group exchange," or "direct medial contact" (always implying human verbal intercourse) the ancient (biblical and Near Eastern) ideas encompass a much wider range of possible participants, including forces and entities of nature, demonic and semi-divine figures and, most notably, a great variety of non-verbal means of signification (musical, ceremonial, gestural, emotional and others). On the other hand, modern conceptualizations of "communication" may easily extend into the life-sciences and into chemistry and physics with their particular modes of systemic exchanges.[2] In this essay I will stay on a middle road, without losing awareness of the broader debate. I hope to gain insight into the ancient means of entering into contact with the gods and thereby access additional information about our forebears' theological conceptualizations.

Thc task at hand is the analysis of some basic patterns of communication with the divine in the Hebrew Bible.[3] To narrow down the choice of examples: no other biblical book offers as much wealth of emotions,

1. Within the humanities there is a great variety of theoretical aspects; see, e.g., E. Griffin, *A First Look at Communication Theory* (7th ed.; New York: McGraw Hill, 2009). There is special emphasis on reader-reception theories; see, e.g., W. Iser, *How to Do Theory* (Malden, Mass.: Blackwell, 2006).

2. Cf. K. L. von Bertalanffy, *General Systems Theory: Foundations, Developments, Applications* (New York: George Braziller, 1968).

3. The Hebrew Bible, not to mention other ancient Near Eastern literature, offers a wide field for research in all kinds of dialogue structures; see, e.g., S. Welke-Holtmann, *Die Kommunikation zwischen Frau und Mann: Dialogstrukturen in den Erzähltexten der Hebräischen Bibel* (Exegese in unserer Zeit 13; Münster: LIT, 2004), and U. Schmidt, *Zentrale Randfiguren: Strukturen der Darstellung von Frauen in den Erzählungen der Königebücher* (Gütersloh: Gütersloher Verlagshaus, 2003).

thoughts or arguments in relation to the divine as the Hebrew Psalter. (In spite of its impressive questioning of divine justice, the book of Job is much more thematically monotonous, engrossed in a single topic and adhering to limited models of argumentation.) Due to the nature of the texts collected in the Psalter we find diverse forms of communication with the divine in these old songs and prayers, deriving from a variety of different life situations.[4] Accordingly the Psalter provides an ideal place to begin searching for parameters of human–divine communication.

By drawing on older studies of the Psalter and applying some common sense we may surmise that, in spite of the great diversity of communications with the divine in the psalms, we may identify a limited number of basic forms of communication.[5] This assumption rests mainly on insights into psalm categories or genres, developed by Hermann Gunkel, Sigmund Mowinckel and others. If the categorization of psalm texts according to genre (and their implied *Sitz im Leben*) is valid, then modes of communicating with the divine seem likely to fall into similar patterns.

It should be clear from the beginning, however, that communication is ritualized almost everywhere in the world, and the means of encountering deities are especially perceived as needing a high level standardization, that is, the cultic ceremony. This holds true also in the Psalter. The poems collected there very likely come from or are part of a variety of liturgies, rituals or ceremonies, in distinction to the spontaneous prose prayers which sometimes appear in narrative contexts, although even these much less formal supplications adhere to some basic structure of petition, reflecting the fundamental elements of the liturgical pieces in the Psalter.[6] There is a great deal of internal and external evidence for the

4. A careful form-critical and genre-oriented analysis of the individual psalms and their life situations is still, despite some opinions, very useful for recognizing the variations of exchange with the divine; see E. S. Gerstenberger, *Psalms, Part I–II* (FOTL 14–15; Grand Rapids, Mich.: Eerdmans, 2001); "The Psalms: Genres, Life Situations, and Theologies—Towards a Hermeneutics of Social Stratification," in *Diachronic and Synchronic: Reading the Psalms in Real Time* (ed. J. S. Burnett, W. H. Bellinger Jr., and W. D. Tucker Jr.; LHBOTS 488; London: T&T Clark International, 2007), 81–92, and "The Psalter," in *The Blackwell Companion to the Hebrew Bible* (ed. L. G. Perdue; Oxford: Blackwell, 2001), 402–17.

5. See E. S. Gerstenberger, *Der bittende Mensch: Bittritual und Klagelied des Einzelnen im Alten Testament* (WMANT 51; Neukirchen–Vluyn: Neukirchener Verlag, 1980; repr. Eugene, Or. Wipf & Stock, 2009), and *Psalms*.

6. Patrick D. Miller has a list of such "prose prayers" which (correctly) leaves out actual psalms quoted in the text (e.g. 2 Sam 22; Isa 38; Jon 2); see P. D. Miller, *They Cried to the Lord: The Form and Theology of Biblical Prayer* (Minneapolis: Fortress, 1994), 337–57.

regular psalms in the Hebrew Bible being genuine ceremonial poems, composed by expert singers for general use in diverse worship or meditative rituals, even if the life situations of determined categories of psalms may have changed over time from a domestic to sanctuary environment or vice versa.[7]

Be this as it may, I propose to look more closely at three of the very basic patterns which form means of communication in the Psalter. The first is connected with prayers of lament, complaint or supplication. Clearly, the conditions of misery, anxiety and sickness which bring about a ritual prayer of this sort under the guidance of a shamanistic expert constitute a very special situation, opportune for developing distinct forms of communication. Secondly, there is the large group of psalms which breathes praise and thanksgiving, a very particular mood and attitude concerning divine beings and divine order. Lastly, the Psalter contains a number of didactic poems, also called wisdom psalms. These are usually attributed to the last stage of psalm collecting and editing and reflect the life and institutions of the post-exilic community. These categories form three principal modes of communication with the divine (whether the number of matrices is sufficient to serve all the extant genres of psalms we will evaluate at the end). For our limited purposes they constitute examples of differentiated ways of approaching the divine realm.

7. Sigmund Mowinckel defended this idea, taking exception only for the "private sapiential poems"; see S. Mowinckel, *The Psalms in Israel's Worship* (2 vols.; New York: Abingdon, 1962), 2:104–24 ("Learned Psalmography"). His notion of "cultic use," however, is too much aligned to temple worship only (ibid., 202–6; cf. also S. Mowinckel, *Religion und Kultus* [Göttingen: Vandenhoeck & Ruprecht, 1953]). On subsequent developments in research, see W. Brueggemann, *The Psalms and the Life of Faith* (ed. P. D. Miller; Minneapolis: Fortress, 1995). Against Mowinckel, Hermann Gunkel considered many psalms "second hand spiritual poetry," modelled along the line of older worship specimens; see H. Gunkel and J. Begrich, *Einleitung in die Psalmen: Die Gattungen der religiösen Lyrik Israels* (HKAT 2; Göttingen: Vandenhoeck & Ruprecht, 1933), 93–94, 261–65, 415–33. "Detachment from any cultic performance" is the main development for him. The strongest arguments for continued cultic use of the psalms can be adduced from the individual complaint genre; aside from the formal liturgical structures, the analogy of Babylonian incantation prayers embedded in extensive ritual prescriptions ought not to be disregarded (cf. Gerstenberger, *Mensch*; S. M. Maul, *Zukunftsbewältigung: Eine Untersuchung altorientalischen Denkens anhand der babylonisch-assyrischen Löserituale [Namburbi]* [Mainz: Zabern, 1994]; Miller, *Lord*, 5–31, 55–134; G. Cunningham, *"Deliver Me from Evil": Mesopotamian Incantations 2500–1500 BC* [StP.SM 17; Rome: Pontifical Biblical Institute, 1997]).

Crying Out from Below

Communication, according to our own conceptualization, always involves two or more parties. The divine being is one active participant whose specific role we must search for: are there special rules and parameters for talking to a deity or listening to his or her voice? We may dismiss this question as insignificant insofar as the discourse of the miserable extant in complaint psalms is pretty much modelled after secular human imprecatory patterns.[8] The problems of communication in the relevant psalms rather lie in the extreme gap (not of the qualitative kind) between sufferer and helper: "Why are you so far from helping me…?" (Ps 22:1[2]) is a reproachful question often used in complaints.[9] The distance in horizontal or vertical ("From the depths I am calling"; cf. Ps 130:1) terms is distressing, as it implies physical and spiritual dimensions and impedes contact with the potential helper. The normal and wholesome relation between supplicant and YHWH would be that of closeness, trust solidarity as is easily recognizable in "affirmations of confidence": the salvific attributes given to YHWH.[10] One outstanding appellation (invocation) of the deity sought suggests a very personal, familial relationship: "My god" ("god of my strength," "refuge," etc.; cf. Pss 22:1[2]; 40:5[6]; 71:3–6).[11] To what extent a wilful absence of a god

8. Cf. Gerstenberger, *Mensch*, 17–63 ("Das alltägliche Bittschema"): customary behaviour and words (i.e. ordinary ritual patterns) determine the behaviour of any person who needs to approach someone else for help. Differences of psalm procedure are principally due to the liturgical framework for which they were made and not to any metaphysical otherness of the divine sphere. Annette Zgoll has very ably drawn on Babylonian audience etiquette to explain prayer postures ("Audienz - Ein Modell zum Verständnis mesopotamischer Handerhebungsrituale: Mit einer Deutung der Novelle vom Armen Mann von Nippur," *BagM* 34 [2005]: 181–203) and Friedhelm Hartenstein refers similarly to royal practices (*Das Angesicht JHWHs: Studien zu seinem höfischen und kultischen Bedeutungshintergrund in den Psalmen und in Exodus 32–34* [FAT 55; Tübingen: Mohr Siebeck, 2008]).

9. Verse numbering is according to NRSV, with MT enumeration in square brackets where applicable.

10. The formal "expression of trust" element in complaint psalms is important; it signals the basis of the mutual reliance between the supplicant and the deity; see the discussions in Gunkel and Begrich, *Einleitung*, 232–36, and Gerstenberger, *Mensch*, 127–30; Miller, *Lord*, 178–232.

11. Cf. E. S. Gerstenberger, *Theologies in the Old Testament* (trans. J. Bowden; Edinburgh: T. & T. Clark, 2002), 25–91. The familial affiliation of this personal deity is the decisive theological feature. Phenomenologically, faith in a familial deity constitutes a particular type of religion, as already A. Alt, *Der Gott der Väter: Ein Beitrag zur Vorgeschichte der israelitischen Religion* (BWANT 48; Stuttgart:

from the downtrodden may be understood as a divine castigation on account of committed sins or some unaccounted for estrangement, possibly caused by mischievous enemies, was a matter to be resolved in each individual case by proper diagnostic analysis.[12] On the whole, we may take the note of complaint—abysmal distance!—to have been the main obstacle to communication in this category of psalms. Yet this distance was considered an anomaly; it had to be overcome in personal confrontation with the protective deity via proper entreaty, possibly accompanied by ablutions, exorcisms, small sacrifices, vows, confessions of guilt or other means of atonement and rehabilitation.

Plaintive, reproachful communication in the Psalter is thus not neutral, but an intentional, partisan affair. It does not purport mere dialogue, exchange of opinions or assertions. In particular, the "cry from below" arises from despair; the communication in such situations aims first of all to overcome the barrier of distance—sometimes due to guilt or misunderstanding—and in the second place targets the power in the divine realm which is handled by a deity potentially willing to step in and save and restore the wretched person.[13] The real aim of supplicants is to regain

Kohlhammer, 1929), maintained. See also R. Albertz, *Persönliche Frömmigkeit und offizielle Religion: Religionsinterner Pluralismus in Israel und Babylon* (Stuttgart: Calwer, 1978), and H. Vorländer, *Mein Gott: Die Vorstellungen vom persönlichen Gott im Alten Orient und im Alten Testament* (AOAT 23; Neukirchen–Vluyn: Neukirchener Verlag, 1975).

12. The problem of enemies or evildoers is a very serious one in the complaint genre. See S. Mowinckel, *Psalmenstudien I. Āwän und die individuellen Klagepsalmen* (Kristiania: Jacob Dybwad, 1921); O. Keel, *Feinde und Gottesleugner: Studien zum Image der Widersacher in den Individualpsalmen* (Stuttgart: Katholisches Bibelwerk, 1969); M. Bauks, *Die Feinde des Psalmisten und die Freunde Ijobs: Untersuchungen zur Freund-Klage im Alten Testament am Beispiel von Ps 22* (SBS 203; Stuttgart: Katholisches Bibelwerk, 2004); P. Riede, *Im Netz des Jägers. Studien zur Feindmetaphorik der Individualpsalmen* (WMANT 85; Neukirchen–Vluyn: Neukirchener Verlag, 2000) and F. van der Velden, *Psalm 109 und die Aussagen zur Feindschädigung in den Psalmen* (SBB 37; Stuttgart: Katholisches Bibelwerk, 1997). Proper diagnosis as an issue in communication with the divine powers sometimes shows up in narratives in the Hebrew Bible (cf. 1 Kgs 14:1–3; 2 Kgs 1:1–2; Num 5:11–31). More extensive procedures are known from ancient Near Eastern sources; see N. P. Heeßel, *Babylonisch-assyrische Diagnostik* (AOAT 43; Münster: Ugarit-Verlag, 2000).

13. In his classic study, C. Barth maintained that the supplicants experienced their precarious situation already as a real death predicament (cf. Ps 88) (*Die Errettung vom Tode in den individuellen Klage- und Dankliedern des Alten Testamentes* [Zollikon: Evangelischer Verlag, 1947]). The supplicant thus requires rescue from this death zone.

power and life; psalms of complaint are intended to reach the deity, secure a benevolent ruling about their misery and thus tap the resources of their god in order to fill the vacuum on the human side. Supplication is a balancing act of power, wrestled from a superior divine being (cf. Gen 32:23–33) who is nevertheless considered responsible for his or her familial clients. It asks for a transfer of divine power to the human end of the spectrum, where there is extreme need of it. In this sense, the cries from below aim to produce a participatory action involving both deity and petitioner and resulting in the wellbeing of the supplicant.

Viewed through the concept of power regulation, we may try to sketch the mechanism of complaint and petition in the Psalter as one of the main types of communication with the divine. There are many variants in the complaint psalms, of course, and due to space we can only look at some basic issues here.[14] First, professional communication with the divine power in the case of a patient fearing for his life would have been no easy task, with intricate and conventionally fixed procedures to be followed. The overall bundle of rites is complex; just like today, the experts needed to clarify causes and consequences of the calamity at hand, determine the powers responsible for sending remedies, prepare proper means and rituals to counteract the evil and so on. All these operations belong to this type of lament-communication, although they are only rarely considered in the context of our topic. Studies on Mesopotamian diagnostics and related subjects already illuminate the general situation.[15] The trajectory of complaint rituals from preparatory rites to thanksgiving conclusion has been outlined and analyzed by a number of scholars.[16] Communication, we may learn, does not go without preparation, nor can it avoid the professional help which itself makes the subjects of communication uncertain: Is it the practitioner or the patient who communicates with the divine?[17]

14. A fairly exhaustive enumeration of the internal structure of complaint may be found in Gunkel and Begrich, *Einleitung*, 240–50, and Mowinckel, *Worship*, 2:1–25, esp. 9–11; my own summary is in *Psalms: Part 1*, 11–14.

15. Cf. Heeßel, *Diagnostics*, 2000; W. Mayer, *Untersuchungen zur Formensprache der babylonischen "Gebetsbeschwörungen"* (StP.SM 5; Rome: Pontifical Biblical Institute, 1976); Cunningham, *Evil*; Gerstenberger, *Mensch*.

16. Cf. Mayer, *Untersuchungen*; Gerstenberger, *Mensch*, 113–60; Maul, *Zukunftsbewältigung*, 29–113; Cunningham, *Evil*; and C. Frechette, *Mesopotamian Ritual Prayers (Šuillas): A Case Study Investigating Idiom, Rubric, Form and Function* (AOAT 379; Münster: Ugarit-Verlag, 2012).

17. Cf. W. P. Brown, "The Psalms and 'I': The Dialogical Self and the Disappearing Psalmist," in Burnett, Bellinger, and Tucker, eds., *Diachronic and Synchronic*, 26–44.

Such verbal acts relating to the divine helper are at least partially transmitted in the psalms. The formulation leaves open the possibility that other words besides the psalms were spoken in healing ceremonies and the possibility that concomitant gestures, movements and interactions may have played a considerable role in complaint ceremonies. Putting all the paraphernalia aside for the moment, however, the complaint psalms reveal a great deal about communication under stressful conditions. Formulas of petition normally begin with an invocation of the deity by name, often connected to an initial plea to be heard. Afterwards follow several elements, mostly in support of the supplication: complaints (including descriptions of sufferings, misdeeds of enemies), affirmations of confidence and maledictions (imprecations) on evildoers. The final supplication is often already implicit in these other elements, but as a rule it is spelled out before YHWH or other gods in the plea for their intervention. The wordings of these prayers are artfully composed to achieve their ends and they are time-honoured by long and efficient use in ceremony.

With regard to communication in the opposite direction, from the deity to the petitioner, psalm interpreters have long asked whether or not the ceremonies allowed room for exchange, or, more precisely, whether the deity was called upon to answer the petition.

This is a major issue in psalm research and is perhaps decisive for our recognition of the dialogical framework of communication. Research on this question of "arguing with the deity" also opens up windows towards wisdom literature in the ancient Near East and related compositions in the Hebrew Bible, such as Job and Ecclesiastes. Even within the psalms, however, we have a considerable amount of impatient, challenging questions, reproachful complaints and protestations of innocence, all directed against the deity who is supposedly leading the investigation into the petitioner's maladies. There are also faint signs that the supplication ceremony could (and would) have been interrupted or concluded by a divine oracle of assurance: "You have been heard" or similar. Psalm 35:3 asks verbatim for such an affirmation—"speak to me: 'I am your salvation'"—while Ps 5:3(4) "watches" for a positive reaction of YHWH and the last word of Ps 22:21(22) may be understood as "you have answered me." Together with the deliverance formula elsewhere in the Hebrew Bible ("Do not fear…," frequently occurring in Deutero-Isaiah) a case may be made for verbal exchange within the complaint ceremony, although the particularities of how the deity would communicate him- or herself are hardly verifiable.[18] The divine partner in this situation is

18. The pioneer study was that of J. Begrich, "Das priesterliche Heilsorakel," *ZAW* 52 (1934): 81–92. The debate about the oracular response in healing rituals has

the personal, familial, client-oriented deity, as presupposed in family-religion, and the basic theological concept in the background is that of familial solidarity.[19] The personal god, possibly inherited from ancestor worship, belongs to the family group; he or she is accessible to personal entreaty and can change his or her mind, because all parameters and connotations of this helpfully close god are oriented to social group ties.

The other question still pending is that of the real subjects in this type of communication. We assume that the ritual expert, a shamanistic healer or conjurer, was the actual performer of functions and the author of the liturgical words. They reflected his expertise and experience and guaranteed, to a certain extent (as these professional guarantees go), the effectiveness of the rites. Yet the supplication ceremony is being executed in the name of the patient. Babylonian prayers which resemble the Hebrew Bible's complaint psalms put an Akkadian N.N.-sign at the beginning of an incantation prayer where the cantor-patient has to insert his own personal name, and the ritual prescriptions in the same texts occasionally advise the performing priest: "Let the patient speak…"[20] This plainly means that communication may occur on concomitant or doubled levels, with the healing experts (diviner, diagnostician, incantation priest, curer) identifying with the person in distress and his intimate group. They take up the advocacy of the endangered supplicants in their professional capacity and co-perform with their paying clients in an effort to win back attention and support from the personal god.[21]

For us the final query must be: How does this kind of communication from the depths come to an end? On the basis of shamanistic activities in more modern times we may conclude that rituals of healing performed by seasoned experts are usually successful; one can find "success rates" in the range of 60 to 80 percent, sometimes equalling the rates of modern medical doctors. When ancient Israelite and Judahite clients were delivered they were obliged to bring a thanksgiving sacrifice or service to YHWH (cf. Ps 107). Returning to the imagery of power transfer, we may

continued ever since; cf. W. A. VanGemeren, "Oracles of Salvation," in *Cracking Old Testament Codes: A Guide to Interpreting the Literary Genres of the Old Testament* (ed. D. B. Sandy and R. L. Giese; Nashville, Tenn.: Broadman & Holman, 1995); Miller, *Lord*, 135–77.

19. Cf. Gerstenberger, *Mensch*, 113–60; Gerstenberger, *Theologies*, 25–91; K. van der Toorn, *Family Religion in Babylonia, Syria, and Israel* (Leiden: Brill, 1996).

20. Cf. Gerstenberger, *Mensch*, 64–112; Miller, *Lord*, 55–134.

21. Maul's thesis that the priest in certain moments takes upon himself the identity and the ill fate of his client the supplicant may, however, be overdrawn (Maul, *Zukunftsbewältigung*, 67–71).

say that the successful petition ceremony supplies new life power into desolation and weakness. The supplicant receives a new chance for (normal, wholesome, un-afflicted) life and a small return in gratitude is in order; part of the blessing is thus reverted to the donor of these good gifts and the balance of energies returns to normal.

Our first basic form for relating to a (personal) deity in situations of danger to life is conceived as a dramatic appeal to the loyal god along well-known lines of human social behaviour (law-suit, argumentative contestation, confession of guilt, plea for mercy). Though the enactment of YHWH's own part in the dialogue may have posed liturgical problems, the idea was that the supplicant—with the help of an expert advocate and ritual performer—approached the deity asking for deliverance and rehabilitation and ready to offer up thanks to a helpful, merciful deity. We may term this model of communication "personal interaction."

Praising from on High

The second type of communication in the Psalter is connected with praise contexts. Naturally, variants of this eulogy type are numerous, but a basic context is discernable for many of them. Praise, as a rule, does not start out from dire need and despair (though there are some thin moorings of hymnic poetry even in petitionary situations).[22] Rather, praise of god from the human side usually presupposes divine power and plenty, as imaginable in the context of yearly seasonal harvest festivities realized on a local or regional basis (cf. Exod 23; 34; Lev 23; Deut 16). The social and ideological context, as a rule, is also different from individual complaint discourse. We may safely imply that hymns were (and are) used usually by collective entities, not by individuals; larger organized groups of some political standing, not isolated families. Correspondingly, the concept of the divine in these communications reflects regional or national interests, is couched in the imagery of royalty and hierarchy

22. Cf. Gerstenberger, "Praise in the Realm of Death: The Dynamics of Hymn-Singing in Ancient Near Eastern Lament Ceremonies," in *Lamentations in Ancient and Contemporary Cultural Contexts* (ed. N. C. Lee and C. Mandolfo; SBLSymS 43; Atlanta: SBL, 2008), 115–24. Many researchers have marvelled that eulogies of the gods addressed in Mesopotamian complaints can be quite strong, in contrast to the Hebrew use of laudatory language with individual supplication; some have gone so far as to denounce the mean, cajoling mind of the Babylonian supplicants. See J. Begrich, "Die Vertrauensäußerungen im israelitischen Klagelied des Einzelnen und in seinem babylonischen Gegenstück," *ZAW* 46 (1928): 221–60; G. Widengren, *The Accadian and Hebrew Psalms of Lamentation as Religious Documents* (Stockholm: Almqvist & Wiksell, 1936); Miller, *Lord*, 14–15.

and deals with a different power structure than those of individual lament. The worldview and the theological horizon which emerge from the praise psalms are those of ancient Near Eastern social organizations; hymns celebrate a god for his or her great deeds and gifts to communities, dynasties and nations. If they involve sentiments of gratitude directly, then the thank-offerings discussed under the first paradigm of communication may take place in analogous manners, but praise is more than offering a god thanks: it means further activating and preserving the power of a benign deity in favour of a determined social group or association.

Again thinking of power balances, there may be a certain lack of equilibrium between a deity's potentialities and human capacities; these latter were, according to ancient Near Eastern conceptions, only a small (but real) fraction of the divine powers. At festive gatherings (e.g. harvest, commemorations of victories, sheep-shearing, building dedications) the worshipping crowd praises the gracious provider, probably led by priest or other cultic functionaries. What happens in this process? The act of praising is a dynamic performance, understood to help produce and sustain the goods for which thanks are given. Praise helps to create and maintain the majesty of YHWH imagined as a flow of power from the human to the divine side. Instances in the psalms alert us to this idea that the gods need the supportive attention of humans. The old Canaanite hymn Ps 29 advises the "sons of god" to bring to YHWH "glory and strength" (v. 1). Rivers and other natural powers are instructed to hail YHWH of the universe (cf. Pss 93 and 96) to stabilize his supreme authority further, and cosmic forces have to sing his ethereal praise (Pss 19; 148). One rather cryptic verse in Ps 22 declares YHWH to be "enthroned over the 'praises of Israel'" (v. 3[4]). The existence of creative power and its workings in the world provokes jubilant outbreaks of praise, periodically refreshed and reiterated: "O sing to YHWH a new song, sing to YHWH all the earth" (Ps 96:1); "Declare his glory among the nations, his marvellous works among all the peoples" (v. 3); "Ascribe to YHWH, O families of the peoples, ascribe to YHWH glory and strength" (v. 7). All humanity is called to sing out to YHWH, with all creation participating:

> Say among the nations, "YHWH is king!
> The world is firmly established; it shall never be moved.
> He will judge the peoples with equity."
> Let the heavens be glad, and let the earth rejoice;
> Let the sea roar, and all that fills it;
> Let the field exult, and everything in it.
> Then shall all the trees of the forest sing for joy

Before the Lord, for he is coming,
For he is coming to judge the earth.
He will judge the world with righteousness,
And the peoples with his truth. (Ps 96:10–13; cf. Ps 98:7–9)

On a truly grandiose scale, Ps 148 enacts an all-encompassing eulogy of the creator by enumerating all those who are to join into this great concert of voices:

Praise YHWH!
Praise YHWH from the heavens; praise him in the heights!
Praise him, all his angels; praise him, all his host!
Praise him, sun and moon; praise him, all you shining stars!
Praise him, you highest heavens, and you waters above the heavens!
Let them praise the name of YHWH, for he commanded and they were created.
He established them forever and ever; he fixed the bounds, which cannot be passed.
Praise YHWH from the earth, you sea monsters and all deeps,
Fire and hail, snow and frost, stormy wind fulfilling his command.
Mountains and all hills, fruit trees and all cedars!
Wild animals and all cattle, creeping things and flying birds!
Kings of the earth and all peoples, princes and all rulers of the earth!
Young men and women alike, old and young together!
Let them praise the name of YHWH, for his name alone is exalted;
His glory is above earth and heaven. He has raised up a horn for his people,
Praise for all his faithful, for the people of Israel who are close to him.
Praise YHWH! (Ps 148:1–14)

These two psalms are impressive in their conception of the divine world as also created by the deity responsible for all existence. They compare thematically to the great speeches of YHWH demonstrating to the rebellious Job what real wisdom and power are like (Job 28; 38–41). This power is real, effective and does not suffer counterargument. The advice of hymn-singers to a congregation of adorers is to join into the chorus of praise from around the world and in the midst of all existence.

Yet what are the concepts of this praise, the perceptive horizons in this almost universal painting? Certainly we are not facing a dreamy, enthusiastic, artful and exuberant admiration of curious bystanders as in some romantic glorification of nature. There is communal and personal involvement discernable in every phrase. Furthermore, because YHWH and other ancient Near Eastern deities are strengthened by the praise of their worshippers in this way, they are not the unmovable mover of Greek philosophy, the absolute good or the overall principle of truth and beauty. The world YHWH created is far from being an utterly harmonious entity, even though it is credited with stability, truth and justice. Behind the scenes there loom forces of destruction, corruptions of order and deviations from the plans of the creator. Psalm 96 pinpoints the defaults in saying that YHWH will "judge" (שפט) the earth, applying "righteousness" (צדק) and "truth" (אמונה; all v. 13).[23] Psalm 148 also has a somewhat hidden reference to the powers of destruction which have been overcome by the good creator: "He has raised up a horn for his people" (v. 14). Within the chorus of jubilant voices who join in praise of the creator there is the necessity of supplying refuge and power (the "horn") to the minority people of YHWH in an oppressive and violent world.[24] The general concept of an ordered world, opposed by destructive chaos powers, pervades ancient Near Eastern mythology and other literature; vestiges of primordial and ongoing battle for the good order are found frequently in the Hebrew Scriptures (cf. Gen 1:1–5; Pss 18:7–15[8–16]; 74:13–15; 77:16–19[17–20]; 89:6–11[7–12]; 93:1–4; 97:1–5; 104:1–9; 114:3–8. etc.).[25] Praise is badly needed to counteract these antagonistic forces of disorder and injustice.

In analogous iconographical material from the human political sphere, iconographic representations show scenes of adoration with the king seated and jubilants standing in awe before him. This same motif can depict the veneration of a deity by a client.[26] This praise is normally combined with song and instrumental music to lend it force. Since the

23. The concept of judging in the Hebrew Bible implies the responsibility of right governance in accordance with the good world order; cf. H. Niehr, "שָׁפַט *šāpaṭ*," *ThWAT* 8:408–28. "Righteousness" and "truth" are the foundational pillars of the universe; they speak to the pervasive concepts of world order in the ancient Near East; cf. H. Ringgren and B. Johnson, "צֶדֶק *ṣædæq*," *ThWAT* 6:898–924; H. H. Schmid, *Gerechtigkeit als Weltordnung: Hintergrund und Geschichte des alttestamentlichen Gerechtigkeitsbegriffes* (BHT 40; Tübingen: Mohr, 1968).

24. The symbolism of the bull or sheep/goat horn is very ancient in the Near East; see B. Kedar-Kopfstein, "קֶרֶן *qæræn*," *ThWAT* 7:181–89. It stands for power, authority and protection. For a form-critical analysis of Ps 148, see Gerstenberger, *Psalms*, 2:447–52.

25. Cf. E. N. Ortlund, *Theophany and Chaoskampf: The Interpretation of Theophanic Imagery in the Baal Epic, Isaiah, and the Twelve* (Gorgias Ugaritic Studies 5; Piscataway, N.J.: Gorgias, 2010), and R. S. Watson, *Chaos Uncreated: A Reassessment of the Theme of Chaos in the Hebrew Bible* (BZAW 341; Berlin: de Gruyter, 2005). There is also a counter-current subjacent in biblical tradition, ably portrayed in W. Brueggemann, *Theology of the Old Testament: Testimony, Dispute, Advocacy* (Minneapolis: Fortress, 1997).

26. For examples of both forms of adoration, see O. Keel, *Die Welt der altorientalischen Bildsymbolik und das Alte Testament, am Beispiel der Psalmen* (Neukirchen–Vluyn: Neukirchener Verlag, 1972).

first half of the third millennium instruments were used to accompany praise of the gods, including drums, stringed instruments, pipes, horns and brass. Their common effect was to enhance the acoustic power of eulogy and make a "loud noise to YHWH" (cf. Ezra 3:10–13; 1 Chr 15:16; 2 Chr 20:19, etc.). Singing and instruments are an important part in collective praise.

Collective praises are indeed the rule, not the exception. Sometimes an individual articulating jubilations all by him- or herself seems to be in the forefront of eulogy (cf. Pss 78; 103), but as a rule even such first-person hymns serve the community. Likewise, a hymn to the glory of an individual person such as Ps 8 (perhaps celebrating his coming of age) is framed by the collective eulogy: "O YHWH, our sovereign, how majestic is your name in all the earth!" (vv. 1, 9[2, 10]). In the same vein Pss 103 and 104 begin in the first person singular, with a self-exhortation of the singer ("Bless YHWH, O my soul...," Ps 103:1–2; 104:1), only to continue explicitly in the first person plural. This is the predominant form for (collective) hymns. The personal laudation of the individual on account of an experienced salvation (thanksgiving song and sacrifice) is quite a different matter.[27] There are numerous poems in the Psalter which testify to their origin in community circles or parochial worship by employing first person plural discourse.[28] This is a strong indication of collective action organized by professional leadership, whether in the temple or other community institutions.

Verbal articulations (presumably accompanied by gestures, mime or corporal enactments like dance) underline the impersonal power aspect of praise. I have elsewhere sketched the verbs used in elevating rituals and the frequent use of magnifying, uplifting, strengthening and empowering language.[29] Suffice it to add that all verbal and corporal expressions in hymnic performance were tuned to the task of strengthening praise. We often misunderstand praise language as mere admiration of what is at hand or in sight in terms of obvious glamour and majesty. This is too short-sighted an interpretation of eulogy. The words, phrases and enactments aim to achieve what they are pronouncing. Hymn singing, as much as any conjuring type of speech, is performative in essence. This quality of discourse has to be taken into account when discussing psalmic praise communication.

27. Ps 107 calls for a thanksgiving service for four particular salvific events; see F. Crüsemenn, *Studien zur Formgeschichte von Hymnus und Danklied in Israel* (WMANT 32; Neukirchen–Vluyn: Neukirchener Verlag, 1969), 210–84.

28. Cf. Gerstenberger, "Psalms," 86–89.

29. Cf. ibid., 123–24.

There is not much importance to be attributed to the different areas of life and thematic specifications of the hymns which appear in the Psalter. Even the object of praise may alternate from YHWH himself to his city, Mount Zion, Torah, commandments and blessings. Praises are enacted in grand processions (cf. Pss 24; 48; 68; 132; 2 Sam 6:14–15) or theophanic events (cf. Pss 18; 47; 98; Hab 3). The topics touched on in the hymns of the Hebrew Bible vary among victories over enemies, creation and subjugation of primeval chaos forces, deliverance of Israel and the promise of the holy land, the gift of Torah and seasonal abundance in crops. Important for us is the underlying scheme, of the people (through its hymnic experts?) reacting to the general benevolence of their god. They offer back some of the power and glory granted them by their deity in order to strengthen his or her potency in every respect and to secure future well-being. From a position of relative strength and happiness, the sung praises initiate a flow of energy towards the deity of all destinies and sustenance.

The crucial question, however, concerns the significance of the aforementioned observations for the praise-model of communication. We ought to be wary of our own understandings of praise, which may be object-centred and fixed on dialogical structures. According to the evidence above, there is no dialogue at all in these eulogies of the beneficial divine presence and action. The creator may withhold his blessings with (or without) understandable reason, but there is no way to negotiate the resumption of grace (cf. Ps 104:27–30). The only means of attempting to secure good life is to sing YHWH's praise and thus ward off the "wicked" (Ps 104:31–35; cf. 139:19–22). Even the imagined interlocution of Job and YHWH (Job 38–42) is based on the presupposition that YHWH's creation and wisdom must not be contested but extolled. We hear frequently the voice of the liturgist summoning the worshippers to praise the great god of creation and sustenance. The praise itself goes on with great noise, not only with words but with music, movements, processions, clapping of hands and shouting, probably including endless repetitions of short formulae like "allelujah," "god is great," "majestic are you," and so on. The liturgical action seems one-sided, with no response of the deity expected at all. Rather, the words and gestures start on the human side, trying to reach the divine font of all good gifts and centralized power. The concept of god which transpires from these hymns has little in common with a dialogue. The creator is a remote figure dedicated to ruling a region, a state or the whole universe. He relates to humans, to be sure, but like a distant king working for his subjects, providing necessities of life and keeping up the overall order of the world for the benefit of creation. The whole praising mechanisms are set up because of these background regulations. Many scholars, including Gerhard von Rad, Patrick D. Miller and Walter Brueggemann, have posited that divine action is an essential presupposition of praise. They do not sufficiently emphasize, however, the inherent mechanisms of the "do ut des" model, that is, the obligatory paying back of some of the gifts received.[30] In fact, the emphasis of praise hymns seems not to be entering into an exchange of words with the eulogized one(s) but to return support in exchange for the received gifts and thus to strengthen the position of the benefactor in the future.

The second type of communication with the divine in the Psalter, then, is distinct from the personal encounter type found in complaints. It arises from a collective setting of worship and is aimed at a distant creator and sustainer. The underlying theological assumption is that the good and just order must be supported by the human recipients of existing fortunes and must be perpetually strengthened against the disruptive forces which are rampant in the world. Praise communication, consequently, enters directly and with powerful performance into the battle for the sustenance of the righteous world, building up the power of the supreme deity him- or herself. Eulogy may thus be identified as the flow of energy from humankind to the divine. Functionally it compares to fans singing their chants in sport arenas: those praised welcome the support they receive, and in the same vein the deity accepts the empowerment without immediate response.

Musings Over the Word

A third sharply distinguished mode of communication with the divine in the Psalter is paid little attention in regular psalm exegeses. This is the large and heterogeneous group of poems called "wisdom" or "didactic" psalms in most modern treatments.[31] Form-critically, it is true we cannot identify a uniform genre among these, but the diverse poems demonstrate a common mental pattern and a way of approaching problems which make them likely products of one and the same social and/or religious

30. The classical study on receiving and giving back is M. Mauss, "Essai sur le don: Forme et raison de l'échange dans les societies archaïques," *L'Année Sociologique* 1 (1923–24): 30–186.

31. Cf. Mowinckel, *Psalms*, 2:104–25; Gunkel and Begrich, *Einleitung*, 391–97; J. L. Crenshaw, *Old Testament Wisdom: An Introduction* (3d ed.; Louisville, Ky.: Westminster John Knox, 2010), 187–94, with further references. For a paradigmatic study of a wisdom psalm, see P. Casetti, *Gibt es ein Leben vor dem Tod?* (OBO 44; Göttingen: Vandenhoeck & Ruprecht, 1992).

group. Their self-reflective attitude is typical for a faith community concerned with the will of YHWH and the destiny of his followers and their opponents (the "just" and "wicked"). It is clear enough that the YHWH-communities of the exilic and post-exilic periods focussed on the written and oral transmission of divine revelation through Moses. Torah (and other writings) being the backbone for this kind of new religious organization (unheard of in pre-exilic times), the life and worship of emerging Judaism really revolved around the "word" of YHWH.[32] Without doubt, this involved extensive studying and memorizing of scripture, institutionalized instruction in the divine will must be presupposed of Jewish congregations in the Persian period.[33] The didactic psalms may have been part of these communal educational efforts in which individuals (in classrooms?) meditated aloud the (written) word of God in order to acquire the holiness and righteousness prescribed by YHWH.

The mode of communication with the divine in these didactic psalms is quite characteristic and particular. It does not fit into the aforementioned schemes of praying from below directly to a personal god nor extolling and strengthening the god of order and creation from above. Rather, the supplicant here is practicing a very quiet soliloquy, meant to be overheard only by the god of wisdom. He or she is meditating, perhaps remembering, reading(?) or listening to the divine words of the Torah. "To meditate the Torah day and night, from sheer joy in the will of the Lord" (paraphrase of Ps 1:2) seems to be not only the acknowledged life situation of Pss 1, 19 and 119 but also of musings like those in Pss 9–10; 37; 39; 49; 73; 90; 95; 139, and so on. The contemplator ponders over diverse subjects connected to his or her attempt to be a faithful adept of YHWH, the universal and merciful god of Israel and source of all knowledge, without entering into a demanding and exacting mood. Thus the transience of human existence is a problem (cf. Pss 39; 90), as is the quest for the impeccable righteousness of God himself (the theodicy problem; cf. Pss 9–10; 33; 37; 49; 94). Personal sin may pose a question but more so from the positive side: How can the righteous live up to the exigencies of the commandments (cf. Pss 1; 19; 119)? The past history of YHWH with his elect people may also be a topic of meditation (cf. Pss 78; 105; 106). In short, there is no lack of themes in the rich tradition of the Yahwistic faith community which may be mused over in individual or collective reflection. But how can we evaluate this particular mode of communication against the previous two?

32. Cf. Gerstenberger, *Theologies*, 207–72.

33. Cf. Gerstenberger, *Israel in der Perserzeit, 5. Und 4. Jahrhundert v.Chr.* (Biblische Enzyklopädie 8; Stuttgart: Kohlhammer, 2005), 292–322, 328–53.

The heart of the matter in these sapiential musings seems to be the exercise of a special spirituality, which grew out of the faith community itself. Allegiance to the Torah implied a complete trust in YHWH's revelation and a firm determination to adhere to the rulings and orientations of this god's benevolently revealed words. Means of reflection on and digestion of the divine will have sprung up together with the public reading of Torah (Neh 8). Reflective exercises, possibly in private but more likely in community gatherings or worship, were probably designed to foster familiarity with and allegiance to the covenant stipulations. Meditation on and in response to written or recited texts thus becomes a new vehicle of communication with the divine. It constructs and maintains a creedal identity and a workable spirituality. The conceptions of god underlying this internal communication are remarkable. We can understand this relationship as a mystical one cultivated by the contemplator of YHWH's ways and human nature. YHWH is not approached directly and personally nor is enhanced as the great creational power but experienced through the inherited traditional revelation; all kinds of spontaneous prophecy has either ceased (cf. Zech 13:2–3) or been transformed into Torah interpretation (cf. Jer 11). Faith in the deity starts to be communicated by the text (continuing down to the present in the Jewish, Christian and Islamic traditions) and, by necessity, the reader's reaction to the divine is channelled through a dialogue with the book rather than confrontations with the divinity directly.

The formal address to YHWH is, as a rule, maintained in the relevant psalms: "YHWH, you have been our dwelling place in all generations…" (Ps 90:1); "O YHWH, you have searched me and known me…" (Ps 139:1); "YHWH, let me know my end…" (Ps 39:4[5]). Yet these appellations or invocations sound abstract and seem more rhetorical than real, at least insofar as they lack the urgency of petition or praise addresses. Even more neutral are the descriptive openings of meditative or exhortative psalms (cf. Pss 14; 37; 49); in these the real partner in dialogue often seems to be the speaker's own self: "I said, 'I will guard my ways…'" (Ps 39:1[2]); "Do not fret because of the wicked…" (Ps 37:1); "How can young people keep their way pure?" (Ps 119:9). YHWH is listening in, eventually giving his opinion via the reflective process, and will ultimately decide the cases requiring decision. The arguments, brought forth by the members of the faith community who composed these psalms, however, are usually not of a controversial type. They re-affirm only that which has been age-old praxis in nature and human society. YHWH appears to be the sovereign, little riled lord of wisdom who administers a stable world with revealed, immovable guidelines (the Torah). His age is measured in aeons (Ps 90), his articulate presence is the written Torah (Pss 1; 19; 119) or the radiating holiness inside the temple (cf. Lev 16). His fame reverberates through the universe in a non-verbal language (Ps 19:1–4[2–5]), and it is the general destiny of all mortals which is the burning question (Pss 39:4–6, 11[5–7, 12]; 90:9–12). The futility of all human endeavour is frustrating ("Mortals cannot abide in their pomp; they are like the animals that perish"; Ps 49:12, 20[13, 21]). How could communication with the deity be possible in this world? It occurs by way of the murmuring of Scriptures and attempting an inner dialogue with oneself and the sages—and thereby with YHWH of the book.

The third mode of communication in the Psalter is a novelty, unprecedented in the history of spirituality of the ancient Near East. Personal exchange with YHWH is by immersion in an inner dialogue via the comparison of passages, addressing the deity by confessing loyalty to and identifying with his revealed will, with all this being done in continuous, permanent meditation and prayer. We may call this communication the "mystical immersion" type, prompted by the spirituality of the post-exilic Jewish community and facilitated by the written tradition.

Communication

The Psalter is the foremost example within the Hebrew Bible of the multi-layered theological conceptions which have grown from diverse spiritual situations in the long history of Israelite religion. Because of this a uniform "theology of the Old Testament" cannot be expected, nor can there be a homogeneous means of communication with the divine.[34] Participants in the dialogue or discourse of heterogeneous social, cultural and religious situations will, by necessity, employ diverse models of communication. The Psalter illustrates the wide range of possibilities in an unsurpassable and superb manner, containing as it does the richest collection of spiritual texts available from Israel's heritage.

The final question to address is whether it is legitimate to single out, as the present study does, only three models of communication to represent an unknown number of ancient parameters. The selection of three exemplary types is arbitrary and restrictive, meant to illuminate the situation but by no means conclude the analysis. Complaint and praise have been long recognized to constitute fundamental means of approaching

34. Cf. E. S. Gerstenberger, "Theologies in the Book of Psalms," in *The Book of Psalms: Composition and Reception* (ed. P. W. Flint and P. D. Miller; VTSup 99; Leiden: Brill, 2005), 603–25, and *Theologies*.

the different deities—for some redactors exclusively YHWH—in the psalms.[35] Yet there are clear differences in the forms of communication in the laments of individuals and those of larger social entities; there are also a great number of variations in the thanksgivings (of which this essay does not consider any) and many diverse praise situations (e.g. victory, seasonal blessings, *rites de passage* etc.). Finally, there is a considerable spectrum of meditative modes of communication, with some musings directly involved with scriptures and others impacted by life problems. Given all these variants, the three selected models may only serve as (prominent) examples of the communicative patterns extant in the Psalter.

Communication is exchange, involvement and discourse with a real partner. In trying to grasp the processes of communication we, unavoidably, start from our own societal experiences: one friend talks to another in vivid interlocution; group interaction proceeds according to specific conventionalized rules. As to the divine, we are confronted with some dimensions which go beyond human experience; the divine transcends human limits of time and space to include larger and extremely large extensions up to the whole of the universe. Yet according to the ancient understanding, as visible in psalmic literature, there is no fundamental difference between inter-human and human–divine communication. The formulaic language used in lament-discourse, for example, is quite congruent in both areas.[36] Praise language in the psalms also resembles and has roots in complementary speech forms in the human realm; the musings of the self in relation to YHWH are intimately intertwined with the human capacity for self-conscious internal dialogue.[37] Thus we must

35. There are a large number of studies portraying laments and eulogy as basic attitudes and ceremonies in the Psalter; see, e.g., C. Westermann, *Praise and Lament in the Psalms* (trans. R. N. Soulen and K. R. Crim; Louisville, Ky.: Westminster, 1987); Brueggemann, *Psalms*.

36. Cf. Gerstenberger, *Mensch*. There I make the point that the rhetoric of supplication in the psalms is derived from the everyday discourse between the needy and the potential helper.

37. Cf. W. Brueggemann, *Israel's Praise: Doxology Against Idolatry and Ideology* (Philadelphia: Fortress, 1988), and Miller, *Lord*, 178–232. Miller emphasizes the absolute divine quality of YHWH's actions which solicit praise but explicitly reject any degradation of human praise. Rather, "[t]he rule of the Lord… is confirmed in the praises of the people" as "praise is fundamentally a social or communal experience…" (Miller, *Lord*, 225, 227). Cf. Brown, *Psalms*. There are literary works from the ancient world which already testify to human internal dialogues; see A. I. Baumgarten et al., eds., *Self, Soul, and Body in Religious Experience* (Leiden: Brill, 1995).

leave behind what philosophers call transcendence and immanence in our evaluation of the forms of communication with the divine in the Hebrew Bible: everything in the Psalter happens on the same plane of reality, not in a world divided between human and divine existences.

In our present parameters of thinking, exchange with the divine is a "fictitious" as well as a real affair. Indeed, all our thinking and imagining is fictitious in contrast to historical positivism of the nineteenth century: it occurs according to how we conceptualize the world we are dealing with. That is, we are dealing with the constructs of world rather than with autonomous facts. There is no way of objectively portraying the reality as it "really is in itself" (*das Ding an sich*).[38] We are leading all the way with conventionalized visions and interpretations of the world and of the divine. Thus, logically, all our interactions with the world and with the larger-than-human reality of the divine also occur within these established parameters (usually religious or confessional creeds). This means that the reality we are describing is a construed one, although as such it is real reality for us. We are, in any case, actively involved in the very formation of the world; we are by no means neutral and outside spectators of developments.

Modern worldviews and analytical tools fit in this general picture. There is a host of theories and methods employed to understand and practice "communication": May the insights gained from these be helpful in the analysis of ancient patterns of communicative exchange?[39] Within the humanities we may distinguish between empirical research—anthropological, sociological, socio-psychological, ritual studies as well as behavioural investigations—and more virtual, theoretical reconstructions (nature of language, discourse, apperception, performance etc.).[40] Keeping in mind that all modern theories and techniques have been achieved on the basis of modern evidence (e.g. anthropological field work, analysis of actual literature) and contemporary philosophies, we realize that they may not be directly usable in relation to ancient literary and ceremonial sources. Still, we may legitimately and cautiously use

38. Cf. I. Kant, *Kritik der reinen Vernunft* (ed. R. Schmidt; Leipzig: Philipp Reclam, 1924), published in English as *Critique of Pure Reason* (trans. M. Weigel; London: Penguin, 2007). Kant argues that the "real things-of-themselves" are inaccessible to empirical knowledge.

39. Numerous fields of study, ranging from the humanities to the natural sciences, contribute to communication research today; see von Bertalanffy, *Systems Theory*.

40. Cf., e.g., J. L. Austin, *How to Do Things with Words: The William James Lectures Delivered at Harvard University in 1955* (Cambridge, Mass.: Harvard University Press, 1962), and J. R. Searle, *Speech Acts: An Essay in the Philosophy of Language* (Cambridge: Cambridge University Press, 1969); Iser, *Theory*.

modern instruments of analysis. Thus, speech act theories, reader response models, ritual studies as well as more virtual constructivist approaches may contribute a good deal of insight to understand better what is going on in human–divine communication within the Psalter. Thus we may realize that the three models of exchange presented above represent typical patterns of human–divine relations in determined social and cultural contexts. The concomitant theological as well as anthropological concepts vary greatly according to the basic set-ups of encountering the world.

Looking at the Psalter in this fashion, the very idea of communication in the Bible and the ancient Near East gains new dimensions, strange as it may seem given that traditional patterns of analysis tend to overshadow and hide ancient conceptualizations. Modern plurality of views and approaches is thus able to liberate even archaic patterns of thinking. These liberated perspectives will undoubtedly also bounce back on the petrified models of communication which may remain in our imagination of divine–human relations.

“To Talk to One’s God”: Penitential Prayers in Mesopotamia

Margaret Jaques

The notion of “religion” as a specific area of human activity is a modern concept. To ask “What is the Sumerians’ religion?” or “How did Akkadians conceive their religion?” is to ask something which the Sumerians and Akkadians could neither have asked nor answered. Nonetheless, all the elements we gather in the category “religion”—prayers, rituals, deities, and so on—were present in Mesopotamia. These elements were intimately linked to other aspects of daily life as well as to literature, and the corpus of Sumerian, Akkadian and bilingual texts are now our only source concerning the religious activities of the Mesopotamians. These allow us to reflect on the nature of religion in ancient Mesopotamia even while we are aware that they give us access to only a small part of a very complex system. Here it seems worthwhile to try to understand the ancient Babylonians’ concept of their relations with their gods via a particular type of text, the penitential prayers.

1. *Hymns and Prayers*

In the texts left by the Sumerians and Akkadians we may distinguish several ways of talking to one’s god. M.-J. Seux summarized these as two categories, *Hymns and Prayers*, although these would have been unrecognizable to the Babylonians themselves.[1] The structure and function of these texts allow us to distinguish roughly between these two categories, though with each category the classification of types according to only the content of the text is difficult. Another classification, using the rubrics of superscription and subscription (or both), is equally possible and is specific to the typology which the ancient Babylonians

1. M.-J. Seux, *Hymnes et Prières aux dieux de Babylonie et d’Assyrie* (LAPO 8; Paris: Cerf, 1976).

themselves provided for the penitential prayers. Hereafter, we will also note the problems arising from hybrid forms.

In this methodological introduction to prayers as a communication device we are also confronted with a question of chronology: When do prayers—which we find mentioned in the literary texts already from an early period—appear as independent texts? At first the question seems clear: no independent written prayers survive previous to the Old Babylonian period, that is, around 1800 B.C.E. Yet, does this reflect ancient reality or does it depend on the vagaries of archeological discovery? Here I investigate individual prayers and will not discuss prayers in literary compositions, like the ones in *Gudea Cylinder*, *Gilgamesh and Huwawa* or the *Epic of Lugalbanda*.

2. *Letter-Prayers and er$_2$-ša$_3$-ḫuĝ-ĝa$_2$ Prayers*

During the Old Babylonian period a special kind of prayer appears which van Dijk describes as "letters addressed to the gods" and which W. Hallo, in his paper concerning this corpus, abbreviated as "letter-prayers."[2] We know these letters mainly thanks to the work of the latter: they are individual prayers in the shape of a letter addressed to a deity. Eleven letters in Sumerian have been identified and there are a number of letters acknowledged in Akkadian. These prayers include an appeal to a deity in a hymnal style, as an introduction, then a description of the state of the praying person in the form of a lament in the first person. In this part there are specific formulas: interrogations such as "why?" or "how long?" and interjections such as "u'a!," meaning "alas!" or "woe!" Finally, the letter includes a request for help, as in a letter of Gudea to an unnamed god (probably his personal god Ningišzida): "My god, I am not someone who slanders, may your affection for me come back to its former state!" The final expression, frequent in these letters, is in Sumerian ša$_3$ ki-be$_2$...gi$_4$ meaning literally "to bring back one's heart to its former state." This expression is especially known through its usage in the conclusion of the er$_2$-ša$_3$-ḫuĝ-ĝa$_2$ prayers ("a lament to sooth the heart [of a god]"). This formula, which we find in both the letter-prayers and the er$_2$-ša$_3$-ḫuĝ-ĝa$_2$ prayers, is for Hallo the first and most fundamental criteria allowing him to compare the two types of prayers. These prayers also have in common the topic of the god's wrath and the man's

2. J. van Dijk, *La sagesse suméro-accadienne: Recherches sur les genres littéraires des textes sapientiaux* (Commentationes Orientales 1; Leiden: Brill, 1953), 13; W. Hallo, "Individual Prayers in Sumerian: The Continuity of a Tradition," *JAOS* 88 (1968): 71–89.

affliction which results from it. Hallo adopts a diachronic point of view, arguing that er$_2$-ša$_3$-ḫuĝ-ĝa$_2$ prayers developed from earlier letter-prayers. The texts of the er$_2$-ša$_3$-ḫuĝ-ĝa$_2$ come mostly from the library of Assurbanipal in Nineveh, dating to the end of the first millennium B.C.E., but since Hallo's article older texts dating to the Old Babylonian period have been discovered as well.

3. *Classification of Prayers*

In the introduction to *Hymnes et Prières* Seux describes the elements which characterize the Mesopotamian prayers and distinguishes three groups. First, there are the letter-prayers and the er$_2$-ša$_3$-ḫuĝ-ĝa$_2$ (Seux reiterates the arguments of Hallo but notes that the er$_2$-ša$_3$-ḫuĝ-ĝa$_2$ prayers are much older than believed in Hallo's day, at least concerning the prototypes from which they derived). Second, there are the šu il$_2$-la$_2$, the "(prayers) with raised hand," also called "prayers used by the conjuror" (Seux), "sacramental prayers" (J. Bottéro) or "incantation-prayers" (W. Mayer).[3] These are prayers with the superscription EN$_2$ or EN$_2$ E$_2$.NU.RU, terms whose meaning is "an incantation of the Enuru."[4] They are signed by "it is a formula word for word of a (prayer) of the raised hand" (KA-inim-ma šu il$_2$-la$_2$-kam). As we can see in this case, the verbal address and the gesture (to raise the hand) are combined in the šu il$_2$-la$_2$.[5] These prayers were used in rituals which have nothing to do with magical practices but to which they have been connected since the edition of W. Kunstmann.[6] Third, prayers to the personal god have the subscription "it is a formula word for word so that the angry god (literally 'the god whose heart is seized') turn back" (KA-inim-ma diĝir

3. Seux, *Hymnes et Prières*, 24–27; J. Bottéro, "Magie," in *Reallexikon der Assyriologie und Vorderasiatischen Archäologie*, vol. 7 (ed. D. O. Edzard et al.; Berlin: de Gruyter, 1990), 214; W. Mayer, *Untersuchungen zur Formensprache der babylonischen "Gebetsbeschwörungen"* (StP.SM; Rome: Biblical Institute, 1976).

4. M. Krebernik, *Die Beschwörungen aus Fara und Ebla: Untersuchungen zur ältesten keilschriftlichen Beschwörungsliteratur* (Hildesheim: Georg Olms, 1984), 197–207, shows that E$_2$.NU.RU was probably a toponym, the name of a temple or part of a temple.

5. A distinction between penitential prayers and šu il$_2$-la$_2$ has been given by A. Zgoll, "Audienz—Ein Modell zum Verständnis mesopotamischer Handerhebungsrituale. Mit einer Deutung der Novelle vom Armen Mann von Nippur," *BagM* 34 (2003): 181–203.

6. W. Kunstmann, *Die babylonische Gebetsbeschwörung* (LSS 2; Leipzig: Hinrichs, 1932).

$šа_3$-dab$_{(5)}$-ba gur-ru-da-kam). I shall later come back to this third group of penitential prayers.

4. *Origin of the Penitential Prayers and the Personal God*

In the framework of even a partial review of the history of research on this subject one must quote the contribution of Klein, whose critical paper on the individual prayers begins not with a study of the prayers but with an analysis of the personal god.[7] Of course, the first indication of a real private religion appears in the literature at the beginning of the second millennium, especially in the letter-prayers but also in a wisdom composition with a penitential theme, the Old Babylonian dialogue between the *"Righteous Sufferer" and His God*.[8] This unique text includes the subscription "it is a lament of the plea to the god of a man" (er$_2$-ša$_3$-ne-ša$_4$-diĝir-lu$_2$-ulu$_3$-kam). The rubric er$_2$-ša$_3$-ne-ša$_4$ comprises the first argument in Klein's discussion, which we will discuss further, but first we must provide a philological explanation. Etymologically, the word ša$_3$-ne-ša$_4$ is not clear. The Sumerian verb ša$_4$ ("to shout, to make a noise"), suggests that the prayer was pronounced orally; it might have been a kind of scream of affliction. The meaning of ne is obscure, and ša$_3$-ne may have nothing to do with ša$_3$ ("heart"), which is otherwise often used in words conveying emotion or thought; ša$_3$-ne-ša$_4$ belongs to the terminology of prayers rather than to the one of emotion and does not belong to the Sumerian vocabulary of compassion (arḫuš, ša$_3$-la$_3$ su$_3$, etc.).[9] It does frequently parallel several forms of invocation. As Maul showed concerning the compound er$_2$-ša$_3$-ne-ša$_4$, it is a lament which belongs to the liturgical songs of the *kalû* priests.[10] The compound

7. J. Klein, "'Personal God' and Individual Prayer in Sumerian Religion," in *Vorträge gehalten auf der 28. Rencontre Assyriologique Internationale in Wien* (ed. H. Hirsch and H. Hunger; AfOB 19; Horn: Berger & Söhne, 1982), 295–306.

8. S. N. Kramer, "Man and His God": A Sumerian Variation on the 'Job' Motif," in *Wisdom in Israel and in the Ancient Near East, Festschrift H. H. Rowley* (ed. M. Noth and D. Winton Thomas; VTSup 3; Leiden: Brill, 1955), 170–82, and the study of J. Klein, "*Man and His God:* A Wisdom Poem or a Cultic Lament?," in *Approaches to Sumerian Literature: Studies in Honour of Stip (H. L. J. Vanstiphout)* (ed. P. Michalowski and N. Veldhuis; CM 35; Leiden: Brill, 2006), 123–43.

9. M. Jaques, *Le vocabulaire des sentiments dans les textes sumériens: Recherche sur le lexique sumérien et akkadien* (AOAT 332; Münster: Ugarit-Verlag, 2006), 237–47.

10. S. M. Maul, *"Herzberuhigungsklagen": Die sumerisch-akkadischen Eršahunga-Gebete* (Wiesbaden: Harrassowitz, 1988), 27 n. 90.

diĝir-ša$_3$-ne-ša$_4$ ("[personal] god beseeching" or "[personal] god of the plea") appears in the cultic terminology of the individual prayer as well. It is attested in three texts of the Neo-Sumerian period: in *Gudea Cylinder B* (i 16–19) and *Šulgi Hymn E* (17–19) as well as a hymn to Inana, named by the scholars *Inninšagurra*, which might have been written by the female priest Enḫeduanna, the daughter of Sargon, king of Akkad (2334–2279). The second element of Klein's argument is the expression ša$_3$ ki-be$_2$...gi$_4$, to which we already referred regarding the letter-prayers and the er$_2$-ša$_3$-ḫuĝ-ĝa$_2$. We find this formula in the conclusion of the dialog between the *"Righteous Sufferer" and His God* as well as—and this is a proof of its ancient origin—in another poem entitled *Ninmešarra* dedicated to Inana and also written by Enḫeduanna. Therefore, if the "(personal) god of the plea" was a concept known in the Neo-Sumerian period and the expression ša$_3$ ki-be$_2$...gi$_4$ appeared in penitential prayers in the literature preceding the Old Babylonian period, then the history of the individual Sumerian prayers as reconstructed by Hallo must be revised. The individual penitential prayer that would have existed independently in the oral tradition would be as old as the concept of the personal god to whom it would have been addressed. As for the letter-prayers, they would not be older compositions from which the penitential prayers stem but the opposite: they would have been composed following the penitential prayers' model. Moreover, it is interesting to note that the first attestations of this kind of prayers in the literature would then appear in the work of Enḫeduanna, a priestess of Akkadian origin.

5. *šigû*

I conclude this short review with some remarks concerning the appended chapter in Karel van der Toorn's *Sin and Sanction in Israel and Mesopotamia.*[11] The author compares two types of prayers: the Akkadian *šigû* and the diĝir ša$_3$ dab$_{(5)}$-ba. Seux had already treated many aspects regarding the Akkadian prayers *šigû.*[12] In short, *šigû* is a word whose meaning and etymology are not known and could be an exclamation: first, because it is indeclinable; second, because it is used as an exclamation in the onomastic record (we find, for example, the proper name *šigû-Gula*); and third, because it is often parallel to *aḫulap*. However, while *aḫulap* is a

11. K. van der Toorn, *Sin and Sanction in Israel and Mesopotamia: A Comparative Study* (Studia semitica neerlandica 22; Assen: Van Gorcum, 1985), 117–24.

12. J.-M. Seux, "šiggayon = šigu ?," in *Mélanges bibliques et orientaux en l'honneur de M. Henri Cazelles* (ed. A. Caquot and M. Delcor; AOAT 212; Neukirchen–Vluyn: Neukirchener Verlag, 1981), 419–38.

plea of pity, quite neutral and frequently attested, *šigû* implies a requirement of forgiveness with almost magical power. Medical texts, divinatory compositions and *Namburbi* rituals all contain *šigû* either as a symptom or as a sign charged with negative meaning. For example, in a divinatory text it is said: "If he is sick for the day and he puts his hands on his belly, screams *šigû* and stretches constantly his hands, he will die."[13] Used in another way, *šigû* can designate a penitential prayer, as the lexical equivalents show: the Sumerian words nam-tag ("sin") and er_2 ("tear, complaint, lament") are the Sumerian equivalent of the Akkadian *šigû*. In an Old Babylonian letter sent to a *nadītu* (a woman dedicated to a god, a kind of nun) in Sippar, a ceremony is mentioned which was taking place on the 27th or 28th of the month *Ulūlu* (August–September in Babylon) and which contained *šigû* prayers.[14] More recent texts show the royal practice of this kind of prayer during very elaborate ceremonies; moreover, these ceremonies could include other penitential prayers such as er_2-$ša_3$-ḫuĝ-$ĝa_2$, er_2-šem-ma, and *taqribtu*. Besides the month *Ulūlu*, the hemerological texts give several fixed dates when one would dedicate oneself to the recitation of *šigû* prayers.

6. *diĝir $ša_3$-$dab_{(5)}$-ba Prayers*

šigû also appears in the enumeration of sins in diĝir $ša_3$-$dab_{(5)}$-ba prayers including, among others, a long prayer in Akkadian from Assurbanipal's library.[15] The diĝir $ša_3$-$dab_{(5)}$-ba are a very interesting category of texts, as they enable us to have a look at a form of popular religion in Mesopotamia: an unofficial—at least in the ancient period—as well as individual kind of faith. This is very rare, as the general population could not write and probably did not need to write, and has accordingly left very few traces. These prayers exist in Sumerian and Akkadian and are addressed to the personal god in the first person, "to sooth his anger," according to the subscription. The first line is typical: "What have I done to my god?" (Sumerian: $ĝe_{26}$-e diĝir-$ĝu_{10}$ a-na i_3-im-ak, corresponding to the

13. H. Hunger, *Spätbabylonische Texte aus Uruk: Teil I* (Aussgrabungen der Deutschen Forschungsgemeinschaft in Uruk-Warka; Berlin: Gebr. Mann, 1976), 45 (No. 37:2).

14. A. Ungnad, *Babylonian Letters of the Hammurapi Period* (Publications of the Babylonian Section 7; Philadelphia: University of Pennsylvania Museum, 1915), No. 114.

15. W. G. Lambert, "Dingir.šà.dib.ba Incantations," *JNES* 33 (1974): 267–322, and M. Jaques *"Mon dieu, qu'ai-je donc fait ?" Les prières pénitentielles (diĝir-$ša_3$-$dab_{(5)}$-ba) et l'expression de la piété privée en Mésopotamie* (OBO; forthcoming).

Akkadian *anāku ana ilīja mīna ēpuš*). It is a request formulated as a familiar question to the deity whose is, however, not followed—as is the custom for named gods—by a long list of epithets. In this case, the content of the prayer enables us to identify the category to which the text belongs, as it is addressed to the personal god who is always unnamed. Moreover, the subscription diĝir ša$_3$-dab$_{(5)}$-ba is qualified by W. Lambert as "largely irrelevant." Indeed, one such prayer is repeated in five parallel texts in the Assyrian collection of diĝir ša$_3$-dab$_{(5)}$-ba prayers. Three of them have different subscription and one is not signed at all.[16] The first text has the subscription diĝir ša$_3$-dab$_{(5)}$-ba, the second one is signed as šu il$_2$-la$_2$ to Sîn, the moon god, and the third one bears the subscription "it is a formula to make beneficent the evil appearance of Sîn" (igi du$_8$-a ^{d}Sîn ḫul sig$_{10}$-ga) during an eclipse. Moreover, several texts whose first line is specific to the diĝir ša$_3$-dab$_{(5)}$-ba prayers also have the subscription er$_2$-ša$_3$-ḫuĝ-ĝa$_2$. These hybrids raise a question about the classification of prayers in Mesopotamian literature, with regard to the penitential prayers, šu il$_2$-la$_2$, as well as the incantations. Either one should presume with Lambert that the subscription "to sooth (the anger of) a god" is too imprecise to allow classification, and accordingly allow the transfer of a text from one category to another, or one should presume that for the ancient scholars these texts did not form a category[17] by themselves but existed only in relation to the function they had in rituals. In other words, the subscription is the subscription to rituals in which a text is used and not the subscription to these texts as a category.

7. *Rituals Series with diĝir ša$_3$-dab$_{(5)}$-ba Prayers*

This picture is made even more complex by the subsequent use of the diĝir ša$_3$-dab$_{(5)}$-ba prayers in various rituals, such as the one called *Bīt rimki* (meaning literally, "bath house"), and the relation between the same prayers and a ritual named *Ilī ul īdi* ("my god, I did not know"). It is not known whether there was a ritual series diĝir ša$_3$-dab$_{(5)}$-ba comparable, for example, to the ritual series *Bīt rimki* or the *Šurpu* ("burning") rituals. Unfortunately, all colophons in the fragments which might have given us more information have disappeared. Indeed, prayers were

16. The fifth prayer bears a broken subscription, [KA.INIM.MA... ^{d}EN.Z]U.KA[M], which might be the same as the third text.

17. This is the conclusion of several studies, including, for example, the one of A. Zgoll, *Kunst des Betens: Form und Funktion, Theologie und Psychagogik in babylonisch-assyrischen Handerhebungsgebeten zu Ištar* (AOAT 308; Münster: Ugarit-Verlag, 2003), 21–22.

collected on separate tablets and not in a set; yet this is not a contradicting argument because one might collect the prayers still in use on a single medium for practical reasons. In both rituals mentioned above, *Bīt rimki* and *Ilī ul īdi*, the diĝir ša$_3$-dab$_{(5)}$-ba prayers appear in groups composed of at least three prayers. Moreover, these rituals suggest a complementarity between these prayers and the ritual of the series *Šurpu* (at the end of *ilī ul īdi* a reference is made to this ritual series). This complementarity is confirmed by the texts of *Šurpu* themselves.

To summarize, all these texts (both ritual series and prayers) have at least one similar goal: to change or cancel the curse contained in the anger of the gods.

8. *Medical Series with diĝir ša$_3$-dab$_{(5)}$-ba Prayers*

We can refine this interpretation with the study of texts in which the use of these prayers was considered necessary, that is, in medical texts. A subscription, a little more elaborate than the usual form, is found in a Late Babylonian text: "it is a formula to recite word for word if a man is always prostrate, in order to sooth the angry god" (KA-inim-ma *šumma amēlu niziqtu irtanašši* diĝir ša$_3$-dab$_{(5)}$-ba gur-ru-da-kam). We might discuss at length the exact meaning of the Akkadian word *niziqtu*, which describes a negative psychological and emotional state and is often found in these medical series parallel to terms with similar meaning, such as *nissatu* ("sadness"), *diliptu* ("insomnia"), *gilittu* ("terror"), *tēšû* ("confusion"), *qūlu* ("silence") and *kūru* ("stupor, prostration").

The subscription diĝir ša$_3$-dab$_{(5)}$-ba gur/bur-ru-da-kam (with the verb gur ["to turn back"] or the variant bur ["to undo"]) is translated in texts of medical diagnostics with the corresponding Akkadian expression *libbi ili kamri (/ kamli) lippašir*. For example, this translation of the Sumerian subscription appears in a medical text, related by its content to the *Ilī ul īdi* rituals: "it is a formula to recite word for word, if a man ate the taboo of the god and his god is angry with him" (KA-inim-ma *šumma amēlu ikkib ili īkul-ma ilšu ittīšu kamil*).[18]

The diĝir ša$_3$-dab$_{(5)}$-ba prayers are also attested in texts of medical diagnostics such as *Die babylonisch-assyrische Medizin in Texten und Untersuchungen* No. 316, which consists of recipes and short rituals to dissolve the effects of divine wrath.[19] It is remarkable that in the list of

18. R. Campbell Thompson, *Assyrian Medical Texts from the Originals in the British Museum* (London: Oxford University Press, 1923), No. 81, 5 rev. 4.

19. F. Köcher, *Die babylonisch-assyrische Medizin in Texten und Untersuchungen* (Keilschrifttexte aus Assur 3; Berlin: de Gruyter, 1964), No. 316.

the patient's disorders, there are no diseases, only financial, social, religious and—above all—psychological problems (lack of sleep, anxiety, lethargy, hysteria, etc.). Saying the diĝir ša$_3$-dab$_{(5)}$-ba prayers in these texts constitutes a form of therapy. In these circumstances it is not surprising to find magic rituals accompanied by diĝir ša$_3$-dab$_{(5)}$-ba prayers; these include the ritual of burning in front of the god the statuette of an ancestor whose past sins still burden the new generation (according to the belief that the current generation inherits the personal god of the father, with the personal god passing from one generation to the next, from the father's body to the son's body). We can see that one could not cure the effects of the wrath of the god through prayer alone but also employed the rituals of magic or medical therapy, using bandages, plants and stones.

9. *Origin of the Concept of Sin*

The penitential prayers raise several theological issues with which I wish to conclude. Over the course of its history Mesopotamian theology has undergone significant changes, which have been subjects of remarkable attempts at modern summaries, such as *The Treasures of Darkness* by Jacobsen or *La plus vieille religion* by Bottéro.[20] Although it has not been proven that religion underwent a true revolution after the middle of the third millennium, it is an undeniable fact that human beings' relationship with the gods has gradually changed throughout history. This change is particularly perceptible in the way the ancient Mesopotamians resolved the question of evil. In the *Dictionary of the History of Ideas* Loemker observed that the problem of evil may be solved in a polytheistic system by a limited number of theories under certain conditions.[21] Among these theories he mentions the "dualistic" theory, which assigns evil to demons or to a god who constitutes the counterpart of the good gods. Does this means of solving the problem of evil hinder other explanations of human affliction, such as reference to sin?

The dualism of demons and gods certainly existed in ancient Mesopotamia. There the response constituted the domain of the Sumerian maš-maš or the Akkadian *āšipu*, that is, the exorcist.

20. T. Jacobsen, *The Treasures of Darkness: A History of Mesopotamian Religion* (New Haven: Yale University Press, 1976); J. Bottéro, *La plus vieille religion: En Mésopotamie* (Collection Folio. Histoire 82; Paris: Gallimard, 1998).

21. L. E. Loemker, "Theodicy," in *Dictionary of the History of Ideas: Studies of Selected Pivotal Ideas*, vol. 4 (ed. P. P. Wiener; New York: Scribner, 1973), 378–84 (379).

The word for sin in Sumerian is nam-tag, corresponding to the Akkadian *arnu*, the etymology of which is obscure. The Sumerian word is attested with certainty already in the archaic royal inscriptions of the city of Lagaš (around 2500 B.C.E.), especially in an inscription of the king Erikagina: "There is no sin on the part of Erikagina, the king of Ĝirsu. May Nisaba, the (personal) goddess of Lugalzagesi, the governor of Umma, do put all the sins on his (= Lugalzagesi's) shoulders." In this excerpt, the speaker asks Nisaba not to blame Erikagina but to shift the blame onto Lugalzagesi, who is her protégé. Already we may see the importance of the gods' actions in the transfer of the sin and in its abolition. We may also see the importance of the personal god who, when he is angry because of a sin, may abandon his protégé to the demons. Certainly the concept of sin is as old as the idea of a personal god; the latter is older than believed by Gladigow, according to whom the personal god could appear only with the birth of human individualistic consciousness.[22]

Penitential prayers, sin and the personal god all belong to the same intellectual environment. However, since there is no longer any discourse on religion by the ancient Mesopotamians themselves, it is difficult to look for the origin of this set, elaborate a theory of evil or speculate why a concept does not appear in certain writings. Rather, when texts such as the dialogue between a *"Righteous Sufferer" and His God* or the letter-prayers appear, one must ask what exactly is appearing: Is it a new theology, a new rhetoric or a new way of talking to one's god? The only thing we may be sure about is the emergence of a speech form which expresses a certain type of relation with the gods; this does not prove, of course, that the relation did not previously exist. It is important for the ancient Near Eastern history of religion to consider all these aspects together, drawing as complete picture as possible of the religious data as expressed and lived by the Mesopotamians. Only such research can produce new comparable categories, theories and questions.

22. B. Gladigow, "Der Sinn der Götter. Zum kognitiven Potential der persönlichen Gottesvorstellung," in *Gottesvorstellung und Gesellschaftsentwicklung* (ed. P. Eicher; Forum Religionswissenschaft 1; Munich: Kösel, 1979), 41–66.

How to Approach a Deity: The Growth of a Prayer Addressed to Ištar

Anna Elise Zernecke

A volume edited by Erich Zenger in 2003 summarizes the discussion of ancient Israelite, ancient Near Eastern, Jewish and Christian prayer texts as "Ritual und Poesie."[1] "Ritual and poetry" represents the controversy between H. Gunkel and S. Mowinckel about the origin of the biblical psalms, either as texts originally written for and used in a cultic setting (Mowinckel) or as "geistliche Dichtung" (spiritual poetry) independent from the cult but influenced by cultic forms (Gunkel).[2] It took biblical scholars of the twentieth century a long time to overcome this dichotomy—even longer than Assyriologists—and to be able to value the objects of their study as poetic texts from cultic settings: both ritual and poetry.[3] For the Akkadian prayers of the lifting of the hand (following their conventional subscription), their quality as poetry—in selected cases—has been analyzed by I. T. Abusch and A. Zgoll.[4] Zgoll has also investigated their ritual setting and interpreted it as staging an audience with the deity, analogous to audiences at human courts.[5] The

1. E. Zenger, "Vorwort," in *Ritual und Poesie: Formen und Orte religiöser Dichtung im Alten Orient, im Judentum und im Christentum* (ed. E. Zenger; HBS 36; Freiburg: Herder, 2003), vii–ix.

2. Ibid., vii.

3. Behind the old dichotomy stands F. Heiler's monograph *Das Gebet: Eine religionsgeschichtliche und religionspsychologische Untersuchung* (5th ed.; Munich: Reinhardt, 1923), with its emphasis on prayer as spontaneous expression of the heart, thus depreciating prayers in set forms and depending on religious and poetic conventions.

4. KA.INIM.MA ŠU.IL$_2$.LA$_2$ ^{d}X.KAM, "wording of the lifted hand(s) to the deity X"; see A. Zgoll, *Die Kunst des Betens: Form und Funktion, Theologie und Psychagogik in babylonisch-assyrischen Handerhebungsgebeten zu Ištar* (AOAT 308; Münster: Ugarit-Verlag, 2003), 21, and I. T. Abusch, "The Form and Meaning of a Babylonian Prayer to Marduk," *JAOS* 103 (1983): 1–15.

5. A. Zgoll, "Audienz—Ein Modell zum Verständnis mesopotamischer Handerhebungsrituale. Mit einer Deutung der Novelle vom *Armen Mann von Nippur*," *BagM* 34 (2003): 181–203.

conventionality of the language of these prayers has been known from the studies of W. G. Kunstmann and W. Mayer for some time already.[6] Today, they may be classified as ritual poetry or as prayers with poetic value, in conventional forms, from a cultic setting.

One way of studying the relation between convention and originality in these prayers has not been tried so far. This is the comparison of different versions of the same text that show its development over time. If there are widely differing versions of one text from different times, their study allows us to observe two things: the development of the text itself (the work of later generations with older material) and the evolution of the conventions governing the relation between the supplicant and the deity addressed. Such an analysis shall be attempted in the present study. The text used for this study is widely known and translations can be found in many collections of Mesopotamian material.[7] Ištar 2 is an Akkadian prayer addressed to the goddess Ištar and was first published in 1902.[8] Eight copies of the Akkadian text are now known, although only two are more than tiny fragments.[9] The best known is a Neo-Babylonian copy, now in the British Museum, which was, according to the colophon,

6. W. G. Kunstmann, *Die babylonische Gebetsbeschwörung* (LSS 2; Leipzig: Hinrichs, 1932); W. Mayer, *Untersuchungen zur Formensprache der babylonischen "Gebetsbeschwörungen"* (StP.SM 5; Rome: Biblical Institute, 1976).

7. H. Zimmern, *Babylonische Hymnen und Gebete in Auswahl* (AO 7; Leipzig: Hinrichs, 1905), 19–22; A. Ungnad, *Die Religion der Babylonier und Assyrer* (Religiöse Stimmen der Völker 3; Jena: Diederichs, 1921), 217–22; F. J. Stephens, "Sumero-Akkadian Hymns and Prayers," in *ANET*, 383–92 (383–85); E. Ebeling, *Die akkadische Gebetsserie "Handerhebung": Von neuem gesammelt und herausgegeben* (Deutsche Akademie der Wissenschaften zu Berlin, Institut für Orientforschung: Veröffentlichung 20; Berlin: Akademie-Verlag, 1953), 130–37; A. Falkenstein and W. von Soden, *Sumerische und akkadische Hymnen und Gebete* (Die Bibliothek der Alten Welt; Zurich: Artemis, 1953), 328–33, 401: M.-J. Seux, *Hymnes et prières aux dieux de Babylonie et d'Assyrie* (LAPO 8; Paris: Cerf, 1976), 186–94; W. Beyerlin, ed., *Religionsgeschichtliches Textbuch zum Alten Testament* (2d ed.; Grundrisse zum Alten Testament 1; Göttingen: Vandenhoeck & Ruprecht, 1985), 133–36; B. R. Foster, *Before the Muses: An Anthology of Akkadian Literature* (3d ed.; Bethesda, Md.: CDL, 2005), 599–605; A. E. Zernecke, "Ishtar 2: The 'Great Ishtar Prayer,'" in *Reading Akkadian Prayers and Hymns: An Introduction* (ed. A. Lenzi; ANEM 3; Atlanta: Society of Biblical Literature, 2011), 257–90.

8. L. W. King, ed., *The Seven Tablets of Creation, or the Babylonian and Assyrian Legends Concerning the Creation of the World and of Mankind*, vol. 2 (London: Luzac, 1902), pl. 75–84.

9. The latest edition of all copies known in 2003 is Zgoll, *Kunst*, 41–67. Recently, two more tiny fragments have been published, in S. Maul and R. Strauss, *Ritualbeschreibungen und Gebete I: Mit Beiträgen von Daniel Schwemer* (WVDOG 133; Wiesbaden: Harrassowitz, 2011), 109–11.

the votive offering of a ritual expert in Esagila, the temple of Marduk in Babylon.[10] If it was indeed found in Babylon is unknown, as archaeological data are not published. The subscript and ritual instructions declare this text to be a prayer of the lifting of the hand addressed to the goddess Ištar.

For a long time prayers of this type were only known from the first millennium B.C.E. It therefore came as a surprise when a copy of the same prayer in Akkadian was unearthed in Boğazköy, in the remains of the Hittite capital, dated to the thirteenth century B.C.E. This copy does not label the prayer as "prayer of the lifting of the hand"; there is no designation at all, as the line with the subscription is broken. Still, it is doubtlessly the same prayer. Even more curiously, a very fragmentary version of the prayer, translated into Hittite, was also found in Boğazköy.[11]

The present study deals with the two Akkadian versions of the prayer: the Neo-Babylonian one, hereafter text A, and the Akkadian version from Boğazköy, hereafter text F.[12]

Text A is perfectly preserved and almost every sign can be read without doubt. Text F, on the contrary, is preserved in three fragments, two of which join directly. There is text missing in the Boğazköy tablet, but not many lines are completely lost: the fragments clearly contain the beginning and the end of the prayer, and between the end of the first fragment and the first line of the second fragment there are only three lines missing when compared to text A. In the second break—between obverse and reverse of the fragment—there are not more than four lines missing. Altogether, not too much text seems to be entirely lost, provided that every line in text F is also contained in text A. As eight of the 50 lines preserved in F have no parallel in A, this cannot be maintained in every case, but most of the two texts do run in parallel.[13] Between the two parallel versions there are differences, however, and these differences are worth looking at.

10. Foster, *Muses*, 599, qualifies this text as Neo-Babylonian. Text A lines 112–113 (colophon): "A copy from Borsippa. According to its original. Nergal-balassu-iqbi, son of Atamar-KAL.ME, ritual expert (*āšipu*), has written (it) for his life, checked (it) through and permanently deposited (it) in Esagila." See also Zernecke, "Ishtar 2," 281.

11. E. Reiner and H. G. Güterbock, "The Great Prayer to Ishtar and Its two Versions from Boğazköy," *JCS* 21 (1967): 255–66.

12. These labels follow the most recent edition of both versions in Zgoll, *Kunst*, 41–67.

13. The lines in F are longer than in A. For the present study, the line numbering of A is used.

Text F was found in Boğazköy, at the periphery of Akkadian textual culture. Therefore, text F is most probably not a direct antecedent of text A, and the relationship between both versions would likely have been anything but direct. As these are the only two versions preserved to such an extent that they can be compared, however, a (nearly) direct development shall be assumed for this argument.

The Disposition of the Versions

The overall development between text F and text A can be described as growth: the version from Boğazköy contains 50 lines of prayer (plus 7 or so lost in the breaks), whereas text A has 105 lines. Text A is thus roughly twice as long as text F, but the text did not grow in all places to the same extent. Text A can be subdivided according to the direction of speech, subject and object and the dominant content into the following sections:

lines 1–41	Invocation and praise of Ištar	41 lines
lines 42–55	First petition	14 lines
lines 56–78	Complaint	23 lines
lines 79–102	Second petition	24 lines
lines 103–105	Final praise of Ištar	3 lines

This does not conform completely to the model organization of prayers of the lifting of the hand, but such prayers are not usually as long as Ištar 2 text A.[14] Text F contains all the main structural elements of text A except for the final praise, which may have been lost: text F ends with a wish for the supplicant which is usual at the end of Akkadian prayers in the context of a promise to praise: *bulliṭannīma* ("let me live").[15] Both editions complete the line with "so that I may praise you."[16]

lines 5′–7″	Invocation and praise of Ištar	37 lines, 1 break (+3?)
lines 8″–11″	First petition	6 lines[17]
lines 12″–2‴	Complaint	3 lines, 1 break (+ 4?)
lines 3‴–6‴	Second petition	4 lines
–	Final praise of Ištar	– (broken?)

14. This is why several authors see this prayer as an atypical handlifting prayer; cf. Mayer, *Untersuchungen*, 28 n. 60, 125; I. T. Abusch, "Prayers, Hymns, Incantations, and Curses," in *Religions of the Ancient World: A Guide* (ed. S. I. Johnston; Cambridge, Mass.: Belknap, 2004), 353–55.

15. Mayer, *Untersuchungen*, 312–13.

16. Zgoll, *Kunst*, 59; cf. Reiner and Güterbock, "Prayer," 263.

17. It is impossible to decide whether line 11″ was part of the first petition or the supplication. Here it is seen as part of the first petition.

The overall disposition of text F is essentially the same as of text A. The development that took place between them is characterized by Foster in this way: "the prototype text was enlarged, although the structure and organization of the original were not greatly affected. Ideas and patterns already in the text were expanded and elaborated." He interprets Ištar 2 as "an excellent case study in how a Mesopotamian literary text could evolve or expand and still remain true in its essentials to the intention of the original author."[18]

This is right and wrong at the same time: the disposition of the text remains the same, but the expansion of each part changes quite a lot. This can be seen in a comparison of the proportions of the parts of the prayers:

	Text A	Text F
Invocation and praise	39 %	74 % + break
First petition	13 %	12 %
Complaint	22 %	6 % + break
Second petition	23 %	8 %
Praise	3 %	– (broken?)

The proportion of the main elements differs widely between both versions: the invocation and praise have approximately the same absolute length (37 lines in F, 41 in A), but the parts of the prayer in which the supplicant is dominant are much shorter in the earlier version. Proportionally, the invocation and praise are much more prominent in the earlier version, more prominent also than in all other prayers of the lifting of the hand addressed to Ištar.[19] As a consequence of the different proportions the supplicant, who is not mentioned in the invocation, is much less important in the text from Boğazköy than in the younger version, where the supplicant dominates 58 percent of the prayer.

In the invocation both versions of the text are very close to each other. In the other parts of the prayer the differences are greater, although text F is here often only fragmentarily preserved. The rest of twelve lines—according to the length of the lines in A—can be read after the end of the first invocation and praise, six of which have no parallel in text A.[20] This is six of eight lines in total that have no parallel. The observation of Foster that "the structure and organization of the original were not greatly affected"[21] is true, but only in a very formalistic sense. If a fragment with

18. Foster, *Muses*, 599; cf. Reiner and Güterbock, "Prayer," 263.

19. Zgoll, *Kunst*, 32.

20. Lines 7″, 10″–11″, 4‴–6‴. Line 5‴ ([…] *īnī nūrki ammar*) is close to line 55 in text A (…*nūrki namru lūmur*) but situated in another part of the prayer.

21. Foster, *Muses*, 599.

only the latter parts of the prayer behind the invocation had been found in Boğazköy, it would probably not have been recognized as a parallel of Ištar 2 text A! Text F ought therefore to be interpreted mainly as a witness to the age of the invocation of Ištar 2.

The "Missing Lines" in the Invocation

The development of the text can best be observed in the variants between the two versions of the invocation, which are of approximately the same absolute length: 41 lines in text A, 37 lines in text F. Most of the text runs parallel, but there are characteristic exceptions. Cases in which one of the versions has a line that is entirely different are more interesting for our present purpose than alternative epithets.[22]

The only place where text F has something A does not have are two lines after line 6 of text A. They are thematically close to the preceding text, highlighting Ištar as the warlike goddess within the pantheon. More important for understanding the development of content and the method of expanding the text are the lines in A that have no parallels in F: independent of the first break, these are lines 17, 25, 26, 35 and 41.[23] This is—partly at least—no coincidence; lines 17, 25, 26 and 41 are crucial for the arrangement of the invocation in its later form and for the integrity of the whole prayer.

Line 17 is the last of three lines beginning with *ēkiam lā*, "where… not"—one of the typical "litanies" of text A (see below): "Where are you not great? Where are you not exalted?" (*ēkiam lā rabâti ēkiam lā ṣīrāti*). It sums up the sequence of lines 15–17 with general adjectives, *rabû*, "great," and *ṣīru*, "exalted," which are used several times for Ištar already at the beginning of the text.[24] Both adjectives in combination occur again only a few lines later—this time also in text F: "you indeed are great and exalted" (*attima rabâti u ṣīrāti*; line 23A / 22′F). Both occurrences, in lines 17 and 23, form a frame for Ištar's exaltation, described in lines 18–22. Although lines 15–16 and 18–23 all already

22. For a comparison of the epithets, see Zernecke, *Gott und Mensch in Klagegebeten aus Israel und Mesopotamien: Die Handerhebungsgebete Ištar 10 und Ištar 2 und die Klagepsalmen Ps 38 und Ps 22 im Vergleich* (AOAT 387; Münster: Ugarit-Verlag, 2011), 163–64.

23. Lines 32–33 are missing because of the first break. Line 34 is very fragmentarily preserved in F. Perhaps the lack of line 35 is also connected to this break.

24. Ends of lines 3–4: *rabāt Igigî*, "greatest of the Igigi" (for the form, cf. Zernecke, "Ishtar 2," 260) and *šumūki ṣīrū*, "your names are exalted"; *rabû*, also as the intensive form *rabbû*, in line 100 and as verb in lines 18, 34; and *ṣīru* in lines 103–104.

exist in text F, this frame is a general structuring element which is only created by the insertion of line 17.

The other pluses of A, lines 25, 26 and 41, are connected to each other. Lines 25, 26 and 40 are the only places in the invocation in which Ištar's actions on behalf of human beings are described, rather than her astral dimensions, cosmic importance or general prowess in war. Only here is she the subject of inflected verbs. The goddess is praised as righteous judge in line 25 ("You render the verdict for subject peoples in righteousness and justice"), while in line 26 she is helping the suffering: "You look upon the wronged and afflicted, you guide [them] aright every day" (*tappallasī ḫablu u šagšu tušteššerī uddakam*). The verb *palāsu* N, "to look at," is used here for the first time. It is central for all the rest of the prayer: Ištar is again the subject of *palāsu* in line 40 ("wherever you look, the dead lives, the sick arises"), and it is part of the most frequent petition of the whole prayer, which is repeated three times (44, 54, 92): *kīniš naplisīnni(ma)*, "Look faithfully upon me." In text F *palāsu* is not so prominent: in line 6″, the partial equivalent of line 40A, the verb is missing. The petition *kīniš naplisīnnima* occurs only once in F, in line 3‴ (parallel to line 92A). But *palāsu* is not the only conspicuous verb in line 26: the use of *ešēru* $Št_2$, "to set aright," here "to guide aright," connects line 26 to the very beginning of the prayer, where Ištar is described as "guiding mankind / the four edges of the world aright" in text F (line 6′) as well as in text A (line 2). *Ešēru* is also used in line 41, the last line of the invocation, for the effect of looking at Ištar's face for a miserable person, and in line 84, where the supplicant uses it in a petition: "Guide my step aright!" Interestingly, both lines are missing in text F. Lines 25 and 26 describe Ištar's actions towards men in life-threatening situations. The use of verbs is certainly intentional: they appear again later in the text in petitions directed to Ištar. These two lines explicitly prepare the following petitions, so it seems to be no accident that they are missing in text F, in which the petitions have much less space and importance.[25]

Line 41 is also missing in text F. This last line of the invocation sums up Ištar's help for the afflicted: *iššir lā išaru āmiru pānīki*, "The one who is not right becomes all right (when) seeing your face." The only striking parallel in the vocabulary is the use of *ešēru*, just discussed, but this line, like the preceding one, speaks of the beneficial aspects of "eye-contact" with the goddess; this motive of seeing and being seen is central for the younger version, pervading all parts of the text.[26]

25. Zernecke, *Gott*, 178, 187–91.

26. Ibid., 187–89. *Palāsu*, just discussed, is only one aspect of this phenomenon.

Connected to these passages which are pluses of the later version is a textual change in line 40A (line 6″F), preceding line 41. In both texts, the meaning is that Ištar helps the afflicted. Interestingly, the second half of the line is not identical: in text A "the sick arises" (*itebbī marṣu*), in text F "the bad disappears" (*iḫalliq lemnu*). The designation of the suffering as "sick" (*marṣu*) in the younger version is again no coincidence: only two lines later, the supplicant presents himself using an intensive form of the same adjective (*šumruṣu*, "suffering") to characterize his problems (line 42: "I appeal to you, your tired, wearied, *suffering* servant"). Forms of the same root are used again in the course of the petitions and the supplications (cf. lines 47, 66). This makes it probable that line 40 was changed with respect to the newer paragraphs of the prayer.[27]

A closer look at the very few lines which are missing in the older version of the invocation—with the exception of line 35 which might be related to the first break—shows that these lines are especially well connected to the parts of the prayer which have a much greater length and importance in the younger version: they refer to other lines and they connect the description of Ištar's actions in the invocation to the petitions, so that the goddess should be moved to act for the supplicant in the way she is known and praised for acting. It is therefore possible to conclude that these lines were inserted deliberately into the younger text, developed out of existing material and serving as internal structuring elements for the text.

The "Litanies"

This development of text from existing material can also be observed in other parts of the prayer. One of the features which led to the qualification of Ištar 2 text A as an "atypical" prayer of the lifting of the hand (see above) is the fact that several subsequent lines begin with the same word: in the invocation, Ištar's might is praised by repeated questions which begin with *ēkiam lā*, "where…not?" (lines 15–17A):

15 Where is not your name? Where are not your ordinances?
16 Where are your plans not implemented? Where are your daises not set up?
17 Where are you not great? Where are you not exalted?[28]

Her mercy is emphasized by repeating her word of pardon, *aḫulap*, with possessive suffix of the second person (lines 27–30A):

27. Ibid., 190.

28. *ēkiam lā šumki ēkiam lā parṣūki / ēkiam lā uṣṣurā uṣurātīki ēkiam lā nadû parakkūki / ēkiam lā rabâti ēkiam lā ṣīrāti.*

27 Your *aḫulap*, Lady of heaven and earth, shepherdess of the numerous people!
28 Your *aḫulap*, Lady of holy Eana, the pure treasury!
29 Your *aḫulap*, Lady—your feet do not tire, your knees are swift!
30 Your *aḫulap*, Lady of all battles (and) combats![29]

Both series of lines exist already in the older version and serve as a source for generating more material for the younger text A. Instead of lines 15–17A, there are only two lines introduced with *ēkiam lā* in F (17′–18′). The last line of the sequence in A (line 17) is one of the "missing lines" in the introduction just analyzed (see above). Though the word *aḫulap* is not preserved in F but only the second part of each line, lines 27–30A parallel lines 24′–27′F. Text A contains more such repetitions in the style of "litanies" in other parts of the text: lines 45–50 in the first petition again begin with *aḫulap*, now with the possessive suffix of the first person:

45 *aḫulap* pronounce for me, and let your feelings become reconciled to me—
46 *aḫulap* for my wretched body which is full of confusion and trouble,
47 *aḫulap* for my suffering heart which is full of tears and sighs,
48 *aḫulap* for my wretched, confused and troubled omens,
49 *aḫulap* for my sleepless house which laments (with) wailing,
50 *aḫulap* for my feelings which persevere (in) tears and sighs![30]

These lines have no parallel in text F. The change of the possessive suffix makes them correspond to the first string of *aḫulap*-lines in the invocation. Here, the text has grown in the first petition by enlarging it with an element of the first invocation.[31]

Another such repetition begins with *adi mati*, "how long?" It can be found in the beginning of the complaint (lines 56, 59).

56 How long, my Lady, will my enemies look malevolently at me…
59 How long, my Lady, will the idiot (and) cripple overtake me?[32]

and in the last petition (lines 93–94),

29. *aḫulapki bēlet šamê u erṣeti rēʾât nišī apâti / aḫulapki bēlet Eanna quddušu šutummu ellu / aḫulapki bēlet ul anīḫā šēpāki lāsimā birkāki / aḫulapki bēlet tāḫāzī kalîšunu tamḫārī.*

30. *aḫulapya qibîma kabattaki lippašra / aḫulap zumrīya nassi ša malû ešâti u dalḫāti / aḫulap libbīya šumruṣu ša malû dimti u tānēḫi / aḫulap têrētīya nassāti ešâti u dalḫāti / aḫulap bītīya šudlupu ša unassasu bikâti / aḫulap kabtatīya ša uštabarrû dimti u tānēḫi.*

31. Zernecke, *Gott*, 167.

32. *adi mati bēltī bēlū dabābīya nekelmûʾinnima / adi mati bēltī lillu akû ibâʾanni.*

93 How long, my Lady, will you be angry and your face be averted?
94 How long, my Lady, will you rage and your feelings be infuriated?[33]

Only line 59—the second line beginning with *adi mati* in the complaint—has a parallel in text F. This line seems to be the kernel from which the sequences are developed.[34] Line 56 was created for its position at the beginning of the complaint (lines 56–78). Its subject of "eye-contact," this time with the malevolent enemies, connects it to the theme of seeing and being seen which is important throughout the whole prayer.[35]

In these sequences, one word or expression is taken and developed into a string of parallel lines. These are among the few instances where it is really possible to observe one of the laws governing the growth of the text.

Conclusions

The observations on the text made so far can be evaluated in two different aspects.

First, there is the relation between the human being and the deity: the analysis of both versions shows that both the younger and the older text are identical in their general disposition, with the exception of the final praise, which is not preserved in text F. In the development of the text, however, the proportion of the parts has shifted: a hymnic praise of Ištar, followed by a few lines of supplication and complaint, has grown into an intricately structured prayer of lament and supplication, whose introductory praise is less than 40 percent of the whole text. The supplicant and his request are now of much greater importance.

Only two second-millennium Akkadian prayers are known which are subscribed as prayers of the lifting of the hand in their later versions.[36] Whether this kind of ritual was already extant when they were used in their earlier form is unknown, as both tablets are broken where a subscription would be expected.[37] The prayers of the lifting of the hand are

33. *adi mati bēltī zenâtima suḫḫurū pānūki / adi mati bēltī ra'bātima uzzuzat kabtatki*.

34. Cf. Reiner and Güterbock, "Prayer," 263.

35. See above and Zernecke, *Gott*, 187–89.

36. The other prayer is Ištar 10 text E; see Zgoll, *Kunst*, 107–26.

37. On F, the beginning of the subscription is preserved in line 7‴, [KA.INIM].MA?; see Zgoll, *Kunst*, 56. C. Frechette doubts that there was a hand-lifting ritual already in the second millennium; see Frechette, "The Name of the Ritual: Investigating Ancient Mesopotamian 'Hand-lifting' Rituals with Implications for the Interpretation of Genre in the Psalms" (Ph.D. diss., Harvard University, 2005), 141–42.

structured as audiences.[38] While this structure remains the same, the supplicant becomes more prominent in the transmission of the text. The addresses for the deity, on the other hand, remain constant: in the hymnic invocation, Ištar is addressed with her name, in A with several names and as "Lady" (*bēlet*).[39] In the petitions and the complaint, the relationship to the supplicant is emphasized with the singular first person possessive suffix: *bēltī*, "my Lady."[40]

This growing importance of the supplicant, in combination with the constant structure and stable relationship between the supplicant and the deity addressed, might be used for a hypothetical reconstruction of the history of hand-lifting rituals in general. There are different types of texts designated as hand-lifting rituals by their subscriptions: most specimens are Akkadian prayers for a single supplicant transmitted and performed by the *āšipu*, but there were also Sumerian and bilingual texts from different ritual contexts, mainly used in the *Mīs pî*-ritual and in the *Akītu*-festival.[41] In the latter context, prayers designated as prayers of the lifting of the hand were recited during the processions to the *akītu*-house and back, especially during the returning of the cult statues to their sanctuary. Their function is interpreted as the greeting of the deity, possibly in analogy to greeting procedures at court.[42] According to Frechette's analysis the gesture of hand-lifting in the context of the Akkadian prayers of the lifting of the hand had the same function.[43]

38. Zgoll, "Audienz."

39. A: *Ištar* (lines 2, 34, 38, 103), *Irnini* (lines 3, 105), *Gušea* (line 12); *bēlet* (lines 8, 29, 104). F: *Inana* (line 7′); *bēlet* (lines 9′, 12′, 26′).

40. *bēltī* A: lines 43, 56, 59, 72, 73, 79, 93, 94. F: line 12‴ (line 59A). An exception is *Irninītu*, in line 51A. Cf. Zernecke, *Gott*, 169–72.

41. C. Frechette, "Shuillas," in Lenzi, ed., *Reading Akkadian Prayers and Hymns*, 24–35 (26–27). For the text of the *Mīs pî*, see C. Walker and M. Dick, *The Induction of the Cult Image in Ancient Mesopotamia: The Mesopotamian Mīs Pî Ritual: Transliteration, Translation, and Commentary* (SAALT 1; Helsinki: The Neo-Assyrian Text Corpus Project, 2001). The ritual has been studied by A. Berlejung, *Die Theologie der Bilder: Herstellung und Einweihung von Kultbildern in Mesopotamien und die alttestamentliche Bilderpolemik* (OBO 162; Göttingen: Vandenhoeck & Ruprecht, 1998).

42. D. Shibata, "Ritual Contexts and Mythological Explanations of the Emesal Šuilla-Prayers in Ancient Mesopotamia," *Orient* 45 (2010): 67–85 (74–75). Shibata assumes a general function as a greeting also for the Akkadian prayers of the lifting of the hand ("Ritual Contexts," 75, 81 n. 45). This does not take into account the prominence of complaints and petitions in these texts.

43. C. Frechette, "Reconsidering ŠU.IL$_2$.LA$_{(2)}$ as a Classifier of the *Āšipu* in Light of the Iconography of Reciprocal Hand-Lifting Gestures," in *Proceedings of*

Even though the texts analyzed aim to induce the deity to act on behalf of the supplicant and therefore are not simply greetings, this observation is instructive for the development of Ištar 2: its older version, with the proportionally longer invocation and the very short petition and complaint, might be a transitory stage between a purely hymnic invocation which might be plausible as a greeting and a full-fledged prayer of supplication in which one person complains to a deity.[44] The hypothesis that the Akkadian prayers of the lifting of the hand were originally a fusion of two different genres, hymn and supplication, would then need to be modified: (some of) these prayers might have been hymns that have grown into prayers of supplication.[45]

Secondly, the growth of this text may be compared to the premises used for literary criticism of the Hebrew Bible. In the methodology developed for the analysis of the Hebrew Bible, literary criticism—in the sense of source criticism—and its counterpart redaction criticism are used to enlighten the history and development of the text. Both methods assume that many texts of the Bible were not written as they are now transmitted, but were subject to—sometimes several—revisions and redactions. In this process of *Fortschreibungen*, as the texts were adapted to new historical situations and contexts, they were changed and revised—so that we often have the text and (one or several layers of) its exegesis within the biblical texts. This process is envisaged mainly as growth of the texts.[46] Though most results of literary criticism are (more

the 51st Rencontre Assyriologique Internationale Held at the Oriental Institute of the University of Chicago (ed. R. Biggs, J. Myers and M. Roth; Studies in Ancient Oriental Civilization 62; Chicago: Oriental Institute, 2008), 41–47 (47).

44. According to Zgoll's analysis of hand-lifting rituals as audiences, the function of the invocation is the greeting of the deity; cf. Zgoll, "Audienz," 197–98. The second fragment from the second millennium with a (later) prayer of the lifting of the hand, Ištar 10 text E, has different proportions: it is much closer to the later version with elaborate petitions and a detailed complaint. This text is closer to the later version, especially in the invocation and its end is shorter. Ištar 10 thus seems to have also grown mainly at the end.

45. This hypothesis needs to be corroborated by more material, as neither of the two later prayers of the lifting of the hand, from the second millennium, is in its older version designated as such (see above). For the unmodified thesis, see T.-H. Lee, "Gattungsvergleich der akkadischen Šu-ila-Gebete mit den biblischen Lobpsalmen" (Ph.D. diss., Westfälische Wilhelms-Universität Münster, 1995), 48, 63, 169.

46. Cf. E. Tov, *Textual Criticism of the Hebrew Bible* (Minneapolis: Fortress, 1992), 169, 313–16; G. J. Norton, "Ancient Versions and Textual Transmission of the Old Testament," in *The Oxford Handbook of Biblical Studies* (ed. J. W. Rogerson and J. M. Lieu; Oxford: Oxford University Press, 2008), 211–36 (212–13); R. G. Kratz, "The Growth of the Old Testament," in Rogerson and Lieu, eds.,

or less) hypothetical, the basic assumptions of the methodology of biblical exegesis can be corroborated by the observations on Ištar 2.

One premise of literary criticism is that texts grow. Ištar 2 in both its stages could be used as a parade example for this principle, as the development between F and A is almost direct growth: where there were 50 lines in text F at Boğazköy, text A has 105. Yet shortenings may also be detected: at least seven lines of F, possibly eight, are missing in A.[47] Nevertheless, the majority of the text continued to be transmitted.

The mechanism of textual growth in Ištar 2 has been studied in two particulars: the "litanies" and the "missing lines" in the invocation of F. The "litanies" are compliant to one of the criteria for textual growth in literary criticism: repetitions and redundancies are "classical" indicators for literary developments—if they are not considered stylistic devices—though they are more meaningful in narrative texts.[48] In Ištar 2 the repetitions are certainly poetic devices; indeed, there were already repetitions in text F (lines 17′–18′, 24′–27′). The comparison of both versions, however, shows that these passages were enlarged in text A (lines 15–17) and further counterparts created (lines 45–50 in relation to lines 27–30). A single complaining question (*adi mati*, line 12″F; because of the following break, the possibility of a repetition cannot be excluded) was developed into a system structuring the long passage of complaint (lines 56, 59) which is taken up again at the end of the prayer (lines 93–94). The premise that the repetitions might be later additions may be confirmed with this text, but the limitations of the process are also emphasized.

By and large, the repetitions and the "missing lines" in the invocation of F show that *Fortschreibungen* were developed from extant material. This is why the elements structuring the whole text—lines 25–26, 41A, referring ahead, and line 17A, as reference backwards—are not yet existing in text F. There are only allusions to the eye-contact with Ištar in F, while it is one of the main themes in A (lines 26, 40–41, 43–44, 53–56, 70–73, 77, 92–93, 95, 100–101): the petition *kīniš naplisīnni*(*ma*)

Handbook, 459–88, especially 468–86. See also the textbooks on exegetical methodology, for example, U. Becker, *Exegese des Alten Testaments. Ein Methoden- und Arbeitsbuch* (2d ed.; UTB 2664; Tübingen: Mohr Siebeck, 2008), 41–65, 79–100; O. H. Steck, *Exegese des Alten Testaments: Leitfaden der Methodik: Ein Arbeitsbuch für Proseminare, Seminare und Vorlesungen* (14th ed.; Neukirchen–Vluyn: Neukirchener Verlag, 1999), 46–62, 76–97.

47. The questionable line is line 5‴F, which might have been parallel to line 55A; see above.

48. E.g. J. P. Floss, "Form, Source and Redaction Criticism," in Rogerson and Lieu, eds., *Handbook*, 591–614 (606–7); Becker, *Exegese*, 57; Steck, *Exegese*, 54–55.

("look faithfully upon me," lines 44, 54, 92A), twice repeated in A, is mentioned only once in F (line 3‴). All in all, the lines creating the structure of the text and those with most cross-references within the text are a result of literary growth.

The soundness of the methodology developed for the Hebrew Bible may thus be corroborated by studies such as this one, though this prayer was never part of a canon. Such a study may also show that, though the methodology is sound, its results are always and necessarily hypothetical: it would not have been possible to reconstruct text F from text A by means of literary criticism.

In this study, it became evident that the conventions of how to approach a deity change in the course of transmission: the relation between supplicant and deity was modified insofar as the supplicant presents himself and his suffering much more directly to the deity in the younger text. The representation of the contact between human being and deity as an audience, structuring the disposition of the text and its ritual as a whole, remains stable in this development. The comparison of several details in both versions showed that the text has grown and, in growing, gained an increase in rhetorical elements and poetic devices, such as repetitions and references backwards and forwards. The study of the repetitions and additions in the invocation confirmed some assumptions of literary criticism as developed for the Hebrew Bible, while underlining the hypothetical character of its results.

Appendix: Both Versions of Ištar 2 in Translation[49]

F		A	
5′	TEXT TO BE RECITED: I pray to you, lady of ladies, goddess [...]	1	TEXT TO BE RECITED: I pray to you, lady of ladies, goddess of goddesses!
6′	Lady of the entire inhabited world, who is guiding the four edges of the world aright,	2	Ištar, queen of the entire inhabited world, who is guiding mankind aright,
7′	[I]nana, noble one, greatest of the Igigû,	3	Irnini, you are noble, greatest of the Igigû.
7′–8′	You are exalted, [8′] you are sovereign, your name is exalted!	4	You are the strong one, you are sovereign, your names are exalted!
8′–9′	You indeed are the luminary of heaven, [9′] capable daughter of Sîn, lady!	5	You indeed are the luminary of heaven and earth, valiant daughter of Sîn!

49. The translation of A is quoted from Zernecke, "Ishtar 2," 282–84, with slight alterations.

9′–10′	Assembling weapons, arranging [10′] […] Fierce one,[50]	6	Wielding weapons, arranging battle,
10′–11′	Most capable one of the Igigû, most valiant one among [11′] [the god]s, her brothers,		–
11′	Concentrating / gathering the entirety of ordinances, taking rulership,	7	Concentrating / gathering the entirety of ordinances, wearing the crown of domination,
12′	[La]dy, resplendent are your great deeds, excellent over all gods!	8	Lady, resplendent are your great deeds, exalted over all gods!
13′	[Sta]r of the battle-cry, making harmonious brothers fight each other,	9	Star of the battle-cry, making harmonious brothers fight each other,
14′	Ever furious of queens,	10	Always giving a friend,
14′	Mighty one, lady of the wind, knocking down mountains!	11	Mighty one, lady of the wasteland, knocking down mountains!
15′	[…] battle, clothed with terror!	12	Gušea, clad in battle, clothed with terror!
15′–16′	You are bringing to conclusion [16′] […deci]sion, the commands for earth and heaven.	13	You are bringing to conclusion judgment and decision, the commands for earth and heaven.
16′–17′	Shrines, chaples, soc[les…] [17′] [are attentive] to you.	14	Shrines, chapels, socles, and daises are attentive to you.
17′	Where is not your name? Where are not your daises?	15	Where is not your name? Where are not your ordinances?
18′	[Where are n]ot your ordinances? Where are not drawn your plans?	16	Where are your plans not implemented? Where are your daises not set up?
	–	17	Where are you not great? Where are you not exalted?
19′	[…ha]ve exalted you, they have made your domination great.	18	Anu, Enlil and Ea have elevated you among the gods, they have made your domination great.
20′	[…amon]g the assembly of the gods, they have made you outstanding.	19	They have exalted you among the entirety of the Igigû, they have made your rank outstanding.
20′	At the mention	20	At the mention of your name, heaven and earth shake,

50. Foster, *Muses*, 599.

21′	[…qua]ke, the Anunnakū tremble,	21	The gods quake, the Anunnakū tremble,
22′	[…] praise the [c]ountries.	22	Humanity praises your terrifying name.
22′	You indeed are great and ex[alted!]	23	You indeed are great and exalted!
23′	[…] x the "herds" of mankind, they praise […]	24	The entirety of the black-headed ones, the "herds" of mankind, they praise your heroic acts.
	–	25	You render the verdict for subject peoples in righteousness and justice.
	–	26	You look upon the wronged and afflicted, you guide (them) aright every day.
24′	[…Lad]y of heaven and earth, shepherdess […]	27	Your *aḫulap*, Lady of heaven and earth, shepherdess of the numerous people!
25′	[…Lad]y of the holy sanctuary […]	28	Your *aḫulap*, Lady of holy Eana, the pure treasury!
26′	[…] your feet do [not] tire […]	29	Your *aḫulap*, Lady—your feet do not tire, your knees are swift!
27′	[…] Lady of beatin[g…]	30	Your *aḫulap*, Lady of all battles (and) combats!
28′	[…of the Ig]igû, making sub[missive?…]	31	Resplendent one, lioness of the Igigû, making submissive the angry gods!
29′	[…] *– broken –*	32	Most powerful of all princes, holding the leading rope of kings!
		33	Opening the veil of all young women!
1″	[…vali]ant Lady […]	34	Raising (or) laying, valiant Ištar, great are your heroic acts!
	–	35	Brightness, torch of heaven and earth, brilliance of the entire inhabited world!
2″	[…] combat!	36	Furious one in irresistible onslaught, powerful one in combat!
2″–3″	Firebrand […] 3″ […contriv]ing disaster […]	37	Firebrand that is ignited against the enemies, contriving disaster for the furious!

4″	[…as]sembling the assembly!	38	Glimmering Ištar, assembling the assembly!
5″	[…n]ot comes to know!	39	Goddess of men, goddess / Ištar of women, whose resolution no-one comes to know!
6″	[…the d]ead, disappears the bad. (erased)	40	Wherever you look, the dead lives, the sick arises.
7″	[…] joy		–
	–	41	The one who is not right becomes all right (when) seeing your face.
	–	42	I appeal to you, your tired, wearied, suffering servant:
	–	43	Look at me, my Lady, and accept my supplication!
	–	44	Look faithfully upon me and listen to my prayer!
	–	45	*aḫulap* pronounce for me, and let your feelings become reconciled to me –
	–	46	*aḫulap* for my wretched body which is full of confusion and trouble,
	–	47	*aḫulap* for my suffering heart which is full of tears and sighs,
	–	48	*aḫulap* for my wretched, confused and troubled omens,
	–	49	*aḫulap* for my sleepless house which laments (with) wailing
	–	50	*aḫulap* for my feelings which persevere (in) tears and sighs!
8″	[…let] your [he]art be at rest with respect to me!	51	Irninītu! The aggressive lion, let your heart be at rest with respect to me!
8″–9″	the wild bull [9″] […let be recon]ciled to me!	52	The furious wild bull, let your feelings be reconciled to me!
9″	Kindness [of] you may exist for me! […]	53	May your kind eye be upon me!
10″	[…] change for me!		–
11″	[…] with me the supplication		–
	–	54	With your bright face look faithfully upon me!
	–	55	Drive away the evil dealings concerning my body, let me see your bright light!

	–	56	How long, my Lady, will my enemies look malevolently at me,
	–	57	(And) with lies and untruths plan evil against me?
	–	58	My persecutors (and) ill-wishers rage against me.
12″	[…How l]ong, my Lady, the idio[t…] *– End of obverse, reverse begins with broken passage –*	59	How long, my Lady, will the idiot (and) cripple overtake me?
		60	The wearied went ahead of me, but I, I lagged far behind.
		61	The weak became strong, I have become weak.
		62	I toss like a wave that an evil wind amasses.
1‴	[…]	63	My heart flies (and) flutters around like a bird of heaven.
2‴	[…n]ight and day	64	I moan like a dove night and day.
	–	65	I "glow / burn" and weep bitterly.
	–	66	In "woe" (and) "alas" my feelings are suffering.
	–	67	What indeed have I done to my god and goddess?
	–	68	I am treated as if I did not fear my god and my goddess!
	–	69	Disease, headache, loss, and disaster are imposed upon me.
	–	70	Terrors, averted faces, and abundance of fury are imposed upon me,
	–	71	Anger, rage, fury of gods and men.
	–	72	I have seen, my Lady, very dark days, gloomy months, years of worry.
	–	73	I have seen, my Lady, judgment, confusion and rebellion.
	–	74	Death and constraint keep hold on me.
	–	75	My shrine is deathly still, my sanctuary is deathly still.

	–	76	Over house, gate (and) my fields, deathly silence is poured out.
	–	77	My god: his face is averted to another place.
	–	78	My clan is scattered, my shelter is broken.
	–	79	I am attentive to my Lady, on you my ears are fixed.
	–	80	I indeed pray to you, absolve my blame!
	–	81	Absolve my guilt, my crime, my sin, and my fault!
	–	82	Disregard my sins (gloss: my confusion), accept my supplication!
	–	83	Release my bonds, secure my freedom!
	–	84	Guide my step aright! Brightly, as a lord may I walk along the street among the living!
	–	85	Speak, so that at your command the angry god may become peaceful,
	–	86	(so that) the goddess who has turned away from me in anger may return to me!
	–	87	Dark (and) smoky, may my brazier become bright!
	–	88	Extinguished, may my torch be ignited!
	–	89	May my scattered clan assemble!
	–	90	May the courtyard widen, my sheepfold increase!
	–	91	Accept my prostration, listen to my prayer!
3‴	Look [faithful]ly upon me!	92	look faithfully upon me […]
4‴	[your] good [winds] were blowing for m[e?…]		
5‴	[…] my eye, I see your light.		
	–	93	How long, my Lady, will you be angry and your face be averted?

	–	94	How long, my Lady, will you rage and your feelings be infuriated?
	–	95	Turn your neck that you had let drop, set your face (on) a good word!
	–	96	Like water "undoing" (?) the river, may your feelings be reconciled to me!
	–	97	May I tread over those furious with me as (over) the ground!
	–	98	Make submissive those angry with me and make them prostrate under me!
	–	99	May my prayers and my supplications come to you!
	–	100	May your very great forgiveness be with me!
	–	101	May those who see me in the street magnify your name,
	–	102	And may I make glorious your divinity and your heroism for the black-headed people:
	–	103	Ištar is exalted, Ištar is queen!
	–	104	The Lady is exalted, the Lady is queen!
	–	105	Irnini, the valiant daughter of Sîn, has no opponents!
6‴	[…m]e, let me live!		–
7‴	[WORD]ING (?)	106	WORDING OF THE LIFTED HAND ADDRESSED TO IŠTAR

Psalm 72 in Its Ancient Syrian Context*

Jan Dietrich

The Hebrew ideology of kingship as presented in Ps 72 has customarily been interpreted as being influenced by the traditions of ancient Egypt and ancient Mesopotamia. The Hebrew words and concepts of משפט, צדק and צדקה (all to be found in vv. 1–3) are paralleled with Akkadian *kittum* and *mīšarum* on the one hand, and Egyptian *maʿat* on the other. Without doubt, the idea of fertility is connected to these traditions: when the ruler is enthroned by a god or gods, he has to ensure both justice and fertility in the land. Nevertheless, the connection between king and fertility seems to have strong similarities not only with Egypt and Mesopotamia but especially with ancient Syrian traditions.

The Concept of Justice and Fertility

In the history of research scholars have emphasized the topic of justice when focusing on Egyptian and Mesopotamian parallels for Ps 72. For example, in Mesopotamia the famous stele of King Hammurapi has been quoted many times when interpreting the concept of investiture and justness in Ps 72. From an iconographical point of view, the investiture of Hammurapi by Šamaš was viewed as similar to the assumed "investiture" of the Israelite king in Ps 72. The text of the stele, below the image, emphasizes the concept of justice being held up by the king:

> At that time Anum and Enlil named me to promote the welfare of the people, me, Hammurabi, the devout, god-fearing prince, to cause justice to prevail in the land, to destroy the wicked and the evil, that the strong might not oppress the weak, to rise like the sun over the black-headed (people), and to light up the land… When Marduk commissioned me to

* This article is an expanded version of a paper delivered at the International SBL Meeting at Tartu, Estonia, 2010. I wish to thank my aunt, Ann Weiland, for improving my English.

> guide the people aright, to direct the land, I established law and justice in the language of the land, thereby promoting the welfare of the people. (CH I 27–44; V 14–23).[1]

This concept of investiture and justice, scholars thought, could also be found in Ps 72, with the psalm being sung at a ritual feast of enthronement and investiture, perhaps repeated every year. An important difference may be noted, however. Hammurapi is invested with kingship and justice (CH XLVIII 95–98) in order to enforce his own laws and judgments (CH V 14–23; XLVIII), whereas "Solomon" is invested with kingship in order to enforce the judgments of YHWH (v. 1).[2]

Scholars searching for parallels from Egypt also focused mostly on the concept of justice and compared the Egyptian concept of *maʿat* with Ps 72. For example, a text from the New Kingdom describes the kingdom as follows:

> Re has enthroned the king N on the earth of the living forever, to dispense justice for the people, to pacify the gods, to fulfill truth (*mʾʿt*), to annihilate evil (*jsft*).[3]

Searching for parallels to the just king in non-biblical Syrian and Palestinian texts only a few examples come to mind. For example, Yeḥimilk of Byblos speaks of himself as a just (צדק) and upright (ישר) king in front of the gods: "as/because (he is) a just king and a righteous/upright king in front of the god(s) of Byblos" (כ מלך צדק ומלך ישר לפן אל גבל; *KAI* 4 6).

A similar emphasis may be found in the inscriptions of the kings Yeḥawmilk (*KAI* 10 9), Azatiwada (*KAI* 26 12), Barrakib (*KAI* 215 1–2) and in biblical texts (e.g. 2 Sam 8:15; 1 Kgs 10:9; Jer 22:3, 11–12). Though the term צדק in these Phoenician and Aramaic inscriptions cannot be restricted to meaning "lawfulness" or "righteousness"—it also implies "loyalty"—it still contains connotations of justice and righteousness in these passages.[4]

1. *ANET* 164–65.
2. B. Janowski, "Die Frucht der Gerechtigkeit: Psalm 72 und die judäische Königsideologie," in *Der Gott des Lebens. Beiträge zur Theologie des Alten Testaments III* (Neukirchen–Vluyn: Neukirchener Verlag, 2003), 157–97 (182–83).
3. J. Assmann, *Der König als Sonnenpriester: Ein kosmographischer Begleittext zur kultischen Sonnenhymnik in thebanischen Tempeln und Gräbern* (ADAIK 7; Glückstadt: Augustin, 1970), 22 (author's translation).
4. H. Niehr, "The Constitutive Principles for Establishing Justice and Order in Northwest Semitic Societies with Special Reference to Ancient Israel and Judah," *ZAR* 3 (1997): 112–30 (116–18).

Next to justice and righteousness, fertility is a main theme of both Ps 72 and the ancient Near Eastern ideology of kingship. Yet this aspect of Ps 72 has never been compared at length with ancient Near Eastern parallels.

By enforcing justice the ruler maintains the world order, accomplishing the fertility of land and people as part of the world's order. Thus in the Hebrew Bible the critique of lawlessness and the hope for justice may be explained in terms of fertility (e.g. Isa 45:8; Hos 10:4, 12; Amos 5:7; 6:12): the king's justice will rise like the morning sun and ensure the fertility of the land (2 Sam 23:3–4).[5] In Ps 72:1–17, we find an alternating structure between justice and fertility:[6]

A	1–4	king and justice
B	5–7	king and life/fertility
C	8–11	king and politics (the king's universal regime)
A	12–14	king and justice
B	16–17	king and life/fertility

The connection between king and fertility is to be found in the ancient Near East as well. So, for example, the Codex Hammurapi declares that "Hammurabi, the shepherd, called by Enlil, am I; the one who makes affluence (*nuḫšu*) and plenty (*ṭuḫu*) abound" (CH I 50–56).[7]

Three main functions of the king's portrayal may also be distinguished iconographically: legitimation by the gods; upkeep of the world order and dominion over the real and mythical enemies; and perpetuation of fertility and prosperity.[8] In Mesopotamia the concept of fertility and the king's responsibility for defending fertility in the land seem to be intimately connected with the so-called sacred tree. This tree can appear in different shapes, sometimes realistic and sometimes artificial, but clearly depicts a plant and symbolizes both the fertility of the land as well as the world's order.[9]

5. K. Koch, "Sädäq und Maʿat: Konnektive Gerechtigkeit in Israel und Ägypten?," in *Gerechtigkeit. Richten und Retten in der abendländischen Tradition und ihren altorientalischen Ursprüngen* (ed. J. Assmann; Munich: Fink, 1998), 37–64 (58–61).

6. Cf. Janowski, "Frucht der Gerechtigkeit," 169.

7. *ANET* 164.

8. R. Schmitt, *Bildhafte Herrscherrepräsentation im eisenzeitlichen Israel* (AOAT 283; Münster: Ugarit Verlag, 2001), 8.

9. For the Assyrian connection between the solar disc, kingship and rain, see R. Mayer-Opificius, "Die *geflügelte Sonne*: Himmels- und Regendarstellungen im Alten Vorderasien," *UF* 16 (1984): 189–236 (201). For the Assyrian portrayals of the king in general, see U. Magen, *Assyrische Königsdarstellungen—Aspekte der*

For example, on the partly preserved stele of Ur-Nammu (Fig. 1), the founder of the third dynasty of Ur (ca. 2060–1955 B.C.E.), the king undertakes a libation in front of a tree and a high god (probably the moon god Nanna).[10] Like on the Hammurapi stele, the god holds a ring and a scepter towards the king to invest him with the symbols of kingship. On his part, the king does his duty by strengthening the sacred tree through libation, thereby strengthening the world order as well as the fertility of the land.

Figure 1. Originally published in C. L. Woolley, "The Expedition to Ur," *The Museum Journal* 16 (1925): 48 (fragment). Drawing taken from O. Keel, *Die Welt der altorientalischen Bildsymbolik und das Alte Testament. Am Beispiel der Psalmen* (5th ed.; Göttingen: Vandenhoeck & Ruprecht, 1996), fig. 180.

The most famous iconographical examples of the so-called sacred tree stem from Assurnaṣirpal's palace in Nimrud (883–859 B.C.E.).[11] The

Herrschaft: eine Typologie (BagF 9; Mainz: Zabern, 1986); for Syro-Palestine see Schmitt, *Herrscherrepräsentation.*

10. On the opposite side of the same register almost the same scene is displayed; cf. J. V. Canby, *The "Ur-Nammu" Stela* (University Museum Monograph 110; Philadelphia: University of Pennsylvania Museum of Archaeology and Anthropology, 2001), pl. 3a-b.

11. Cf. J. B. Stearns, *Reliefs from the Palace of Ashurnaṣirpal II* (AfOB 15; Graz: Weidner, 1961). For the floral motifs of the Neo-Assyrian reliefs in general, cf. E. Bleibtreu, *Die Flora der neuassyrischen Reliefs. Eine Untersuchung zu den Orthostatenreliefs des 9.–7. Jahrhunderts v. Chr.* (WZKMS 1; Vienna: Instituts für Orientalistik der Universität Wien, 1980). There has been an ongoing debate in recent years about the nature of the Assyrian tree, depicted as a palmette. The debate concerns whether the palmette images derive from the date palm or whether they

images of the sacred tree at Nimrud depict a palmette which is flanked usually by protective genii holding a bucket in one hand and a cone in the other. In some cases the king may appear in place of the genii, while in others he may even be substituted for the palmette itself (Fig. 2a-b). Simo Parpola deduced from the last example, that "the king is portrayed as the human personification of the Tree."[12] I, however, doubt this and prefer to stress the function of the substitution rather than the phenomenological identification, namely that the palmette achieves protection and purification rites in the same way that the king does.

Figure 2a–b. J. B. Stearns, *Reliefs from the Palace of Ashurnaṣirpal II.* (AfOB 15; Graz: Weidner, 1961), pl. 91 (details).

have nothing to do with date palms and trees, but depict an artificial cult object called [GI]*uriggallu* that was used to demarcate a sacred area (see U. Seidl and W. Sallaberger, "Der 'Heilige Baum'," *AfO* 51 [2005–2006]: 54–74). Whether the Assyrian palmette depicts a date palm or an *uriggallu*, it clearly refers to a plant since *uriggallū* were made of reed (hence the determinative GI); cf. F. A. M. Wiggermann, *Mesopotamian Protective Spirits: The Ritual Texts* (CM 1; Groningen: Styx & PP, 1992), 70–73; B. Pongratz-Leisten, "Mesopotamische Standarten in literarischen Zeugnissen," *BaMi* 23 (1992): 299–340 (306–8, 318–30).

12. S. Parpola, "The Assyrian Tree of Life: Tracing the Origins of Jewish Monotheism and Greek Philosophy," *JNES* 52 (1993): 161–208 (167).

Be this as it may, the topos of fertility spoken of several times in Ps 72 is not limited to the Mesopotamian material but may be traced also in the Syrian and Palestinian sources, where it is even more frequently compared to the concept of justice. To start with the epigraphic material, King Ittobaal pronounces the following curse to any future ruler who tries to open the sarcophagus of King Ahiram: "May the scepter of his reign be stripped off (its leaves), may the throne of his kingship be overturned" (תחתסף חטר משפטה תהתפך כסא מלכה; *KAI* 1 2).[13]

This is not just a metaphorical idiom. When in the Aqhat Epic of Ugarit the king's son was murdered and the kingdom endangered, the text describes the consequences as follows:

wbmt[ ]mṣṣ[ ]/	And by his death […],
[p]rʿ.qẓ.[ ]	the first fruit of summer [declines],
šblt/[b]ǵlph.	the ear [in] its husk […].
(…)	(…)
[ ]/bgrn.yḫrb	[The grain] on the threshing floor shrivels,
[ ]/yǵly.	[the fruit] withers,
yḫsp.ib[ ]/	the bu[ll] droops. (*KTU* 1.19 I 17–19, 29–31)

In both cases the destruction of kingship is described in terms of decline of fertility.[14] This is not merely metaphorical in meaning, nor do vv. 6–7, 16–17 in Ps 72 have a purely symbolic value when emphasizing the fecund and fertile virtues of the king. Like in 2 Sam 21 and other texts, the king is responsible for upholding fertility in the land.[15]

The iconographical sources of Syria and Palestine support this view. On the famous mural painting from Mari in eastern Syria (Fig. 3), the

13. For a new transcription and translation of this text and for the interpretation of the medio-reflexive resp. passive verbs, cf. R. G. Lehmann, *Dynastensarkophage mit szenischen Reliefs aus Byblos und Zypern, Teil 1.2: Die Inschrift(en) des Aḥīrōm-Sarkophags und die Schachtinschrift des Grabes V in Jbeil (Byblos)* (Forschungen zur phönizisch-punischen und zyprischen Plastik: Sepulkral- und Votivdenkmäler als Zeugnisse kultureller Identitäten und Affinitäten II.1.2; Mainz am Rhein: Zabern, 2005), 32, 38, and "Calligraphy and Craftsmanship in the Aḥīrōm Inscription: Considerations on Skilled Linear Flat Writing in Early First Millennium Byblos," *Maarav* 15, no. 2 (2008): 119–64, 217–22 (164).

14. For a similar Neo-Assyrian text commemorating the death of an Assyrian king (K 7856), see T. Kwasman, "A Neo-Assyrian Royal Funerary Text," in *Of God(s), Trees, Kings, and Scholars: Neo-Assyrian and Related Studies in Honour of Simo Parpola* (ed. M. Luukko, S. Svärd and R. Mattila; StOr 106; Helsinki: Finnish Oriental Society, 2009), 111–25 (114).

15. R. Kessler, "Gott und König, Grundeigentum und Fruchtbarkeit," *ZAW* 108 (1996): 214–32 (225–31).

investiture of King Zimri-Lim in the upper register goes hand in hand with the flourishing of nature in the second register. Fertility goddesses hold vases out of which plants, water and fish flow.

Figure 3. Originally published in A. Parrot, "Les Peintures du Palais de Mari," *Syria* 18 (1937): pl. 39. Drawing taken from O. Keel, *Die Welt der altorientalischen Bildsymbolik und das Alte Testament. Am Beispiel der Psalmen* (5th ed.; Göttingen: Vandenhoeck & Ruprecht, 1996), fig. 191.

Palestinian seals may be interpreted in a similar way. On a seal from the Middle Bronze Age (Fig. 4), a palmette is depicted below the Egyptian sign *anch* for life. It is flanked by the Mesopotamian protective goddess Lamma on the right and the ruler in his beaded mantle on the left, the latter holding a kind of *Krummholz* above the tree. On another Old Syrian seal the king appears in front of the sacred tree, depicted in Mittanian style, next to a goddess.[16] Other seals display almost the same constellation, but with the Mesopotamian sun-disc above the tree (instead of the *anch*) and with the ruler blessing and worshipping the tree.[17] (On the second seal, from Karnak, the stylized tree is growing out

16. U. Winter, *Frau und Göttin: Exegetische und ikonographische Studien zum weiblichen Gottesbild im Alten Israel und in dessen Umwelt* (OBO 53; Göttingen: Vandenhoeck & Ruprecht, 1983), fig. 445.

17. O. Keel, "Zur Identifikation des Falkenköpfigen auf den Skarabäen der ausgehenden 13. und der 15. Dynastie," in *Studien zu den Stempelsiegeln aus Palästina/Israel II* (ed. O. Keel, H. Keel-Leu and S. Schroer; OBO 88; Göttingen:

of the head of a Hathor-goddess. Its inscription reads "Seal of Hammurapi of the treasure house," therefore probably belonging to a treasurer named Hammurapi of a North Syrian kingdom.[18])

Figure 4. Originally published in H. El-Safadi, "Die Entstehung der syrischen Glyptik und ihre Entwicklung in der Zeit von Zimrilim bis Amanitaçumma: Teil 1," *UF* 6 (1974): 313–52, pls. 15, 108. Drawing taken from O. Keel, "Zur Identifikation des Falkenköpfigen auf den Skarabäen der ausgehenden 13. und der 15. Dynastie," in *Studien zu den Stempelsiegeln aus Palästina/Israel 2* (ed. O. Keel, H. Keel-Leu and S. Schroer; OBO 88; Göttingen: Vandenhoeck & Ruprecht, 1989), fig. 19.

On two other seals, the king is flanking the tree from both sides, either touching the tree or pointing towards it.[19] And on still another Old Syrian seal (Fig. 5), the ruler appears in front of the water-pouring and plant-growing goddess in her falbala-cloth. Also, two Syrian ivory tablets from Hadatu (Arslan Tash) of about 800 B.C.E. depict a Syrian ruler touching and pointing towards the sacred tree in a kind of *ubāna tarāṣu*-gesture (originally probably from both sides) respectively a Syrian king head-on between growing lotus-stems (Fig. 6).[20]

Vandenhoeck & Ruprecht, 1989), fig. 21, and O. Keel, *Goddesses and Trees, New Moon and Yahweh: Ancient Near Eastern Art and the Hebrew Bible* (JSOTSup 261; Sheffield: Sheffield Academic, 1998), fig. 16.

18. E. Porada, "Syrian Seal from Karnak," *JSSEA* 13 (1983): 237–40 (237).

19. Keel, "Identifikation des Falkenköpfigen," fig. 22–23.

20. W. Orthmann, *Der alte Orient* (Propyläen Kunstgeschichte, 14; Berlin: Propyläen), 1975, fig. 431a. For the *ubāna tarāṣu*-gesture, see Magen, *Assyrische Königsdarstellungen*, 45–55 and pl. 8–9.

Figure 5. Originally published in E. Porada, *Corpus of Ancient Near Eastern Seals in North American Collections*. Vol. 1, *The Collection of the Pierpont Morgan Library* (Washington, D.C.: Pantheon, 1948), no. 929. Drawing taken from U. Winter, *Frau und Göttin. Exegetische und ikonographische Studien zum weiblichen Gottesbild im Alten Israel und in dessen Umwelt* (OBO 53; Göttingen: Vandenhoeck & Ruprecht, 1983), fig. 441.

Figure 6. F. Thureau-Dangin, A. Barrois, G. Dossin, and M. Dunand, *Arslan-Tash: Texte* (Bibliothèque archéologique et historique 16; Paris: Geuthner, 1931), pl. XXXIII no. 43.

In these images the sacred tree as a symbol of fertility and order is entrusted to the care of the king. The king, on the one hand, receives his regalia from the gods and is, on the other hand, responsible for maintaining the world order and the fertility of the land: he is the intimate connection between fertility and order. Thus at Ugarit the king is depicted on a cultic stand which connects the stylized crown of the palmette under him with the winged sun-disc above him (Fig. 7), displaying the connection between fertility, king, and cosmic order.

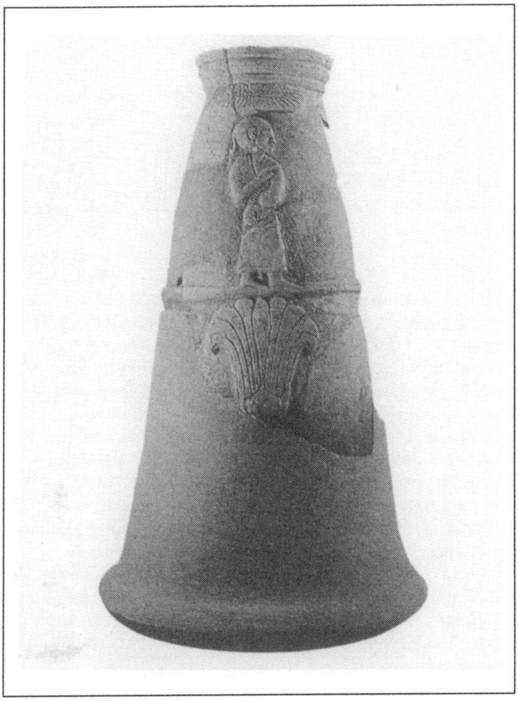

Figure 7. I. Cornelius and H. Niehr, *Götter und Kulte in Ugarit. Kultur und Religion einer nordsyrischen Königsstadt in der Spätbronzezeit* (Mainz: Zabern, 2004), fig. 98.

The king is both a receiver of blessing, fertility and thriving as well as a dispenser of these same virtues. Several portrayals of an enthroned ruler with a flower, most often a lotus, in one of his hands have been found in Syro-Palestine. The context is mostly a banquet- or tribute-scene.[21] Is the flower in the hand of the king just a symbol without

21. E.g. O. Keel and C. Uehlinger, *Gods, Goddesses, and Images of God in Ancient Israel* (Minneapolis: Fortress, 1998), fig. 65, 67–68a, and O. Keel, *Die Welt*

specific meaning? Or does it simply denote the wish for the flourishing of the king's life or a symbol for the flourishing wealth of the banquet or tribute? On an ivory-carving from Samaria of the eighth century B.C.E. there appears a king or queen, with a lotus-tree behind.[22] Three Old Syrian seals (Fig. 8) display rulers sitting on a kind of New-Sumerian façade throne and holding a leafy twig in their hand.[23] As a royal figure also appears on his throne in front of the sacred tree on several cylinder seals, two from Ugarit, one from Tell es-Saᶜidiyeh and another from Tell el-ᶜAğul, in my opinion the twig as well as the lotus in the hand of a king on his throne expresses not only the wish for the life and thriving of the ruler, but for his governed land as well.[24]

Figure 8. Originally published in C. H. Gordon, "Western Asiatic Seals in the Walters Art Gallery," *Iraq* 6 (1939): 3–34, pls. 5, 37. Drawing taken from O. Keel, "Zur Identifikation des Falkenköpfigen auf den Skarabäen der ausgehenden 13. und der 15. Dynastie," in *Studien zu den Stempelsiegeln aus Palästina/Israel 2* (ed. O. Keel, H. Keel-Leu and S. Schroer; OBO 88; Göttingen: Vandenhoeck & Ruprecht, 1989), fig. 62.

We have already discussed the Nimrud palace reliefs in which the Assyrian king appears in place of the sacred tree. The same substitution occurs in an ivory from Nimrud (Fig. 9)—carved in a Syrian style adapted to Assyrian iconography—and displays a king sitting on his throne receiving a long-stemmed lily growing out of the earth in front of

der altorientalischen Bildsymbolik und das Alte Testament: Am Beispiel der Psalmen (5th ed.; Göttingen: Vandenhoeck & Ruprecht, 1996), fig. 331.

22. Keel and Uehlinger, *Gods*, fig. 239.
23. See also Keel, "Identifikation des Falkenköpfigen," fig. 63–64.
24. Keel, *Goddesses and Trees*, fig. 88–89, 91–92.

him while receiving purification rites by the *abkallū*-griffins.[25] The scene depicts the king receiving purification and life. On another seal (Fig. 10), a striking and fighting royal figure may be seen as enforcing the fertility which is depicted by leafy twigs and a flower (cf. a seal from Avaris with the striking king, wearing a red crown and a twig as scepter).[26] Here the king ensures fertility.

Figure 9. M. E. L. Mallowan, *Nimrud and Its Remains*, vol. 2 (London: Collins, 1966), fig. 483.

Coming back to Ps 72, in v. 6 the king is identified with abundant showers. One Old Syrian seal displays a king flanked by two water-gods—one even a naked fertility goddess—while another shows a king flanked by Lamma and a god or hero with water running out of his shoulders into two jars (Fig. 11).[27] These pictures suggest the ruler's responsibility for water, which is not only mentioned in Ps 72, but also expressed by the mural painting from Mari and by the semantic iconography of these seals.

In sum, it has been seen from Ps 72 and from these various images that it is part of the ideology of kingship in Syro-Palestine to achieve and ensure fertility.

25. M. E. L. Mallowan, *Nimrud and Its Remains II* (London: Collins, 1966), 481–82, 487, and Schmitt, *Bildhafte Herrscherrepräsentation*, 81.

26. Keel, "Identifikation des Falkenköpfigen," fig. 75.

27. S. Schroer, *Die Ikonographie Palästinas/Israels und der Alte Orient: Eine Religionsgeschichte in Bildern II: Die Mittelbronzezeit* (IPIAO 2; Fribourg: Academic, 2008), fig. 513.

Figure 10. O. Keel, *Corpus der Stempelsiegel-Amulette aus Palästina/ Israel: Von den Anfängen bis zur Perserzeit. Einleitung* (OBO.SA 10; Göttingen: Vandenhoeck & Ruprecht, 1995), fig. 486.

Figure 11. Originally published in K. M. Kenyon and T. A. Holland, *The Excavations at Jericho*. Vol. 5, *The Pottery Phases of the Tell and Other Finds* (London: British School of Archeology in Jerusalem, 1983), fig. 354, pl. 38d. Drawing taken from Schroer, *Die Ikonographie Palästinas/ Israels und der Alte Orient: Eine Religionsgeschichte in Bildern II: Die Mittelbronzezeit* (IPIAO 2; Fribourg: Academic, 2008), fig. 509.

The Difficult Verses 5 and 15

We come now to the difficult vv. 5 and 15 of Ps 72. In v. 5 the text should be amended following the LXX, from ירא to ארך Hiphil. To live long and to have one's days lengthened by the gods and "in front of" the gods is a typical phrase in Akkadian literature (e.g. *ša šarru turiki ūmēšu*, "you make long the days of the king").[28] A Sumerian and Akkadian

28. Cf. CAD s.v. *arāku/urruku/šūruku*; see also O. Loretz, *Die Königspsalmen, Teil I: Ps. 20; 21; 72; 101 und 144, Mit einem Beitrag von Ingo Kottsieper zu Papyrus Amherst* (UBL 6; Münster: Ugarit-Verlag, 1988), 120, and E. Lipiński,

coronation(?)-hymn found at both Syrian Emar and Ugarit states, for example: "Live, my master! Your days may be long!" (*bu-luṭ be-li* $\mathrm{U}_4^{\mathrm{ME\check{S}}}$*-kà li-ri-ku*).[29] Yet this is also a typical phrase in Phoenician and Old Aramaic inscriptions, using ארך.[30] Thus:

> May the master of heaven and the mistress of Byblos and the assembly of the holy gods of Byblos make long the days of Yeḥimilk and his years over Byblos (יארך בעל שמם ובעל[ת] גבל ומפחרת אל גבל קדשם ימת יחמלך ושנתו על גבל; *KAI* 4 3–6)[31]

> May the mistress of Byblos make long the days of Elibaal and his years over Byblos (תארך בעלת [גבל] [ימת א]לבעל ושנתו על [גבל]; *KAI* 6 2–3)

> May the mistress of Byblos make long the days of Sipitbaal and his years over Byblos (תארך בעלת גבל ימת שפטבעל ושנתו על גבל; *KAI* 7 4–5)

In the Tell Fekheriye inscription King Haddu-Yascha erects a stele in front of Hadad which twice contains a Peal infinitive of ארך: "and to make long his days and to multiply his years (…) and to lengthen his life" (ולמארך יומוה ולכבר שנוה [...] ולמארך חיוה; *KAI* 309 7–8, 14).[32]

"The Bilingual Inscription from Tell Fekheriye," in *Studies in Aramaic Inscriptions and Onomastics II* (ed. E. Lipiński; OLA 57; Leuven: Peeters, 1994), 19–81 (41).

29. Emar 6/4 Nr. 775:1, cf. T. R. Kämmerer, *šimâ milka: Induktion und Reception der mittelbabylonischen Dichtung von Ugarit, Emār und Tell el-ʻAmārna* (AOAT 251; Münster: Ugarit-Verlag, 1998), 216–17, and M. Dietrich, "*buluṭ bēlī* 'Lebe, mein König!' Ein Krönungshymnus aus Emar und Ugarit und sein Verhältnis zu mesopotamischen und westlichen Inthronisationsliedern," *UF* 30 (1998): 155–200 (158). The text ends with a long wish for the fertility of the land and finally with a wish for a long-lasting kingship. Interestingly enough, the Ugaritic text expands the wish for fertility by five more colons; cf. Dietrich, "*buluṭ bēlī*," 162 n. 40 and 163.

30. Cf. J. Hoftijzer and K. Jongeling, *Dictionary of the North-West Semitic Inscriptions* (HO 1/21; Leiden: Brill, 1995), 108. For similar biblical phrases in connection with the king or a kingly figure, cf. Deut 17:20; 1 Kgs 3:14; Isa 53:10; Prov 28:16. On the Ugaritic letter *KTU* 2.23 20–22, see further below.

31. For comparison with Ps 72, cf. M. Arneth, *Sonne der Gerechtigkeit: Studien zur Solarisierung der Jahwe-Religion im Lichte von Psalm 72* (ZARB 1; Wiesbaden: Harrassowitz, 2000), 115–16.

32. A. Abou-Assaf, P. Bordreuil and A. R. Millard, *La Statue de Tell Fekherye et son inscription bilingue assyro-araméenne* (Etudes Assyriologiques 7; Paris: ERC, 1982); Lipiński, "Bilingual"; C. Leonhard, "Die literarische Struktur der Bilingue vom Tell Fakheriyeh," *WZKM* 85 (1995): 157–79. For the Peal infinitive with m-prefix, see T. Muraoka, "The Tell-Fekherye Bilingual Inscription and Early Aramaic," *Abr-Nahrain* 22 (1983–84): 79–117 (98–99), and Lipiński, "Bilingual," 58–59. In the Akkadian version of Tell Fekheriye, lines 10–11 are *ana buluṭ*^{ut} *napšāti-šú urruk ūmē-šú šúm-ud šanāti-šú*, "to enliven his soul, to lengthen his days,

In the bilingual Karatepe inscriptions King Azatiwada hopes that "Baal KRNTRYS and all gods of the city (may give) Azatiwada longevity of days and multitude of years" (בעל כרנתריש וכל אלן קרת לאזתוד ארך ימם ורב שנת; *KAI* 26 A III 4–6).[33] Some hundred years later, King Yeḥawmilk asked, "May the mistress of Byblos bless Yeḥawmilk, king of Byblos, and may she enliven him and make long his days and his years over Byblos" (תברך בעלת גבל אית יחומלך מלך גבל ותחוו ותארך ימו ושנתו על גבל; *KAI* 10 8–9).[34] And, last but not least, in line 58 of the broken Aramaic text of the Behistun inscription is the benediction "and your days will be long lasting" (ויומיך יארכון; Behistun 58/72).[35]

Figure 12. Originally published in C. L. Woolley, *Alalakh: An Account of the Excavations at Tell Atchana in the Hatay 1937–1949* (Reports of the Research Committee of the Society of Antiquaries of London 18; Oxford: Society of Antiquaries, 1955), pls. 60.9, 67.150. Drawing taken from D. Collon, *The Seal Impressions from Tell Atchana/Alalakh* (AOAT 27; Kevelaer: Butzon & Bercker, 1975), no. 12.

to multiply his years." Cf. also the Aramaic inscription of the priest Si Gibbor of Neirab; he thanks Šaḥar and says בצדקתי קדמוה שמני שם טב והארך יומי ("By my righteousness in front of him, he gave me a good name and made long my days"; *KAI* 226 2–3; Lipiński, "Bilingual," 36, 40–41).

33. M. L. Barré, "An Analysis of the Royal Blessing in the Karatepe Inscription," *Maarav* 3 (1982): 177–94 (178–86).

34. For comparison with Ps 72, cf. Arneth, *Sonne der Gerechtigkeit*, 116–17.

35. A. Cowley, *Aramaic Papyri of the Fifth Century B.C. Edited, with Translations and Notes* (Oxford: Clarendon, 1923), 253, 259, and J. C. Greenfield and B. Porten, *The Bisitun Inscription of Darius the Great: Aramaic Version* (CII 1/5/1; London: Lund Humphries, 1982), 50, 68.

In these Syrian inscriptions the gods grant life and lengthen the days of the king. This same idea may also be seen on Old Syrian seals which depict the ruler in front of a god or goddess and the Egyptian sign *anch* ("life") next to the king (e.g. once above the tree of life [Fig. 4] or several times behind the ruler on a seal from Alalach [Fig. 12]).

The particular crux in Ps 72 may also be resolved by reference to these Syrian materials, namely why the king of Ps 72 has his days lengthened "in front of" the sun and the moon (cf. Ps 89:37–38). Shalom Paul once proposed, on the basis of parallels from Phoenician and Aramaic inscriptions using the comparative preposition *k* or *km* together with sun and moon, that עם שמש in Ps 72:5 ought to be translated as a comparison.[36] It is preferable, however, to translate the term עם שמש literally, on the basis of the spatial prepositions לפני ירח in the same verse, לפני שמש in v. 17 and Ugaritic parallels.[37] Thus in a Ugaritic letter the writer pronounces his wish to his master: "And length of days to my master in front of Amon and in front of the gods of Egypt" (*w urk ym bʿly lpn amn w lpn il mṣrm*; *KTU* 2.23 20–22).[38] Similarly, in the Aqhat Epic Anat promises Aqhat lengthening of days "in front of" Baal if he is willing to give her his bow: "I will make you count in front of Baal years, in front of the son of El you will enumerate months" (*ašsprk ʿm bʿl šnt ʿm bn il tspr yrḫm*; *KTU* 1.17 VI 28–29).

These Ugaritic parallels, compared with the prepositions in Ps 72:5, suggest that the king's name shall flourish literally "in front of" the sun; this may even imply in front of YHWH as the sun. The preposition עם ("in front of") means, like its parallel לפני in Ps 72:5 as well as in the Ugaritic parallels, a lengthening of days literally "vis-à-vis" or "face to face with" the sun and moon respectively, that is, the god(s), with the Ugaritic cases probably implying face to face with a cultic statue. Thus the difficult v. 5 should be translated: "He may live long vis-à-vis the sun, and face to face with the moon throughout all generations."[39] This

36. S. Paul, "Psalm 72:5—A Traditional Blessing for the Long Life of the King," *JNES* 31 (1972): 351–55 (353).

37. M. Dietrich and O. Loretz, "Von hebräisch *ʾm*/*lpny* (Ps 72,5) zu ugaritisch *ʿm* 'vor,'" in *Orbis Ugariticus: Ausgewählte Beiträge von Manfried Dietrich und Oswald Loretz* (Festschrift O. Loretz; ed. M. Dietrich; Münster: Ugarit-Verlag, 2008 [1988]), 65–70 (68–69).

38. P. Xella, "Baal Safon in KTU 2.23: Osservazioni Epigrafiche," *Rivista di studi fenici* 15 (1987): 111–14.

39. Concerning the so-called solarization process in Israel, cf. O. Keel, *Die Geschichte Jerusalems und die Geschichte des Monotheismus* (OLB 4/1; Göttingen: Vandenhoeck & Ruprecht, 2007), 284–86, 380–85, 416–20. For the importance of the moon god in Israel, see G. Theuer, *Der Mondgott in den Religionen*

translation is confirmed by the Syrian iconography: it is a typical motif also on Old Syrian seals to have the sun and moon disc or a winged sun disc appearing above the ruler's head or between the ruler and the deity (Fig. 11).[40] The sun and moon represent continuance, duration and stability of the cosmos and the king's reign.

Finally, we come to the difficult v. 15. Like the term "lengthening the days" in v. 5, there appears the sentence "and he may live," followed by the wish of receiving gold, in v. 15. It has never been clear who the subject of this verse is: the king or the humbled?[41] Comparing the parallel wish in v. 5, the wish for life most sensibly addresses the king, while the humbled probably does not have gold to give. The king's concern with the humbled need not be a late post-exilic concept: it is part of the royal ideology and legitimation to give gold to the humbled.[42] So, for example, in the Kulamuwa inscription King Kulamuwa boasts about helping the *muškabīm* (probably some poor and indigenous people from Samᶜal).[43] Lines 11–12 declare: "And who did not see the face of an ox (i.e. did not possess an ox), I made owner of a herd and owner of silver and master of gold" (ומי בל חז פן אלף שתי בעל בקר ובעל כסף ובעל חרץ; *KAI* 24 11–12).

As these many examples indicate, scholars need not look far, to Mesopotamia and Egypt, for ancient Near Eastern parallels to Ps 72 and its intimate connection between kingdom and fertility: there are close parallels in Syria as well as in Palestine itself.

Syrien-Palästinas. Unter besonderer Berücksichtigung von KTU 1.24 (OBO 173; Göttingen: Vandenhoeck & Ruprecht, 2000). For example, a wish for the eternal duration of the kingship of Azatiwada, כם שם שמש וירח, occurs in *KAI* 26A/B IV 2–3, *KAI* 26 C IV 5 and *KAI* 26 C V 5–7; see Theuer, *Mondgott*, 311–12, 444.

40. Cf. also Schroer, *Ikonographie*, fig. 528; B. Teissier, *Egyptian Iconography on Syro-Palestinian Cylinder Seals of the Middle Bronze Age* (OBO.SA 11; Göttingen: Vandenhoeck & Ruprecht, 1996), fig. 184–86.

41. Cf. Arneth, *Sonne der Gerechtigkeit*, 47–48; E. Zenger, "Psalm 72," in F.-L. Hossfeld and E. Zenger, *Psalmen 51–100* (HThKAT; Freiburg: Herder, 2000), 302–30 (306–7).

42. For a late post-exilic dating, cf. U. Becker, "Psalm 72 und der Alte Orient: Grenzen und Chancen eines Vergleichs," in *Mensch und König: Studien zur Anthropologie des Alten Testaments* (Festschrift R. Lux; ed. A. Berlejung and R. Heckl; HBS 53; Freiburg, 2008), 123–40 (127–29, 136–37).

43. Cf. J. Tropper, *Die Inschriften von Zincirli: Neue Edition und vergleichende Grammatik des phönizischen, sam'alischen und aramäischen Textkorpus* (ALASPM 6; Münster: Ugarit-Verlag, 1993), 27–46.

Bibliography

Abou-Assaf, A., P. Bordreuil and A. R. Millard. *La Statue de Tell Fekherye et son inscription bilingue assyro-araméenne*. Etudes Assyriologiques 7. Paris: ERC, 1982.

Abusch, I. T. "*Alaktu* and *Halakhah*: Oracular Decision, Divine Revelation." *HTR* 80 (1987): 15–42.

———. "The Form and Meaning of a Babylonian Prayer to Marduk." *JAOS* 103 (1983): 1–15.

———. "Prayers, Hymns, Incantations, and Curses." Pages 353–55 in *Religions of the Ancient World: A Guide*. Edited by S. I. Johnston. Cambridge, Mass.: Belknap, 2004.

Albertz, R. "*Ludlul bēl nēmeqi*—eine Lehrdichtung zur Ausbreitung und Vertiefung der persönlichen Mardukfrömmigkeit." Pages 85–105 in *Geschichte und Theologie: Studien zur Exegese des Alten Testaments und zur Religionsgeschichte Israels*. Edited by R. Albertz. BZAW 326. Berlin: de Gruyter, 2003.

———. *Persönliche Frömmigkeit und offizielle Religion. Religionsinterner Pluralismus in Israel und Babylon*. Stuttgart: Calwer, 1978.

Alt, A. *Der Gott der Väter. Ein Beitrag zur Vorgeschichte der israelitischen Religion*. BWANT 48. Stuttgart: Kohlhammer, 1929. Repr. pages 1–78 in *Kleine Schriften zur Geschichte Israels*, vol. 1. Munich: Beck, 1953.

Ambos, C. "Types of Ritual Failure and Mistakes in Ritual Cuneiform Sources." Pages 25–47 in *When Rituals Go Wrong: Mistakes, Failure, and the Dynamics of Ritual*. Edited by U. Hüsken. Numen Book Series: Studies in the History of Religions 115. Leiden: Brill, 2007.

Annus, A., and A. Lenzi. *Ludlul bēl nēmeqi: The Standard Babylonian Poem of the Righteous Sufferer*. SAACT 7. Helsinki: Neo-Assyrian Text Corpus Project, 2010.

Arneth, M. *Sonne der Gerechtigkeit: Studien zur Solarisierung der Jahwe-Religion im Lichte von Psalm 72*. ZARB 1. Wiesbaden: Harrassowitz, 2000.

Aro, J. "Remarks on the Practice of Extispicy in the Time of Esarhaddon and Assurbanipal." Pages 109–17 in *La Divination en Mésopotamie ancienne, et dans les Régions voisines, XIVe RAI (Strasbourg, 2–6 juillet 1965)*. Paris: Presses Universitaires de France, 1966.

Assmann, J. *Der König als Sonnenpriester: Ein kosmographischer Begleittext zur kultischen Sonnenhymnik in thebanischen Tempeln und Gräbern*. ADAIK 7. Glückstadt: Augustin, 1970.

———. *Moses the Egyptian: The Memory of Egypt in Western Monotheism*. London: Harvard University Press, 1997.

———. *Of God and Gods: Egypt, Israel, and the Rise of Monotheism*. Madison: University of Wisconsin Press, 2008.

———. *The Price of Monotheism*. Translated by R. Savage. Stanford, Calif.: Stanford University Press, 2010.

Austin, J. L. *How to Do Things with Words: The William James Lectures Delivered at Harvard University in 1955*. Edited by J. O. Urmson and M. Sbisa. 2d ed. Oxford: Oxford University Press, 1976.

Barré, M. L. "An Analysis of the Royal Blessing in the Karatepe Inscription." *Maarav* 3 (1982): 177–94.

Barstad, H. M. "No Prophets? Recent Developments in Biblical Prophetic Research and Ancient Near Eastern Prophecy." *JSOT* 37 (1993): 39–60.

Barth, C. *Die Errettung vom Tode in den individuellen Klage- und Dankliedern des Alten Testamentes*. Edited by B. Janowski. 2d ed. Stuttgart: Kohlhammer, 1997.

Bauks, M. *Die Feinde des Psalmisten und die Freunde Ijobs: Untersuchungen zur Freund-Klage im Alten Testament am Beispiel von Ps 22*. SBS 203. Stuttgart: Katholisches Bibelwerk, 2004.

Baumgarten, A. I. et al., eds. *Self, Soul, and Body in Religious Experience*. Leiden: Brill, 1995.

Beard, M. "Writing and Religion: Ancient Literacy and the Function of the Written Word in Roman Religion." Pages 35–58 in *Literacy in the Roman World*. Edited by J. H. Humphrey. Journal of Roman Archaeology Supplementary Series 3. Ann Arbor: Journal of Roman Archaeology, 1991.

Beaulieu, P.-A. "The Social and Intellectual Setting of Babylonian Wisdom Literature." Pages 3–19 in *Wisdom Literature in Mesopotamia and Israel*. Edited by R. J. Clifford. SBLSymS 36. Atlanta: SBL, 2007.

Becker, U. *Exegese des Alten Testaments: Ein Methoden- und Arbeitsbuch*. 2d ed. UTB 2664. Tübingen: Mohr Siebeck, 2008.

———. "Psalm 72 und der Alte Orient: Grenzen und Chancen eines Vergleichs." Pages 123–40 in *Mensch und König: Studien zur Anthropologie des Alten Testaments: Rüdiger Lux zum 60. Geburtstag*. Edited by A. Berlejung and R. Heckl. HBS 53. Freiburg: Herder, 2008.

Becking, B. "Do the Earliest Samaritan Inscriptions Already Indicate a Parting of the Ways?" Pages 213–22 in Lipschits, Knoppers and Albertz, eds., *Judah and the Judeans in the Fourth Century B.C.E.*

Beckman, G. *Hittite Diplomatic Texts*. 2d ed. SBLWAW 7. Atlanta: SBL, 1999.

Begrich, J. "Das priesterliche Heilsorakel." *ZAW* 52 (1934): 81–92. Repr. pages 217–31 in *Gesammelte Studien*.

———. 1964. *Gesammelte Studien zum Alten Testament*. Edited by W. Zimmerli. ThB 21. Munich: Kaiser.

———. "Die Vertrauensäußerungen im israelitischen Klagelied des Einzelnen und in seinem babylonischen Gegenstück." *ZAW* 46 (1928): 221–60. Repr. pages 128–216 in *Gesammelte Studien*.

Berlejung, A. *Die Theologie der Bilder: Herstellung und Einweihung von Kultbildern in Mesopotamien und die alttestamentliche Bilderpolemik*. OBO 162. Freiburg: Universitätsverlag. Göttingen: Vandenhoeck & Ruprecht, 1998.

Bertalanffy, K. L., von. *General Systems Theory: Foundations, Developments, Applications*. Rev. ed. New York: George Braziller, 1976.

Beyerlin, W., ed. *Religionsgeschichtliches Textbuch zum Alten Testament*. Göttingen: Vandenhoeck & Ruprecht, 1975.

Biggs, R. "*Qutnu*, *maṣraḫu* and Related Terms in Extispicy." *RA* 63 (1969): 159–67.

Bleibtreu, E. *Die Flora der neuassyrischen Reliefs: Eine Untersuchung zu den Orthostatenreliefs des 9.–7. Jahrhunderts v. Chr.* WZKMS 1. Vienna: Instituts für Orientalistik der Universität Wien, 1980.

Blum, E. "Die Kombination I der Wandinschrift vom Tell Deir ʿAlla: Vorschläge zur Rekonstruktion mit historisch-kritischen Anmerkungen." Pages 573–601 in *Berührungspunkte: Studien zur Sozial- und Religionsgeschichte Israels und seiner Umwelt: Festschrift für Rainer Albertz zu seinem 65. Geburtstag*. Edited by Kottsieper et al. AOAT 350. Münster: Ugarit-Verlag, 2008.

Böck, B. *Das Handbuch Muššuʾu "Einreibung": Eine Serie sumerischer und akkadischer Beschwörungen aus dem 1. Jt. vor Chr.* Biblioteca del Próximo Oriente Antiguo 3. Madrid: Consejo Superior de Investigaciones Científicas, 2007.

Bodel, J. "'Sacred Dedications': A Problem of Definitions." Pages 17–30 in *Dediche Sacre Nel Mondo Greco-Romano: Diffusione, funzioni, tipologie*. Edited by J. Bodel and M. Kajava. Acta Instituti Romani Finlandiae 35. Rome: Institutum Romanum Finlandiae, 2009.

Bottéro, J. "Magie: A in Mesopotamien." Pages 200–234 in *Reallexikon der Assyriologie und Vorderasiatischen Archäologie*, vol. 7. Edited by D. O. Edzard et al. Berlin: de Gruyter, 1990.

———. *La plus vieille religion: En Mésopotamie*. Collection Folio. Histoire 82. Paris: Gallimard, 1998.

Bourdieu, P. *The Logic of Practice*. Translated by R. Nice. Cambridge: Polity, 1980.

Bremer, J.-M. "The Reciprocity of Giving and Thanksgiving in Greek Worship." Pages 127–37 in Gill, Postlethwaite and Seaford, eds., *Reciprocity in Ancient Greece*.

Brown, W. P. "The Psalms and 'I': The Dialogical Self and the Disappearing Psalmist." Pages 26–44 in Burnett, Bellinger and Tucker, eds., *Diachronic and Synchronic*.

Brueggemann, W. *Israel's Praise: Doxology Against Idolatry and Ideology*. Philadelphia: Fortress, 1988.

———. *The Psalms and the Life of Faith*. Edited by P. D. Miller. Minneapolis: Fortress, 1995.

———. *Theology of the Old Testament: Testimony, Dispute, Advocacy*. Minneapolis: Fortress, 1997.

Buchler, J. *The Philosophical Writings of Peirce*. New York: Dover, 1955.

Burkert, W. "Offerings in Perspective: Surrender, Distribution, Exchange." Pages 43–50 in Linders and Nordquist, eds., *Gifts to the Gods*.

Burnett, J. S., W. H. Bellinger and W. D. Tucker, eds. *Diachronic and Synchronic: Reading the Psalms in Real Time*. LHBOTS 488. London: T&T Clark International, 2007.

Butler, S. A. L. *Mesopotamian Conceptions of Dreams and Dream Rituals*. AOAT 258. Münster: Ugarit-Verlag, 1998.

Campbell Thomson, R. *Assyrian Medical Texts from the Originals in the British Museum*. London: Oxford University Press, 1923.

Canby, J. V. *The "Ur-Nammu" Stela*. University Museum Monograph 110. Philadelphia: University of Pennsylvania Museum of Archaeology and Anthropology, 2001.

Cancik-Kirschbaum, E. "Prophetismus und Divination—ein Blick auf die keilschriftlichen Quellen." Pages 33–53 in Köckert and Nissinen, eds., *Propheten in Mari*.

Carroll, R. P. *Jeremiah: A Commentary*, vol. 1. OTL. London: SCM, 1986.

Casetti, P. *Gibt es ein Leben vor dem Tod? Eine Auslegung von Psalm 49*. OBO 44. Göttingen: Vandenhoeck & Ruprecht, 1982.

Charpin, D. *Archives épistolaires de Mari II*. ARM 26/II. Paris: ERC, 1988.
Charpin, D., and N. Ziegler. *Florilegium marianum V: Mari et le Proche-Orient à l'époque Amorrite: Essai d'histoire politique*. MNABU 6. Paris: SEPOA, 2003.
Childs, B. S. *Memory and Tradition in Israel*. London: SCM, 1962.
Cohen, M. E. *The Canonical Lamentations of Ancient Mesopotamia*. 2 vols. Potomac, Md.: Capital Decisions, 1988.
Connelly, J. B. "Standing Before One's God: Votive Sculpture and the Cypriot Religious Tradition." *BA* 52 (1989): 210–18.
Cowley, A. *Aramaic Papyri of the Fifth Century B.C. Edited, with Translations and Notes*. Oxford: Clarendon, 1923.
Crenshaw, J. L. *Old Testament Wisdom: An Introduction*. 3d ed. Louisville, Ky.: Westminster John Knox, 2010.
Crüsemann, F. *Studien zur Formgeschichte von Hymnus und Danklied in Israel*. WMANT 32. Neukirchen–Vluyn: Neukirchener Verlag, 1969.
Cryer, F. H. "Der Prophet und der Magier: Bemerkungen anhand einer überholten Diskussion." Pages 79–88 in *Prophetie und geschichtliche Wirklichkeit im alten Israel: Festschrift für Siegfried Herrmann zum 65. Geburtstag*. Edited by R. Liwak and S. Wagner. Stuttgart: Kohlhammer, 1991.
Cunningham, G. *"Deliver Me from Evil": Mesopotamian Incantations 2500–1500 BC*. StP.SM 17. Rome: Pontifical Biblical Institute, 1997.
Derks, T. *Gods, Temples and Ritual Practices: The Transformation of Religious Ideas and Values in Roman Gaul*. Amsterdam Archaeological Studies 2. Amsterdam: Amsterdam University Press, 1998.
Dietrich, C. *Asyl: Vergleichende Untersuchung zu einer Rechtsinstitution im Alten Israel und seiner Umwelt*. BWANT 182. Stuttgart: Kohlhammer, 2008.
Dietrich, M. "*buluṭbēlī* 'Lebe, mein König!' Ein Krönungshymnus aus Emar und Ugarit und sein Verhältnis zu mesopotamischen und westlichen Inthronisationsliedern." *UF* 30 (1998): 155–200.
Dietrich, M., and O. Loretz. "Von hebräisch *ʾm* // *lpny* (Ps 72,5) zu ugaritisch *ʿm* 'vor'." Pages 65–70 in *Orbis Ugariticus: Ausgewählte Beiträge von Manfried Dietrich und Oswald Loretz*. Festschrift O. Loretz. Edited by M. Dietrich. Münster: Ugarit-Verlag, 2008.
Dijk, J., van. *La sagesse suméro-accadienne: Recherches sur les genres littéraires des textes sapientiaux*. Commentationes Orientales 1. Leiden: Brill, 1953.
Dijkstra, K. *Life and Loyalty: A Study in the Socio-religious Culture of Syria and Mesopotamia in the Graeco-Roman Period Based on Epigraphical Evidence*. Leiden: Brill, 1995.
Dirven, L. "Aspects of Hatrene Religion: A Note on the Statues of Kings and Nobles from Hatra." Pages 209–46 in *The Variety of Local Religious Life in the Near East in the Hellenistic and Roman Periods*. Edited by T. Kaizer. Leiden: Brill, 2008.
Donald, M. "Material Culture and Cognition: Concluding Thoughts." Pages in 181–87 *Cognition and Material Culture: The Archaeology of Symbolic Storage*. Edited by C. Renfrew and C. Scarre. Cambridge: McDonald Institute for Archaeological Research, 1998.
Dossin, G. "Les archives épistolaires du Palais de Mari." *Syria* 19 (1938): 105–26. Repr. 102–32 in *Recueil Georges Dossin: Melanges d'Assyriologie (1934–1959)*. Akkadica, Supplementum 1. Leuven: Peeters, 1983.

Dubovský, P. *Hezekiah and the Assyrian Spies: Reconstruction of the Neo-Assyrian Intelligence Services and Its Significance for 2 Kings 18–19*. Rome: Pontifical Biblical Institute, 2006.

Durand, J.-M. *Archives épistolaires de Mari I*. ARM 26/I. Paris: ERC, 1988.

———. *Florilegium marianum VII: Le culte d'Addu d'Alep et l'affaire d'Alahtum*. MNABU 8. Paris: SEPOA, 2002.

———. *Florilegium marianum VIII: Le culte des pierres et les monuments commémoratifs en Syrie amorrite*. MNABU 9. Paris: SEPOA, 2005.

———. "La religion amorrite en Syrie à l'époque des Archives de Mari." Pages 161–703 in *Mythologie et Religion des Sémites Occidentaux*. Vol. 1, *Ébla, Mari*. Edited by G. del Olmo Lete. OLA 162. Leuven: Peeters, 2008.

Ebeling, E. *Die akkadische Gebetsserie "Handerhebung": Von neuem gesammelt und herausgegeben*. Deutsche Akademie der Wissenschaften zu Berlin, Institut für Orientforschung: Veröffentlichung 20. Berlin: Akademie-Verlag, 1953.

Ellis, M. deJong. "Observations on Mesopotamian Oracles and Prophetic Texts: Literary and Historiographic Considerations." *JCS* 41 (1989): 127–86.

Eshel, H. "Hellenism in the Land of Israel from the Fifth to the Second Centuries BCE in Light of Semitic Epigraphy." Pages 16–124 in *A Time of Change: Judah and Its Neighbours in the Persian and Early Hellenistic Periods*. Edited by Y. Levin. London: T&T Clark International, 2007.

Falkenstein, A., and W. von Soden. *Sumerische und akkadische Hymnen und Gebete*. Die Bibliothek der Alten Welt. Zurich: Artemis, 1953.

Farber, W. "Witchcraft, Magic, and Divination in Ancient Mesopotamia." Pages 1895–1909 in Sasson et al., eds., *Civilizations of the Ancient Near East*, vol. 3.

Fincke, J. C. "Ist die mesopotamische Opferschau ein nächtliches Ritual?" *BiOr* 66 (2009): 520–77.

Finkel, I. L. "A New Piece of Libanomancy." *AfO* 29–30 (1983–84): 50–55.

Fleming, D. E. "The Rituals from Emar: Evolution of an Indigenous Tradition in Second-Millenium Syria." Pages 51–61 in *New Horizons in the Study of Ancient Syria*. Edited by M. W. Chavalas and J. L. Hayes. Bibliotheca Mesopotamica 25. Malibu, Calif.: Undena, 1992.

———. *Time at Emar: The Cultic Calendar and the Rituals from the Diviner's Archive*. MC 11. Winona Lake, Ind.: Eisenbrauns, 2000.

Floss, J. P. "Form, Source and Redaction Criticism." Pages 591–614 in Rogerson and Lieu, eds., *The Oxford Handbook of Biblical Studies*.

Foster, B. R. *Before the Muses: An Anthology of Akkadian Literature*. 3d ed. Bethesda, Md.: CDL, 2005.

Frahm, E. "Hochverrat in Assur." Pages 89–137 in *Assur-Forschungen: Arbeiten aus der Forschungsstelle "Edition literarischer Keilschrifttexte aus Assur" der Heidelberger Akademie der Wissenschaften*. Edited by S. M. Maul and N. P. Heeßel. Wiesbaden: Harrassowitz, 2010.

Frankena, R. *Tākultu: De sacrale maaltijd in het assyrische Ritueel, met een overzicht over de in Assur vereerde goden*. Leiden: Brill, 1954.

Frechette, C. *Die akkadische Gebetsserie "Handerhebung": Von neuem gesammelt und herausgegeben*. Deutsche Akademie der Wissenschaften zu Berlin, Institut für Orientforschung: Veröffentlichung 20. Berlin: Akademie-Verlag, 1953.

———. *Mesopotamian Ritual Prayers (Šuillas): A Case Study Investigating Idiom, Rubric, Form and Function*. AOAT 379. Münster: Ugarit-Verlag, 2012.

———. "The Name of the Ritual: Investigating Ancient Mesopotamian 'Hand-lifting' Rituals with Implications for the Interpretation of Genre in the Psalms." Ph.D. diss., Harvard University, 2005.

———. "Reconsidering ŠU.IL$_2$.LA$_{(2)}$ as a Classifier of the *Āšipu* in Light of the Iconography of Reciprocal Hand-Lifting Gestures." Pages 41–47 in *Proceedings of the 51st Rencontre Assyriologique Internationale Held at the Oriental Institute of the University of Chicago*. Edited by R. D. Biggs, J. Myers and M. T. Roth. Studies in Ancient Oriental Civilization 62. Chicago: Oriental Institute of the University of Chicago.

———. "Shuillas." Pages 24–35 in Lenzi, ed., *Reading Akkadian Prayers and Hymns*.

Geller, M. J. "Incipits and Rubrics." Pages 225–58 in *Wisdom, Gods, and Literature: Studies in Assyriology in Honour of W. G. Lambert*. Edited by A. R. George and I. L. Finkel. Winona Lake, Ind.: Eisenbrauns, 2000.

George, A. R. *Babylonian Topographical Texts*. OLA 40. Leuven: Peeters, 1992.

George, A. R., and F. N. H. Al-Rawi. "Tablets from the Sippar Library: VII: Three Wisdom Texts." *Iraq* 60 (1998): 187–206.

Gerstenberger, E. S. *Der bittende Mensch: Bittritual und Klagelied des Einzelnen im Alten Testament*. WMANT 51. Neukirchen–Vluyn: Neukirchener Verlag, 1980; repr. Eugene, Or. Wipf & Stock, 2009.

———. *Israel in der Perserzeit, 5. Und 4. Jahrhundert v.Chr.* Biblische Enzyklopädie 8. Stuttgart: Kohlhammer, 2005.

———. "Praise in the Realm of Death: The Dynamics of Hymn-Singing in Ancient Near Eastern Lament Ceremonies." Pages 115–24 in *Lamentations in Ancient and Contemporary Cultural Contexts*. Edited by N. C. Lee and C. Mandolfo. SBLSymS 43. Atlanta: SBL, 2008.

———. "The Psalms: Genres, Life Situations, and Theologies: Towards a Hermeneutics of Social Stratification." Pages 81–92 in Burnett, Bellinger and Tucker, eds., *Diachronic and Synchronic*.

———. *Psalms, Part I–II*. FOTL 14–15. Grand Rapids: Eerdmans, 2001.

———. "The Psalter." Pages in 402–17 *The Blackwell Companion to the Hebrew Bible*. Edited by L. G. Perdue. Oxford: Blackwell, 2001.

———. "Theologies in the Book of Psalms." Pages 603–25 in *The Book of Psalms: Composition and Reception*. Edited by P. W. Flint and P. D. Miller. VTSup 99. Leiden: Brill.

———. *Theologies in the Old Testament*. Translated by J. Bowden. Edinburgh: T. & T. Clark, 2002.

Gesche, P. D. *Schulunterricht in Babylonien im ersten Jahrtausend v. Chr.* AOAT 275. Münster: Ugarit-Verlag, 2001.

Gibson, J. C. L. *Textbook of Syrian Semitic Inscriptions*. Vol. 2, *Aramaic Inscriptions Including Inscriptions in the Dialect of Zenjirli*. Oxford: Clarendon, 1975.

Gill, C., N. Postlethwaite and R. Seaford, eds. *Reciprocity in Ancient Greece*. Oxford: Oxford University Press, 1998.

Gladigow, B. "Der Sinn der Götter: Zum kognitiven Potential der persönlichen Gottesvorstellung." Pages 41–66 in *Gottesvorstellung und Gesellschaftsentwicklung*. Edited by P. Eicher. Forum Religionswissenschaft 1. Munich: Kösel, 1979.

Gorman, F. H., Jr. *The Ideology of Ritual: Space, Time and Status in the Priestly Theology*. Sheffield: Sheffield Academic, 1990.

Grabbe, L. L. *Priests, Prophets, Diviners, Sages: A Socio-Historical Study of Religious Specialists in Ancient Israel*. Valley Forge, Pa.: Trinity Press International, 1995.

Greenfield, J. C., and B. Porten. *The Bisitun Inscription of Darius the Great: Aramaic Version*. CII 1,5,1. London: Lund Humphries, 1982.

Griffin, E. *A First Look at Communication Theory*. 7th ed. New York: McGraw Hill, 2009.

Grottanelli, C. "Do ut Des?" *Scienze Dell'antichità: Storia Archeologia Antropologia* 3–4 (1989–1990): 45–54.

Gudme, A. K. de H. "Barter Deal or Friend-Making Gift? A Reconsideration of the Conditional Vow in the Hebrew Bible." In *The Gift in Antiquity*. Edited by M. Satlow. Oxford: Blackwell, forthcoming.

———. "How Should We Read Hebrew Bible Ritual Texts? A Ritualistic Reading of the Law of the Nazirite (Num 6:1–21)." *SJOT* 23 (2009): 64–84.

Gunkel, H., and J. Begrich. *Einleitung in die Psalmen: Die Gattungen der religiösen Lyrik Israels*. HKAT 2. Göttingen: Vandenhoeck & Ruprecht, 1933.

———. *Introduction to the Psalms: The Genres of the Religious Lyric of Israel*. Translated by J. D. Nogalski. Atlanta: Mercer University Press, 1998.

Hackett, J. A. *The Balaam Text from Deir ʿAllā*. HSM 31. Chico, Calif.: Scholars, 1984.

Hallo, W. "Individual Prayers in Sumerian: The Continuity of A Tradition." *JAOS* 88 (1968): 71–89.

Hartenstein, F. *Das Angesicht JHWHs: Studien zu seinem höfischen und kultischen Bedeutungshintergrund in den Psalmen und in Exodus 32–34*. FAT 55. Tübingen: Mohr Siebeck, 2008.

Hayward, R. *The Targum of Jeremiah, Translated with a Critical Introduction, Apparatus and Notes*. The Aramaic Bible 12. Wilmington, Del.: Michael Glazier, 1987.

Healey, J. F. " 'May He Be Remembered for Good': An Aramaic Formula." Pages 177–86 in *Targumic and Cognate Studies: Essays in Honour of Martin McNamara*. Edited by K. J. Cathcart and M. Maher. Sheffield: Sheffield Academic, 1996.

Heeßel, N. P. *Babylonisch-assyrische Diagnostik*. AOAT 43. Münster: Ugarit-Verlag, 2000.

———. "The Calculation of the Stipulated Term in Extispicy." Pages 163–75 in *Divination and Interpretation of Signs in the Ancient World*. Edited by A. Annus. Oriental Institute Seminars 6. Chicago: Oriental Institute of the University of Chicago, 2010.

———. *Divinatorische Texte I: Terrestrische, teratologische, physiognomische und oneiromantische Omina*. Keilschrifttexte aus Assur literarischen Inhalts 1. WVDOG 116. Wiesbaden: Harrassowitz, 2007.

———. *Divinatorische Texte II: Opferschau-Omina*. Keilschrifttexte aus Assur literarischen Inhalts 5. WVDOG. Wiesbaden: Harrassowitz, 2012.

Heiler, F. *Das Gebet: Eine religionsgeschichtliche und religionspsychologische Untersuchung*. 5th ed. Munich: Reinhardt, 1923.

Heimpel, W. *Letters to the King of Mari: A New Translation with Historical Introduction, Notes, and Commentary*. Mesopotamian Civilizations 12. Winona Lake, Ind.: Eisenbrauns, 2003.

Hillers, D. R., and L. Cussini. *Palmyrene Aramaic Texts*. Baltimore, Md.: The Johns Hopkins University Press, 1996.

Hjelm, I. "Changing Paradigms: Judean and Samarian Histories in Light of Recent Research." Pages 161–79 in *Historie og Konstruktion: Festskrift til Niels Peter Lemche I anledning af 60 års fødselsdagen den 6. September 2005*. Edited by M. Müller and T. L. Thompson. Copenhagen: Museum Tusculanum, 2005.

Hoftijzer, J., and K. Jongeling. *Dictionary of the North-West Semitic Inscriptions*. HO 1/21. Leiden: Brill, 1995.

Huffmon, H. B. "The Treaty Background of Hebrew *Yādaᶜ*." *BASOR* 181 (1966): 31–37.

Huffmon, H. B., and S.B. Parker. "A Further Note on the Treaty Background of Hebrew *Yādaᶜ*." *BASOR* 184 (1966): 36–38.

Hunger, H. *Spätbabylonische Texte aus Uruk: Teil I*. Aussgrabungen der Deutschen Forschungsgemeinschaft in Uruk-Warka. Berlin: Gebr. Mann, 1976.

Iser, W. *How to Do Theory*. Malden, Mass.: Blackwell, 2006.

Jacobsen, T. *The Treasures of Darkness: A History of Mesopotamian Religion*. New Haven: Yale University Press, 1976.

Janowski, B. "Die Frucht der Gerechtigkeit: Psalm 72 und die judäische Königsideologie." Pages 157–97 in *Der Gott des Lebens. Beiträge zur Theologie des Alten Testaments III*. Neukirchen–Vluyn: Neukirchener Verlag, 2003.

Japhet, S. *I & II Chronicles: A Commentary*. Louisville, Ky.: Westminster John Knox, 1993.

Jaques, M. *"Mon dieu, qu'ai-je donc fait ?" Les prières pénitentielles (diĝir-ša$_3$-dab$_{(5)}$-ba) et l'expression de la piété privée en Mésopotamie*. OBO. Forthcoming.

———. *Le vocabulaire des sentiments dans les textes sumériens. Recherche sur le lexique sumérien et akkadien*. AOAT 332. Münster: Ugarit-Verlag, 2006.

Jeyes, U. "Divination as a Science in Ancient Mesopotamia." *JEOL* 33 (1991–92): 23–41.

———. *Old Babylonian Extispicy: Omen Texts in the British Museum*. Istanbul: Nederlands Historisch-Archaeologisch Instituut te Istanbul, 1989.

Jones, A. *Memory and Material Culture*. Cambridge: Cambridge University Press, 2007.

Kämmerer, T. R. *šimâ milka: Induktion und Reception der mittelbabylonischen Dichtung von Ugarit, Emār und Tell el-ᶜAmārna*. AOAT 251. Münster: Ugarit-Verlag, 1998.

Kant, I. *Kritik der reinen Vernunft*. Edited by R. Schmidt. Leipzig: Philipp Reclam, 1924. Published in English as *Critique of Pure Reason*. Translated by M. Weigel. London: Penguin, 2007.

Kartveit, M. *The Origin of the Samaritans*. Leiden: Brill, 2009.

Kedar-Kopfstein, B. "קֶרֶן *qæræn*." *ThWAT* 7:181–89.

Keel, O. "Die Brusttasche des Hohenpriesters als Element priesterschriftlicher Theologie." Pages 379–91 in *Das Manna fällt auch heute noch: Beiträge zur Geschichte und Theologie des Alten, Ersten Testament. Festschrift für Erich Zenger*. Edited by F. L. Hossfeld and L. Schwienhorst-Schönberger. Freiburg: Herder, 2004.

———. *Corpus der Stempelsiegel-Amulette aus Palästina/Israel: Von den Anfängen bis zur Perserzeit: Einleitung*. OBO.SA 10. Göttingen: Vandenhoeck & Ruprecht, 1995.

———. *Feinde und Gottesleugner: Studien zum Image der Widersacher in den Individualpsalmen*. Stuttgart: Katholisches Bibelwerk, 1969.

———. *Die Geschichte Jerusalems und die Geschichte des Monotheismus*. OLB 4/1. Göttingen: Vandenhoeck & Ruprecht, 2007.

———. *Goddesses and Trees, New Moon and Yahweh: Ancient Near Eastern Art and the Hebrew Bible*. JSOTSup 261. Sheffield: Sheffield Academic, 1998.

———. *The Symbolism of the Biblical World: Ancient Near Eastern Iconography and the Book of Psalms*. Translated by T. J. Hallet. Winona Lake, Ind.: Eisenbrauns, 1997.

———. *Die Welt der altorientalischen Bildsymbolik und das Alte Testament: Am Beispiel der Psalmen*. 5th ed. Göttingen: Vandenhoeck & Ruprecht, 1996.

———. "Zur Identifikation des Falkenköpfigen auf den Skarabäen der ausgehenden 13. und der 15. Dynastie." Pages 281–323 in *Studien zu den Stempelsiegeln aus Palästina/Israel II*. Edited by O. Keel, H. Keel-Leu and S. Schroer. OBO 88. Göttingen: Vandenhoeck & Ruprecht, 1989.

Keel, O., and C. Uehlinger. *Gods, Goddesses, and Images of God in Ancient Israel*. Minneapolis: Fortress, 1998.

Kessler, R. "Gott und König, Grundeigentum und Fruchtbarkeit." *ZAW* 108 (1996): 214–32.

King, L.W. *The Seven Tablets of Creation, or the Babylonian and Assyrian Legends Concerning the Creation of the World and of Mankind*. 2 vols. London: Luzac, 1902.

Klauber, E. G. *Politisch-religiöse Texte aus der Sargonidenzeit*. Leipzig: Pfeiffer, 1913.

Klein, J. "*Man and His God:* A Wisdom Poem or a Cultic Lament?" Pages 123–43 in *Approaches to Sumerian Literature: Studies in Honour of Stip (H. L. J. Vanstiphout)*. Edited by P. Michalowski and N. Veldhuis. CM 35. Leiden: Brill, 2006.

———. " 'Personal God' and Individual Prayer in Sumerian Religion." Pages 295–306 in *Vorträge gehalten auf der 28. Rencontre Assyriologique Internationale in Wien*. Edited by H. Hirsch and H. Hunger. AfOB 19. Horn: Berger & Söhne, 1982.

Koch, K. "Sädäq und Maʾat: Konnektive Gerechtigkeit in Israel und Ägypten?" Pages 37–64 in *Gerechtigkeit: Richten und Retten in der abendländischen Tradition und ihren altorientalischen Ursprüngen*. Edited by J. Assmann. Munich: Fink, 1998.

Koch, U. S. *Secrets of Extispicy: The Chapter Multābiltu of the Babylonian Extispicy Series and Niṣirti bārûti Texts Mainly from Aššurbanipal's Library*. AOAT 326. Münster: Ugarit-Verlag, 2005.

Koch-Westenholz, U. *Babylonian Liver Omens: The Chapters* Manzāzu, Padānu *and* Pān Tākalti *of the Babylonian Extispicy Series Mainly from Aššurbanipal's Library*. Carsten Niebuhr Institute Publications 25. Copenhagen: Museum Tusculanum Press, 2000.

Köcher, F. *Die babylonisch-assyrische Medizin in Texten und Untersuchungen 3*. Keilschrifttexte aus Assur 3. Berlin: de Gruyter, 1964.

Köckert, M., and M. Nissinen, eds. *Propheten in Mari, Assyrien und Israel*. FRLANT 201. Göttingen: Vandenhoeck & Ruprecht, 2003.

Kramer, S. N. " 'Man and His God': A Sumerian Variation on the 'Job' Motif." Pages 170–82 in *Wisdom in Israel and in the Ancient Near East, Festschrift H. H. Rowley*. Edited by M. Noth and D. Winton Thomas. VTSup 3. Leiden: Brill, 1955.

Kratz, R. G. "The Growth of the Old Testament." Pages 459–88 in Rogerson and Lieu, eds., *The Oxford Handbook of Biblical Studies*.

Krebernik, M. *Die Beschwörungen aus Fara und Ebla: Untersuchungen zur ältesten keilschriftlichen Beschwörungsliteratur*. Hildesheim: Georg Olms, 1984.

Kunstmann, W. G. *Die babylonische Gebetsbeschwörung*. LSS 2. Leipzig: Hinrichs, 1932.

Kwasman, T. "A Neo-Assyrian Royal Funerary Text." Pages 111–25 in *Of God(s), Trees, Kings, and Scholars: Neo-Assyrian and Related Studies in Honour of Simo Parpola*. Edited by M. Luukko, S. Svärd and R. Mattila. StOr 106. Helsinki: Finnish Oriental Society, 2009.

Lambert, W. G. *Babylonian Wisdom Literature*. Oxford: Clarendon, 1960. Repr. Winona Lake, Ind.: Eisenbrauns, 1996.

———. "A Catalogue of Texts and Authors." *JCS* 16 (1962): 59–77.

———. "Dingir.šà.dib.ba Incantations." *JNES* 33 (1974): 267–322.

———. "The Qualifications of Babylonian Diviners." Pages 141–58 in *Festschrift für Rykle Borger zu seinem 65. Geburtstag am 24. Mai 1994.* tikip santakki mala bašmu… Cuneiform Monographs 10. Edited by S. Maul. Groningen: Styx, 1998.

Lawson, T. E., and R. N. McCauley. *Rethinking Religion: Connecting Cognition and Culture*. Cambridge: Cambridge University Press, 1990.

Lee, T.-H. "Gattungsvergleich der akkadischen Šu-ila-Gebete mit den biblischen Lobpsalmen." Ph.D. diss., Westfälische Wilhelms-Universität Münster, 1995.

Lehmann, R. G. "Calligraphy and Craftsmanship in the Aḥīrōm Inscription: Considerations on Skilled Linear Flat Writing in Early First Millennium Byblos." *Maarav* 15, no. 2 (2008): 119–64 and 217–22.

———. *Dynastensarkophage mit szenischen Reliefs aus Byblos und Zypern. Teil 1.2. Die Inschrift(en) des Aḥīrōm-Sarkophags und die Schachtinschrift des Grabes V in Jbeil (Byblos).* Forschungen zur phönizisch-punischen und zyprischen Plastik: Sepulkral- und Votivdenkmäler als Zeugnisse kultureller Identitäten und Affinitäten II/1/2. Mainz am Rhein: Zabern, 2005.

Leiderer, R. *Anatomie der Schafsleber im babylonischen Leberorakel: Eine makroskopisch-analytische Studie*. Munich: Zuckschwerdt, 1990.

Lenzi, A., ed. *Reading Akkadian Prayers and Hymns: An Introduction*. ANEM 3. Atlanta: SBL, 2011.

———. *Secrecy and the Gods: Secret Knowledge in Ancient Mesopotamia and Biblical Israel*. SAAS 19. Helsinki: The Neo-Assyrian Text Corpus Project, 2008.

Leonhard, C. "Die literarische Struktur der Bilingue vom Tell Fakheriyeh." *WZKM* 85 (1995): 157–79.

Lidzbarski, M. *Handbuch der Nordsemitischen Epigraphik nebst Ausgewählten Inschriften*. Vol. 1, *Text*. Weimar: Emil Felber, 1898.

Lincoln, B. "Theses on Method." *Method & Theory in the Study of Religion* 8 (1996): 225–27. Repr. in *Method & Theory in the Study of Religion* 17 (2005): 8–10.

Linders, T. "Gods, Gifts, Society." Pages 115–22 in Linders and Nordquist, eds., *Gifts to the Gods*.

Linders, T., and G. Nordquist, eds. *Gifts to the Gods*: *Proceedings of the Uppsala Symposium 1985*. Uppsala: Academia Ubsaliensis, 1987.

Lipiński, E. "The Bilingual Inscription from Tell Fekheriye." Pages 19–81 in *Studies in Aramaic Inscriptions and Onomastics II*. Edited by E. Lipiński. OLA 57. Leuven: Peeters.

Lipschits, O., G. N. Knoppers and R. Albertz, eds. *Judah and the Judeans in the Fourth Century B.C.E.* Winona Lake, Ind.: Eisenbrauns, 2007.

Livingstone, A. "The Case of the Hemerologies: Official Cult, Learned Formulation and Popular Practice." Pages 97–113 in *Official Cult and Popular Religion in the Ancient Near East*. Edited by E. Matsushima. Heidelberg: Winter, 1993.

———. "New Dimensions in the Study of Assyrian Religion." Pages 165–77 in *Assyria 1995: Proceedings of the 10th Anniversary Symposium of the Neo-Assyrian Text Corpus Project Helsinki, September 7–11, 1995*. Edited by S. Parpola and R. M. Whiting. Helsinki: Helsinki University Press, 1997.

Loemker, L. E. "Theodicy." Pages 378–84 in *Dictionary of the History of Ideas: Studies of Selected Pivotal Ideas*, vol. 4. Edited by P. P. Wiener. New York: Scribner, 1973.

Loretz, O. *Die Königspsalmen, Teil I: Ps. 20. 21. 72. 101 und 144, Mit einem Beitrag von Ingo Kottsieper zu Papyrus Amherst*. UBL 6. Münster: Ugarit-Verlag, 1988.

Lundager Jensen, H. J. *Den Fortærende Ild: Strukturelle analyser af narrative og rituelle tekster i Det Gamle Testamente*. Aarhus: Aarhus Universitetsforlag, 2000.

Luukko, M., and G. Van Buylaere, with S. Parpola. *The Political Correspondence of Esarhaddon*. SAA 16. Helsinki: Helsinki University Press, 2002.

Magen, U. *Assyrische Königsdarstellungen—Aspekte der Herrschaft: eine Typologie*. BAF 9. Mainz: Zabern, 1986.

Magen, Y. "The Dating of the First Phase of the Samaritan Temple on Mount Gerizim in Light of the Archaeological Evidence." Pages 157–211 in Lipschits, Knoppers and Albertz, eds., *Judah and the Judeans in the Fourth Century B.C.E.*

———. *Mount Gerizim Excavations*. Vol. 2, *A Temple City*. Judea and Samaria Publications 8. Jerusalem: Israel Antiquities Authority, 2008.

———. *The Samaritans and the Good Samaritan*. Judea and Samaria Publications 7. Jerusalem: Israel Antiquities Authority, 2008.

Magen, Y., H. Misgav and L. Tsfania. *Mount Gerizim Excavations*. Vol. 1, *The Aramaic Hebrew and Samaritan Inscriptions*. Judeaea and Samaria Publications 2. Jerusalem: Israel Antiquities Authority, 2004.

Mallowan, M. E. L. *Nimrud and Its Remains II*. London: Collins, 1966.

Maul, S. M. *"Herzberuhigungsklagen": Die sumerisch-akkadischen Eršahunga-Gebete*. Wiesbaden: Harrassowitz, 1988.

———. "Omina und Orakel: A. Mesopotamien." Pages 45–88 in *Reallexikon der Assyriologie und Vorderasiatischen Archäologie*, vol. 10. Edited by D. O. Edzard. Berlin: de Gruyter, 2003–2005.

———. *Zukunftsbewältigung: Eine Untersuchung altorientalischen Denkens anhand der babylonisch-assyrischen Löserituale (Namburbi)*. BagF 18. Mainz: Zabern, 1994.

Maul, S., and R. Strauss. *Ritualbeschreibungen und Gebete I: Mit Beiträgen von Daniel Schwemer*. WVDOG 133. Wiesbaden: Harrassowitz, 2011.

Mauss, M. "Essai sur le don: Forme et raison de l'échange dans les societies archaïques." *L'Année Sociologique* 1 (1923–24): 30–186.

———. *The Gift: Forms and Functions of Exchange in Archaic Societies*. Translated by W. D. Halls. Abingdon: Routledge, 2002.

Mayer, W. *Untersuchungen zur Formensprache der babylonischen "Gebetsbeschwörungen"*. StP.SM 5. Rome: Pontifical Biblical Institute, 1976.

Mayer-Opificius, R. "Die *geflügelte Sonne*. Himmels- und Regendarstellungen im Alten Vorderasien." *UF* 16 (1984): 189–236.

McLean, B. H. *An Introduction to Greek Epigraphy of the Hellenistic and Roman Periods from Alexander the Great Down to the Reign of Constantine (323 B.C.–A.D. 337)*. Ann Arbor: University of Michigan Press, 2002.

Mendenhall, G. E. *Ancient Israel's Faith and History: An Introduction to the Bible in Context*. Edited by G. A. Herrion. Louisville, Ky.: Westminster John Knox, 2001.

———. "Covenant Forms in Israelite Tradition." *BA* 17, no. 3 (1968): 50–73.

Meyer, J.-W. *Untersuchungen zu den Tonlebermodellen aus dem Alten Orient*. AOAT 39. Neukirchen–Vluyn: Neukirchener-Verlag, 1987.

Milgrom, J. *Leviticus 1–16*. AB 3. New York: Doubleday, 1991.

Miller, P. D. *They Cried to the Lord: The Form and Theology of Biblical Prayer*. Minneapolis: Fortress, 1994.

Moran, W. L. "The Babylonian Job." Pages 182–200 in *The Most Magic Words: Essays on Babylonian and Biblical Literature*. Edited by R. S. Hendel. CBQMS 35. Washington, D.C.: Catholic Biblical Association of America, 2002.

Mowinckel, S. *Psalmenstudien I: Āwän und die individuellen Klagepsalmen*. Amsterdam: Schippers, 1961.

———. *The Psalms in Israel's Worship*. 2 vols. New York: Abingdon, 1962.

———. *Religion und Kultus*. Göttingen: Vandenhoeck & Ruprecht, 1953.

Muraoka, T. "The Tell-Fekherye Bilingual Inscription and Early Aramaic." *Abr-Nahrain* 22 (1983–84): 79–117.

Naiden, F. S. "Rejected Sacrifice in Greek and Hebrew Religion." *JANER* 6 (2006): 186–90.

Naveh, J. "Graffiti and Dedications." *BASOR* 235 (1979): 27–30.

Naveh, J., and Y. Magen. "Aramaic and Hebrew Inscriptions of the Second-Century BCE at Mount Gerizim." *Atiqot* 32 (1997): 9*–17*.

Niehr, H. "The Constitutive Principles for Establishing Justice and Order in Northwest Semitic Societies with Special Reference to Ancient Israel and Judah." *ZAR* 3 (1997): 112–30.

———. "שפט *šāpaṭ*." *ThWAT* 8:408–28.

Nissinen, M. "Das kritische Potential in der altorientalischen Prophetie." Pages 1–33 in Köckert and Nissinen, eds., *Propheten in Mari*.

———. "Falsche Prophetie in neuassyrischer und deuteronomistischer Darstellung." Pages 172–95 in *Das Deuteronomium und seine Querbeziehungen*. Edited by T. Veijola. Schriften der Finnischen Exegetischen Gesellschaft 62. Helsinki: Finnische Exegetische Gesellschaft, 1996.

———. "Prophecy Against the King in Neo-Assyrian Sources." Pages 157–70 in *"Lasset uns Brücken bauen…": Collected Communications to the XVth Congress of the IOSOT, Cambridge 1995*. Edited by K.-D. Schunck and M. Augustin. Frankfurt am Main: Lang, 1998.

———. "Prophecy and Omen Divination: Two Sides of the Same Coin." Pages 341–51 in *Divination and Interpretation of Signs in the Ancient World*. Edited by A. Annus. Oriental Institute Seminar Series 6. Chicago: Oriental Institute of the University of Chicago, 2010.

———. *References to Prophecy in Neo-Assyrian Sources*. SAAS 7. Helsinki: The Neo-Assyrian Text Corpus Project, 1998.

———. "What Is Prophecy? An Ancient Near Eastern Perspective." Pages 17–37 in *Inspired Speech: Prophecy in the Ancient Near East: Essays in Honour of Herbert B. Huffmon*. Edited by J. Kaltner and L. Stulman. JSOTSup 378. London: T&T Clark International, 2004.

Nissinen, M., with C. L. Seow and R. K. Ritner. *Prophets and Prophecy in the Ancient Near East*. SBLWAW 12. Atlanta: SBL, 2003.

Noegel, S. B. "Dreams and Dream Interpreters in Mesopotamia and in the Hebrew Bible [Old Testament]." Pages 45–71 in *Dreams: A Reader on Religious, Cultural, and Psychological Dimensions of Dreaming*. Edited by K. Bulkeley. Hampshire: Palgrave-St. Martin's, 2001.

Norton, G. J. "Ancient Versions and Textual Transmission of the Old Testament." Pages 211–36 in Rogerson and Lieu, eds., *The Oxford Handbook of Biblical Studies*.

Nougayrol, J. "Choix de textes littéraires: 162: (Juste) suffrant (R.S. 25.460)." *Ugaritica* 5 (1968): 265–73 with plate on 435.

———. " 'Oiseau' ou oiseau?" *RA* 61 (1967): 23–38.

———. "Textes hépatoscopiques d'époque ancienne conservés au musée du Louvre (II)." *RA* 40 (1945–46): 56–97.

———. "Trente ans de recherches sur la divination babylonienne (1935–1965)." Pages 5–19 in *La Divination en Mésopotamie ancienne, et dans les Régions voisines, XIVe RAI (Strasbourg, 2–6 juillet 1965)*. Paris: Presses Universitaires de France 1966.

Oppenheim, A. L. *Ancient Mesopotamia: Portrait of a Dead Civilization*. Rev. ed. Chicago: University of Chicago Press, 1996.

———. *The Interpretation of Dreams in the Ancient Near East, with a Translation of an Assyrian Dream Book*. TAPS 46/2. Philadelphia: American Philosophical Society, 1956.

Orthmann, W. *Der alte Orient*. Propyläen Kunstgeschichte 14. Berlin: Propyläen, 1975.

Ortlund, E. N. *Theophany and Chaoskampf: The Interpretation of Theophanic Imagery in the Baal Epic, Isaiah, and the Twelve*. Gorgias Ugaritic Studies 5. Piscataway, N.J.: Gorgias, 2010.

Osborne, R. "Hoards, Votives, Offerings: The Archaeology of the Dedicated Object." *World Archaeology* 36 (2004): 1–10.

Overholt, T. W. *Channels of Prophecy: The Social Dynamics of Prophetic Activity*. Minneapolis: Fortress, 1989.

Parker, R. "Pleasing Thighs: Reciprocity in Greek Religion." Pages 105–26 in Gill, Postlethwaite and Seaford, eds., *Reciprocity in Ancient Greece*.

Parpola, S. *Assyrian Prophecies*. SAA 9. Helsinki: Helsinki University Press, 1997.

———. "The Assyrian Tree of Life: Tracing the Origins of Jewish Monotheism and Greek Philosophy." *JNES* 52 (1993): 161–208.

———. *Letters from Assyrian and Babylonian Scholars*. SAA 10. Helsinki: Helsinki University Press, 1993.

———. *Letters from Assyrian Scholars to the Kings Esarhaddon and Assurbanipal*. 2 vols. AOAT 5A. Neukirchen–Vluyn: Neukirchener Verlag, 1970–83.

———. "A Man Without a Scribe." Pages 315–24 in Ana šadî Labnāni lū allik: *Beiträge zu altorientalischen und mittelmeerischen Kulturen: Festschrift für Wolfgang Röllig*. Edited by B. Pongratz-Leisten et al. AOAT 247: Neukirchen–Vluyn: Neukirchener Verlag, 1997.

Parpola, S., and K. Watanabe. *Neo-Assyrian Treaties and Loyalty Oaths*. SAA 2. Helsinki: Helsinki University Press, 1988.

Paul, S. "Psalm 72:5—A Traditional Blessing for the Long Life of the King." *JNES* 31 (1972): 351–55.

Peirce, C. S. *The Collected Papers of Charles Sanders Peirce*. Edited by C. Hartshorne and P. Weiss. Cambridge, Mass.: Harvard University Press, 1960.

Pongratz-Leisten, B. "From Ritual to Text to Intertext: A New Look on the Dreams in *Ludlul Bēl Nēmeqi*." Pages 139–57 in *In the Second Degree: Paratextual Literature in Ancient Near Eastern and Ancient Mediterranean Culture and Its Reflections in Medieval Literature*. Edited by P. Alexander, A. Lange and R. Pillinger. Leiden: Brill, 2010.

———. *Herrschaftswissen in Mesopotamien: Formen der Kommunikation zwischen Gott und König im 2. und 1. Jahrtausend v. Chr.* SAAS 10. Helsinki: The Neo-Assyrian Text Corpus Project, 1999.

———. “Mesopotamische Standarten in literarischen Zeugnissen.” *BagM* 23 (1992): 299–340.

Porada, E. “Syrian Seal from Karnak.” *JSSEA* 13 (1983): 237–40.

Porter, B. N., ed. *One God or Many? Concepts of Divinity in the Ancient World.* TCBAI 1. Chebeague, Maine: Casco Bay Assyriological Institute, 2000.

Postgate, J. N. “Text and Figure in Ancient Mesopotamia: Match and Mismatch.” Pages 176–84 in *The Ancient Mind: Elements of Cognitive Archaeology*. Edited by C. Renfrew and E. B. W. Zubrow. Cambridge: Cambridge University Press, 1994.

Puëch, E. “Balaᶜam and Deir ᶜAlla.” Pages 25–47 in *The Prestige of the Pagan Prophet Balaam in Judaism, Early Christianity and Islam.* Edited by G. H. van Kooten and J. van Ruiten. Themes in Biblical Narrative 11. Leiden: Brill, 2008.

Pummer, R. “Samaritanism: A Jewish Sect or an Independent Form of Yahwism?” Pages 1–24 in *Samaritans: Past and Present: Current Studies.* Edited by M. Mor and F. V. Reiterer. Berlin: de Gruyter, 2010.

Rabinowitz, I. “Aramaic Inscriptions of the Fifth Century B.C.E. from a North-Arab Shrine in Egypt.” *JNES* 15 (1956): 1–9.

Rad, G., von. *Old Testament Theology*. Vol. 1, *The Theology of Israel’s Historical Traditions*. Edinburgh: Oliver & Boyd, 1963.

———. *Theologie des Alten Testaments, Band 1: Die Theologie der geschichtlichen Überlieferungen Israels*. Munich: Kaiser, 1957.

Radner, K. *Die Macht des Namens: Altorientalische Strategien zur Selbsterhaltung.* Wiesbaden: Harrasowitz, 2005.

Rappaport, R. A. *Ritual and Religion in the Making of Humanity*. Cambridge: Cambridge University Press, 1999.

Reiner, E., and H. G. Güterbock. “The Great Prayer to Ishtar and Its Two Versions from Boğazköy.” *JCS* 21 (1967): 255–66.

Renfrew, C. *The Archaeology of Cult: The Sanctuary at Phylakopi*. London: Thames & Hudson, 1985.

Richter, T. “Untersuchungen zum Opferschauwesen I: Überlegungen zur Rekonstruktion der altbabylonischen *bārûtum*-Serie.” *Or* 62 (1993): 121–41.

———. “Untersuchungen zum Opferschauwesen III: Drei übersehene Opferschau-protokolle aus altbabylonischer Zeit.” Pages 399–414 in *Munuscula Mesopotamica: Festschrift für Johannes Renger*. Edited by B. Böck, E. C. Cancik-Kirschbaum and T. Richter. AOAT 267. Münster: Ugarit-Verlag, 1999.

Riede, P. *Im Netz des Jägers: Studien zur Feindmetaphorik der Individualpsalmen.* WMANT 85. Neukirchen–Vluyn: Neukirchener Verlag, 2000.

Ringgren, H., and B. Johnson. “צדק *ṣædæq*.” *ThWAT* 6:898–924.

Roberts, J. J. M. “Does God Lie? Divine Deceit as a Theological Problem in Israelite Prophetic Literature.” Pages 211–20 in *Congress Volume: Jerusalem, 1986*. Edited by J. A. Emerton. Leiden: Brill, 1988.

Rochberg-Halton, F. *The Heavenly Writing: Divination, Horoscopy, and Astronomy in Mesopotamian Culture*. Cambridge: Cambridge University Press, 2005.

Rogerson, J. W., and J. M. Lieu, eds. *The Oxford Handbook of Biblical Studies*. Oxford: Oxford University Press, 2008.

Sarna, N. "The Abortive Insurrection in Zedekiah's Day (Jer. 27–29)," *Eretz Israel* 14 (1978): 89*–96*.

Sasson, J. M. "The King and I." *JAOS* 118 (1998): 453–70.

Sasson, J. M. et al., eds. *Civilizations of the Ancient Near East*, vol. 3. Peabody, Mass.: Hendrickson, 1995.

Satlow, M. "Giving for a Return: Jewish Votive Offerings in Late Antiquity." Pages 91–108 in *Religion and the Self in Antiquity*. Edited by D. Brakke, M. Satlow and S. Weitzman. Bloomington: Indiana University Press, 2005.

Schenker, A. "Nebukadnezzars Metamorphose vom Unterjocher zum Gottesknecht in den beiden Jeremia-Rezensionen." *RB* 89 (1982): 498–527.

Schmid, H. H. *Gerechtigkeit als Weltordnung: Hintergrund und Geschichte des alttestamentlichen Gerechtigkeitsbegriffes*. BHT 40. Tübingen: Mohr, 1968.

Schmid, K. "Nebukadnezars Antritt der Weltherrschaft und der Abbruch der Davidsdyanstie." Pages 150–66 in *Die Textualisierung der Religion*. Edited by J. Schaper. FAT 62. Tübingen: Mohr Siebeck, 2009.

Schmidt, U. *Zentrale Randfiguren: Strukturen der Darstellung von Frauen in den Erzählungen der Königebücher*. Gütersloh: Gütersloher Verlagshaus, 2003.

Schmitt, R. *Bildhafte Herrscherrepräsentation im eisenzeitlichen Israel*. AOAT 283. Münster: Ugarit-Verlag, 2001.

Schottroff, W. *"Gedenken" im Alten Orient und im Alten Testament: Die Wurzel Zakar im Semitischen Sprachkreis*. WMANT 15. Neukirchen–Vluyn: Neukirchener Verlag, 1964.

Schroer, S. *Die Ikonographie Palästinas/Israels und der Alte Orient: Eine Religionsgeschichte in Bildern II: Die Mittelbronzezeit*. IPIAO 2. Fribourg: Academic, 2008.

Searle, J. R. *Speech Acts: An Essay in the Philosophy of Language*. Cambridge: Cambridge University Press, 1969.

Seidl, U., and W. Sallaberger. "Der 'Heilige Baum'." *AfO* 51 (2005–6): 54–74.

Seux, M.-J. *Hymnes et Prières aux dieux de Babylonie et d'Assyrie*. LAPO 8. Paris: Cerf, 1976.

———. "šiggayon = šigu ?" Pages 419–38 in *Mélanges bibliques et orientaux en l'honneur de M. Henri Cazelles*. Edited by A. Caquot and A. Delcor. AOAT 212. Neukirchen–Vluyn: Neukirchener Verlag, 1981.

Shibata, D. "Ritual Contexts and Mythological Explanations of the Emesal Šuilla-Prayers in Ancient Mesopotamia." *Orient* 45 (2010): 67–85.

Smith, M. *Palestinian Parties and Politics That Shaped the Old Testament*. Corrected ed. London: SCM, 1987.

Smith, M. S. *God in Translation: Deities in Cross-Cultural Discourse in the Biblical World*. FAT 57. Tübingen: Mohr Siebeck, 2008.

Soden, W., von. "Weisheitstexte in akkadischer Sprache, 1. Der leidende Gerechte." Pages 110–35 in *Texte aus der Umwelt des Alten Testaments: Band III Weisheitstexte, Mythen und Epen: Lieferung 1 Weisheitstexte*. Edited by O. Kaiser. Gütersloh: Gütersloh Verlagshaus Gerd Mohn, 1990.

Starr, I. "Extispicy Reports from the Old Babylonian and Sargonid Periods." Pages 201–8 in *Essays on the Ancient Near East in Memory of Jacob Joel Finkelstein*. Edited by M. de Jong Ellis. Hamden, Conn.: Archon, 1977.

———. "In Search of Principles of Prognostication in Extispicy." *HUCA* 45 (1974): 17–23.

———. *Queries to the Sungod: Divination and Politics in Sargonid Assyria.* SAA 4. Helsinki: Helsinki University Press, 1990.

———. *The Rituals of the Diviner.* Bibliotheca Mesopotamica 12. Malibu, Calif.: Undena, 1983.

Stearns, J. B. *Reliefs from the Palace of Ashurnaṣirpal II.* AfOB 15. Graz: Weidner, 1961.

Steck, O. H. *Exegese des Alten Testaments: Leitfaden der Methodik: Ein Arbeitsbuch für Proseminare, Seminare und Vorlesungen.* 14th ed. Neukirchen–Vluyn: Neukirchener Verlag, 1999.

Steinkeller, P. "Of Stars and Men: The Conceptual and Mythological Setup of Babylonian Extispicy." Pages 11–47 in *Biblical and Oriental Essays in Memory of William L. Moran.* Edited by Gianto. BibOr 48. Pontifical Biblical Institute, 2005.

Stephens, F. J. "Sumero-Akkadian Hymns and Prayers." Pages 383–92 in *Ancient Near Eastern Texts Relating to the Old Testament.* Edited by J. B. Pritchard. 3d ed. Princeton, N.J.: Princeton University Press, 1969.

Stökl, J. "The Villain King: Nebuchadnezzar in Jewish Memory in the Persian and Hellenistic Periods." In *Bringing the Past to the Present in the Late Persian and Early Hellenistic Period: Images of Central Figures.* Edited by E. Ben Zvi and D. V. Edelman. Forthcoming.

Stowers, S. "The Religion of Plant and Animal Offerings Versus the Religion of Meanings, Essences, and Textual Mysteries." Pages 35–56 in *Ancient Mediterranean Sacrifice: Images, Acts, Meanings.* Edited by J. W. Knust and Z. Varhelyi. Oxford: Oxford University Press, 2011.

Teissier, B. *Egyptian Iconography on Syro-Palestinian Cylinder Seals of the Middle Bronze Age.* OBO.SA 11. Göttingen: Vandenhoeck & Ruprecht, 1996.

Temple, R. K. G. "An Anatomical Verification of the Reading of a Term in Extispicy." *JCS* 34 (1982): 19–27.

Theuer, G. *Der Mondgott in den Religionen Syrien-Palästinas: Unter besonderer Berücksichtigung von KTU 1.24.* OBO 173. Göttingen: Vandenhoeck & Ruprecht, 2000.

Timm, S. "Wird Nebukadnezar entlastet? Zu 2Kön 18,24–25,21." Pages 359–89 in *"Sieben Augen auf einem Stein" (Sach 3,9): Studien zur Literatur des Zweiten Tempels. Festschrift für Ina Willi-Plein zum 65. Geburtstag.* Edited by F. Hartenstein and M. Pietsch. Neukirchen–Vluyn: Neukirchener Verlag, 2007.

Toorn, K., van der. *Family Religion in Babylonia, Syria, and Israel.* Leiden: Brill, 1996.

———. "L'oracle de victoire comme expression prophétique au Proche-Orient ancien." *RB* 94 (1987): 63–97.

———. *Scribal Culture and the Making of the Hebrew Bible.* Cambridge, Mass.: Harvard University Press, 2007.

———. *Sin and Sanction in Israel and Mesopotamia: A Comparative Study.* Studia semitica neerlandica 22. Assen: Van Gorcum, 1985.

———. "Theodicy in Akkadian Literature." Pages 57–89 in *Theodicy in the World of the Bible: The Goodness of God and the Problem of Evil.* Edited by A. Laato and J. C. de Moor. Leiden: Brill, 2003.

Tov, E. "The Literary History of the Book of Jeremiah in Light of Its Textual History." Pages 363–84 in *The Greek and Hebrew Bible: Collected Essays on the Septuagint.* Edited by E. Tov. VTSup 72. Leiden: Brill, 1999.

———. *The Septuagint Translation of Jeremiah and Baruch: A Discussion of an Early Revision of the LXX of Jeremiah 29–52 and Baruch 1:1–3:8*. HSM 8. Missoula, Mont.: Scholars Press, 1976.

———. *Textual Criticism of the Hebrew Bible*. Minneapolis: Fortress, 1992.

———. "A Textual-Exegetical Commentary on Three Chapters in the Septuagint." Pages 275–90 in *Scripture in Transition: Essays on Septuagint, Hebrew Bible, and Dead Sea Scrolls in Honour of Raija Sollamo*. Edited by A. Voitila and J. Jokiranta. JSJSup 126. Leiden: Brill, 2008.

Tropper, J. *Die Inschriften von Zincirli: Neue Edition und vergleichende Grammatik des phönizischen, samʾalischen und aramäischen Textkorpus*. ALASP 6. Münster: Ugarit-Verlag, 1993.

Ullucci, D. "The End of Animal Sacrifice." Ph.D. diss., Brown University, 2009.

Ungnad, A. *Babylonian Letters of the Hammurapi Period*. Publications of the Babylonian Section 7. Philadelphia: University of Pennsylvania Museum, 1915.

———. *Die Religion der Babylonier und Assyrer*. Religiöse Stimmen der Völker 3. Jena: Diederichs, 1921.

Van Baal, J. "Offering, Sacrifice and Gift." *Numen* 23 (1976): 161–78.

Van Straten, F. "Gifts for the Gods." Pages 65–151 in *Faith, Hope and Worship: Aspects of Religious Mentality in the Ancient World*. Edited by H. S. Versnel. Leiden: Brill, 1981.

VanderKam, J. C. "Prophecy and Apocalyptics in the ANE." Pages 2083–94 in Sasson et al., eds., *Civilizations of the Ancient Near East*, vol. 3.

VanGemeren, W. A. "Oracles of Salvation." Pages 139–76 in *Cracking Old Testament Codes: A Guide to Interpreting the Literary Genres of the Old Testament*. Edited by S. D. Brent and R. L. Giese. Nashville: Broadman & Holman, 1995.

Velden, F., van der. *Psalm 109 und die Aussagen zur Feindschädigung in den Psalmen*. SBB 37. Stuttgart: Katholisches Bibelwerk, 1997.

Vorländer, H. *Mein Gott: Die Vorstellungen vom persönlichen Gott im Alten Orient und im Alten Testament*. AOAT 23. Neukirchen–Vluyn: Neukirchener Verlag, 1975.

Walker, C., and M. Dick, *The Induction of the Cult Image in Ancient Mesopotamia: The Mesopotamian Mīs Pî Ritual: Transliteration, Translation, and Commentary*. SAALT 1. Helsinki: The Neo-Assyrian Text Corpus Project, 2001.

Watanabe, K. *Die adê-Vereidigung anlässlich der Thronfolgeregelung Asarhaddons*. BagM 3. Berlin: Mann, 1987.

Watson, R. S. *Chaos Uncreated: A Reassessment of the Theme of Chaos in the Hebrew Bible*. BZAW 341. Berlin: de Gruyter, 2005.

Welke-Holtmann, S. *Die Kommunikation zwischen Frau und Mann: Dialogstrukturen in den Erzähltexten der Hebräischen Bibel*. Exegese in unserer Zeit 13. Münster: LIT, 2004.

Westermann, C. *Praise and Lament in the Psalms*. Translated by R. N. Soulen and K. R. Crim. Louisville, Ky.: Westminster, 1987.

Widengren, G. *The Accadian and Hebrew Psalms of Lamentation as Religious Documents*. Stockholm: Almqvist & Wiksell, 1936.

Wiggermann, F. A. M. *Mesopotamian Protective Spirits: The Ritual Texts*. CM 1. Groningen: Styx, 1992.

Winter, U. *Frau und Göttin: Exegetische und ikonographische Studien zum weiblichen Gottesbild im Alten Israel und in dessen Umwelt*. OBO 53. Göttingen: Vandenhoeck & Ruprecht, 1983.

Xella, P. "Baal Safon in KTU 2.23: Osservazioni Epigrafiche." *Rivista di studi fenici* 15 (1987): 111–14.

Zenger, E. "Psalm 72." Pages 302–30 in Zenger and Hossfeld, *Psalmen 51–100*. HThKAT. Freiburg: Herder, 2000.

———. "Vorwort." Pages in vii–ix. *Ritual und Poesie: Formen und Orte religiöser Dichtung im Alten Orient, im Judentum und im Christentum*. Edited by E. Zenger. HBS 36. Freiburg: Herder, 2003.

Zernecke, A. E. *Gott und Mensch in Klagegebeten aus Israel und Mesopotamien: Die Handerhebungsgebete Ištar 10 und Ištar 2 und die Klagepsalmen Ps 38 und Ps 22 im Vergleich*. AOAT 387. Münster: Ugarit-Verlag, 2011.

———. "Ishtar 2: The 'Great Ishtar Prayer'." Pages 257–90 in Lenzi, ed., *Reading Akkadian Prayers and Hymns*.

Zgoll, A. "Audienz—Ein Modell zum Verständnis mesopotamischer Handerhebungsrituale. Mit einer Deutung der Novelle vom Armen Mann von Nippur." *BagM* 34 (2005): 181–203.

———. "Der betende Mensch: Zur Anthropologie in Mesopotamien." Pages 121–40 in *Der Mensch im Alten Israel: Neue Forschungen zur alttestamentlichen Anthropologie*. Edited by B. Janowski and K. Liess. HBS 59. Freiburg im Breisgau: Herder, 2009.

———. *Die Kunst des Betens: Form und Funktion, Theologie und Psychagogik in babylonisch-assyrischen Handerhebungsgebeten zu Ištar*. AOAT 308. Münster: Ugarit-Verlag, 2003.

———. *Traum und Welterleben im antiken Mesopotamien: Traumtheorie und Traumpraxis im 3.–1. Jahrtausend v. Chr. als Horizont einer Kulturgeschichte des Träumens*. AOAT 333. Münster: Ugarit-Verlag, 2006.

Zimmern, H. *Babylonische Hymnen und Gebete in Auswahl*. AO 7. Leipzig: Hinrichs, 1905.

Indexes

Index of References

Index of Authors